750+ MATCHING

Based Questions for NEET

BIOLOGY

Corporate Office

DISHA PUBLICATION
45, 2nd Floor, Maharishi Dayanand Marg, Corner Market, Malviya Nagar, New Delhi - 110017
Tel : 49842349 / 49842350

Typeset by Disha DTP Team

www.dishapublication.com
Books & ebooks for School & Competitive Exams

www.mylearninggraph.com
Etests for Competitive Exams

Write to us at **feedback_disha@aiets.co.in**

CONTENTS

The Living World

1. Match the following columns.

	Column I		Column II
A.	Linnaeus	1.	Living species of today
B.	John Ray	2.	Father of taxonomy
C.	Synchronic species	3.	Coined the term species
D.	Neontological species	4.	Species belonging to same time period

   Codes

	A	B	C	D			A	B	C	D
(a)	2	3	4	1	(b)		1	3	2	4
(c)	4	3	2	1	(d)		1	2	3	4

2. Match the following columns.

	Column I		Column II
A.	Numerical taxonomy	1.	Nuclear and chromosomal studies
B.	Classical taxonomy	2.	Number of shared characters
C.	Practical taxonomy	3.	Utility of organism
D.	Karyotaxonomy	4.	a-taxonomy

   Codes

	A	B	C	D			A	B	C	D
(a)	2	4	3	1	(b)		1	3	2	4
(c)	4	2	3	1	(d)		1	2	4	3

3. Match the column I with column II :

	Herbarium		Location
(A)	Royal Botanical Garden	(i)	Paris
(B)	Conservation and Botanical Garden	(ii)	St. Petersburg
(C)	Herbarium of forest Reseach Institute	(iii)	London
(D)	British Museum of Natural History	(iv)	Kolkata
(E)	Museum of Natural History	(v)	Kew
		(vi)	Dehradun
		(vii)	Geneva

   (a) A-(v), B-(vii), C-(vi), D-(iii), E-(i)
   (b) A-(ii), B-(iv), C-(v), D-(i), E-(iii)
   (c) A-(vi), B-(v), C-(vii), D-(iii), E-(ii)
   (d) A-(iii), B-(ii), C-(i), D-(iv), E-(vii)

4. Match the Coloumn I with Column II :

	Museums		Locations
(A)	Zoology Museum	(i)	Mumbai
(B)	Natural History Museum	(ii)	Delhi
(C)	Prince of klales Museum	(iii)	Chicago (USA)
(D)	National Museum of National History	(iv)	
(E)	Field Museum of Natural History	(v)	
		(vi)	London
		(vii)	Amesterdam

   (a) A-(vi), B-(vii), C-(ii), D-(i), E-(iv)
   (b) A-(ii), B-(iii), C-(vii), D-(vi), E-(v)
   (c) A-(iv), B-(vi), C-(iii), D-(i), E-(v)
   (d) A-(vii), B-(vi), C-(i), D-(ii), E-(iii)

5. Match the following columns and select the correct option.

	Column I		Column II
A.	*Panthera tigris*	(i)	Mango
B.	*Mangifera indica*	(ii)	Common Indian frog
C.	*Musca domestica*	(iii)	Cockroach
D.	*Periplaneta americana*	(iv)	Tiger
E.	*Rana tigerina*	(v)	House fly

(a) A-(ii), B-(v), C-(i), D-(iii), E-(iv)
(b) A-(iv), B-(i), C-(v), D-(iii), E-(ii)
(c) A-(ii), B-(v), C-(iii), D-(i), E-(iv)
(d) A-(iv), B-(i), C-(v), D-(ii), E-(iii)

6. Match each item in Column-I with one in Column-II and choose your answer from the codes given below:

Column-I Taxonomical Aid	Column-II Feature
I. Flora	1. Useful in providing information for identification of names of species found in an area
II. Manuals	2. Contains the actual account of habitat and distribution of plants of a given area.
III. Monographs	3. Contain information on any one taxon

	I	II	III			I	II	III
(a)	1	2	3		(b)	3	2	1
(c)	2	1	3		(d)	2	3	1

7. Match Column-I with Column-II for housefully classification and select the correct option using the codes given below:

Column-I	Column-II
A. Family	1. Diptera
B. Order	2. Arthropoda
C. Class	3. Muscidae
D. Phylum	4. Insecta

Codes

	A	B	C	D			A	B	C	D
(a)	3	1	4	2		(b)	3	2	4	1
(c)	4	3	2	1		(d)	4	2	1	3

8. Which of the following taxonomic categories are correctly matched to their standard termination of names with respect to biological classification of plants?

I.	Division	–	phyta
II.	Class	–	opsida
III.	Order	–	ales
IV.	Family	–	idae

(a) I, II, IV   (b) II, III, IV
(c) II, III, IV   (d) I, II, III, IV

9. The living organisms can be unexceptionally distinguished from the non-living things on the basis of their ability for:
(a) responsiveness to touch
(b) interaction with the environment and progressive evolution
(c) reproduction
(d) growth and movement

10. Herbarium sheet gives information about
(a) Date and place of collection only
(b) English and local names only
(c) Collector's name only
(d) Not a single option with correct information

11. Match Column-I with Column-II and choose the correct option

Column-I	Column-II
A. Ex-situ conservation	(i) Central National Herbarium
B. Quick referral system	(ii) Museum
C. Preserved plants and animals	(iii) Flora
D. Actual account of habitat and distribution of plants in a given area	(iv) Royal Botanical

(a) A-(ii), B-(iii), C-(iv), D-(i)
(b) A-(i), B-(iv), C-(ii), D-(iii)
(c) A-(iv), B-(i), C-(iii), D-(ii)
(d) A-(iv), B-(i), C-(ii), D-(iii)

12. Match Column-I with Column-II and select the correct option from the codes given below.

Column-I	Column-II
A. Binomial nomenclature	(i) Hippocrates
B. The Darwin of the 20th century	(ii) Earnst Mayr
C. Father of Botany	(iii) Linnaeus
D. Father of medicine	(iv) Theopharastus

(a) A-(iii), B-(ii), C-(iv), D-(i)
(b) A-(iii), B-(ii), C-(i), D-(iv)
(c) A-(i), B-(ii), C-(iii), D-(iv)
(d) A-(ii), B-(iii), (i) C-(iv), D-(i)

13. Which of the following is a mismatched pair of common name and biological name of an organism?
(a) Para rubber – *Hevea brasiliensis*
(b) Tea – *Thea chinesis*
(c) Earthworm – *Pheretima posthuma*
(d) Frog – *Bufo melanostictus*

14. Match Column-I with Column-II and select the correct option from codes given below.

Column-I	Column-II
A. John Ray	(i) Gave the concept of new systematics.
B. C. Linnaeus	(ii) First described species as a unit of classification
C. Aristotle	(iii) Father of Zoology
D. Julian Huxley	(iv) Introduced binomial nomenclature

(a) A-(i), B-(ii), C-(iii), D-(iv)
(b) A-(iv), B-(ii), C-(iii), D-(i)
(c) A-(ii), B-(iii), C-(i), D-(iv)
(d) A-(ii), B-(iv), C-(iii), D-(i)

15. Match Column-I with Column-II and select the correct option from the codes given below.

Column-I	Column-II
A. Ecology	(i) Relationships of organisms and environment
B. Herbarium	(ii) Original specimen cited by an author
C. Holotype	(iii) A hierarchical unit
D. Taxon	(iv) Collection of wild and domestic plants

(a) A-(i), B-(ii), C-(iii), D-(iv)
(b) A-(i), B-(ii), C-(iv), D-(iii)
(c) A-(i), B-(iv), C-(ii), D-(iii)
(d) A-(iv), B-(ii), C-(iii), D-(i)

16. Select the mismatched pair.
(a) *Panthera leo* — Belongs to class Mammalia
(b) *Musca domestica* — The common house lizard, a reptile
(c) *Entamoeba coli* — Commonly occurring protozoan in human intestine
(d) *Solanum tuberosum* — A dicotyledonous plant

17. Select the correct option to complete the given table:

Common name	Biological name	Phylum/ Division	Class	Order	Family	Genus
Man	*Homo sapiens*	Chordata	Mammalia	Primata	(i)	*Homo*
Housefly	*Musca domestica*	Arthropoda	Insecta	(ii)	Muscidae	*Musca*
Mango	*Mangifera indica*	Angiospermae	(iii)	Sapindales	Anacardiaceae	*Mangifera*
Wheat	*Triticum aestivum*	(iv)	Monocotyledonae	Poales	Poaceae	*Triticum*

(a) (i) – Hominidae, (ii) – Diptera, (iii) – Dicotyledonae, (iv) – Angiospermae
(b) (i) – Hominidae, (ii) – Dicotyledonae, (iii) – Diptera, (iv) – Angiospermae
(c) (i) – Hominidae, (ii) – Diptera, (iii) – Angiospermae, (iv) – Dicotyledonae
(d) (i) – Hominidae, (ii) – Dicotyledonae, (iii) – Angiospermae, (iv) – Diptera

18. Select the incorrect set from the following:
(a) Polymoniales – Convolvulaceae, Solanaceae.
(b) Primata – gorilla, gibbon
(c) Felidae – cat, dog
(d) Panthera – leopard, tiger

Solutions

1. (a) 2. (a) 3. (a) 4. (d) 5. (b)
6. (c) 7. (a) 8. (d) 9. (c) 10. (a)
11. (d) 12. (c)

13. (d) *Bufo melanostictus* is a biological name of toads. Bufo is a genus of true toads in the amphibian family Bufonidae.

14. (d)

15. (a) A particular specimen or illustration designated by the author to represent the type of a species is referred to as holotype. It is now essential to designate a holotype when publishing a new species.

16. (b) 17. (a)

18. (c) Cat belongs to family Felidae and dog belongs to Family Canidae.

Biological Classification 

1. Match the following Columns.

Column I	Column II
A. Artificial system	1. AW Eichler
B. Phylogenetic system	2. Peter Sneath
C. Phenetic system	3. C Linnaeus
D. *Systema Naturae*	4. Theophrastus

Codes

	A	B	C	D		A	B	C	D
(a)	4	1	2	3	(b)	1	2	3	4
(c)	4	3	2	1	(d)	2	4	1	3

2. Match the following Columans.

Column I	Column II
A. Animalia	1. Unicellular prokaryotes
B. Monera	2. Multicellular and prokaryotes
C. Protista	3. Unicellular eukaryotes
D. Plantae	4. Multicelluar ingestive heterotrophs

Codes

	A	B	C	D		A	B	C	D
(a)	4	3	1	2	(b)	4	1	3	2
(c)	1	2	4	3	(d)	2	3	1	4

3. Match the following Coumns.

Column I	Column II
A. Plant virus	1. Potato spindle tuber disease
B. Animal virus	2. Kuru disease
C. Viroid	3. Tobacco necrosis disease
D. Prions	4. Polio

Codes

	A	B	C	D		A	B	C	D
(a)	2	1	3	4	(b)	3	4	1	2
(c)	4	3	2	1	(d)	1	2	3	4

4. Match the following Coumns.

Column I	Column II
A. Flex d'Herelle	1. Bacteriophage
B. Loeffler and Frosch	2. Foot and mouth disease
C. Robert Gallo	3. Prions
D. Stanley Prusiner	4. HIV

Codes

	A	B	C	D		A	B	C	D
(a)	1	2	3	4	(b)	4	3	2	1
(c)	2	1	3	4	(d)	1	2	4	3

5. Match the following Coumns.

Column I	Column II
A. Filovirus	1. Mumps
B. Paramyxoviridae	2. Ebola
C. Deltaviridae	3. Influenza virus
D. Orthomyxoviridae	4. Hepatitis-D

Codes

	A	B	C	D		A	B	C	D
(a)	2	1	4	3	(b)	3	4	1	2
(c)	1	2	3	4	(d)	2	3	4	1

6. Select the correct difference between bacteriophage and animal virus multiplication.

	Bacteriophage	Animal viruses
I.	Biosynthesis occur in cytoplasm.	Biosynthesis occur in nucleus (DNA viruses) or cytoplams (RNA viruses).

II. Tail fibres attach to thecell wall proteins. — Attachment sites are plasma membrane proteins or glycoproteins.

III. Uncoating is necesary. — Uncoating is not necessary.

IV. Viral DNA enters into host cell endocytosis. — Viral DNA injected into host cell.

Choose the correct option from the codes given below.

(a) I and II   (b) III and IV
(c) II, III and IV   (d) I, II, III and IV

7. Consider the following given bacteria and classify them as Gram positive (+) and Gram negative (–) bacteria.

Choose the correct option from the codes that follow.

I. Acetobacter   II. Escherichia
III. Vibrio   IV. Salmonella
V. Streptococcus   VI. Mycobacterium
VII. Enterocococus   VIII. Pneumococcus

	Gram positive	Gram negative
(a)	V, VI,VII, VIII	I, II, III, IV
(b)	I, II, III, IV	V, VI,VII, VIII
(c)	II, IV, VIII	I, III, V, VI, VII
(d)	I, VIII, III, II	IV, V, VI, VII

8. In the following table identify the correct matching of the crop, its disease and the corresponding pathogen

	Crop	Disease	Pathogen
(a)	Citrus	Canker	*Pseudomonas rubrilineans*
(b)	Potato	Late blight	*Fusarium udum*
(c)	Brinjal	Root-knot	*Meloidogyne incogita*
(d)	Pigeon Pea	Seed gall	*Pytopthora infestons*

9. Match the following Columns.

Column I		Column II
A. *Nitrobacter*	1.	Free-living aerobic nitrogen-fixer
B. *Clostridium*	2.	Converts ammonia into nitrite
C. *Nitrosococcus*	3.	Changes nitrite to nitrate
D. *Azotobacter*	4.	Free-living anaerobic nitrogen-fixer

Codes

	A	B	C	D
(a)	2	4	3	1
(b)	3	4	2	1
(c)	4	2	1	3
(d)	1	2	3	4

10. Match the following Columns.

Column I		Column II
A. Actinomycin-D	1.	Inhibits mRNA synthesis
B. Tetracycline	2.	Inhibits 50S subunits of robosomes
C. Streptomycin	3.	Inhibits binding of tRNA with ribosomes
D. Chloramphenicol	4.	Alters 30S Subunits of ribosomes

Codes

	A	B	C	D
(a)	1	2	3	4
(b)	3	4	2	1
(c)	1	3	2	4
(d)	1	3	4	2

11.

	Column I		Column II		Column III
A.	Obligate aerobes	1.	Respire anaerobically under normal condition, but can respire aerobically when oxygen is available	(i)	*Bacillus subtilis*
B.	Facultative anaerobes	2.	Respire only anaerobically	(ii)	Halophiles
C.	Obligate anaerobes	3.	Generally respire aerobically, but switch over to anaerobic mode of respiration if oxygen becomes deficient	(iii)	*Clostridium botulinum*
D.	Facultative aerobes	4.	Respire only aerobically	(iv)	Rhodopseudomonas

Codes

	A	B	C	D
(a)	4-(i)	3-(iii)	1-(iv)	3-(ii)
(b)	4-(i)	3-(ii)	2-(iii)	1-(iv)
(c)	1-(ii)	2-(i)	3-(iv)	4-(iii)
(d)	4-(iii)	3-(iv)	2-(i)	1-(ii)

12. Match the following Columns.

	Column I		Column II
A.	Mycoplasma	1.	Ether linked lipids
B.	Transduction	2.	Sex pili
C.	Conjugation	3.	Requires virus
D.	Thermophiles	4.	Cell wall-less bacteria

Codes

	A	B	C	D
(a)	4	3	2	1
(b)	1	2	3	4
(c)	2	3	4	1
(d)	3	4	1	2

13. Match the following Columns.

	Column I		Column II
A.	Archaebacteria	1.	Do not possess photosynthetic pigments
B.	Mesosomes	2.	Atrichous
C.	Pili	3.	More prominent in Gram negative bacteria
D.	Cocci bacteria	4.	One or two per cell
E.	Chemosynthetic	5.	Lack peptidoglycan in cell wall bacteria

Codes

	A	B	C	D	E
(a)	5	3	4	2	1
(b)	1	2	3	4	5
(c)	4	2	1	3	5
(d)	5	4	3	2	1

14. Match the type of flagellar arrangement in Column I with their correct names in Coulmn II and mark the right code.

	Column I		Column II
A.		1.	Cephalotrichous
B.		2.	Lophotrichous
C.		3.	Atrichous
D.		4.	Peritrichous
E.		5.	Amphitrichous

Codes

	A	B	C	D	E
(a)	4	2	5	3	1
(b)	4	1	5	3	2
(c)	4	3	5	1	2
(d)	4	1	5	2	3

15. Match the following Columns.

Column I		Column II
A.	Syphilis	1.	*Acetobacter*
B.	Pathogen of Cattle	2.	*Agrobacterium*
C.	Crown gall of apple	3.	*Corynebacterium*
D.	Diphtheria	4.	*Mycobacterium*
		5.	*Treponema*

Codes

	A	B	C	D		A	B	C	D
(a)	3	1	4	2	(b)	5	4	2	3
(c)	5	3	2	1	(d)	2	4	5	3

16. Match the following Columns.

Column I	Column II
(Type of pseudopodia)	(Protozoan species)
A. Lobopodia	1. Euglypha
B. Filopodia	2. *Globigerina* (Forminiferans)
C. Reticulopodia	3. Amoeba
D. Axopodia	4. *Actinophyrus*

Codes

	A	B	C	D		A	B	C	D
(a)	3	1	2	4	(b)	4	3	2	1
(c)	1	2	3	4	(d)	2	4	1	3

17. Match the following Columns.

Column I	Column II
(Structures)	(Features)
A. Magna form	1. Precystic stage of Entamoeba.
B. Minuta form	2. Most active form of Entamoeba.
C. Trophozoite	3. Infective stage of *Entamoeba histolytica*.
D. Tetranucleate cyst	4. The normal trophozoites in *Entamoeba histolytica*.

Codes

	A	B	C	D
(a)	1	2	3	4
(b)	4	1	3	2
(c)	4	1	2	3
(d)	3	4	1	2

18. Match the following Columns.

Column I	Column II
A. Dinoflagellate	1. *Dicyostelium*
B. *Plasmodium*	2. *Noctiluca*
C. Myxomycota	3. Slime mould
D. Acrasiomycota	4. *Fuligo*

Codes

	A	B	C	D		A	B	C	D
(a)	3	2	1	4	(b)	1	4	3	2
(c)	2	3	4	1	(d)	4	3	1	2

19. Match the following Columns.

Column I	Column II
A. *Entamoeba histolytic*	1. Cytozoic parasite
B. *Plamodium*	2. Coelozoic parasite
C. *Wuchereria*	3. Rhabditiform larva
D. Extraintestinal migration	4. Monogenic parasite
	5. Lymphadenitis

Codes

	A	B	C	D		A	B	C	D
(a)	4	2	1	3	(b)	4	1	5	3
(c)	5	1	2	3	(d)	4	2	5	1

20. Which of the following is not matched correctly?

(a) *Anabaena*   – Cyanobacteria
(b) *Amoeba*   – Protozoa
(c) *Gonyaulax*   – Dinoflagellated
(d) *Thermoacidophiles* – Archaebacteria
(e) *Albugo*   – Chrysophytes

21. Match the following Columns.

Column I	Column II
A. *E. histolytica*	1. Kala-azar
B. *E. gingivalis*	2. Sleeping sickness
C. *P. vivax*	3. Amoebic dysentery
D. *T. gambiense*	4. Malaria
	5. Pyorrhoea

Codes

	A	B	C	D
(a)	4	3	2	1
(b)	3	4	5	1
(c)	3	5	4	2
(d)	3	5	2	1

22. Match the following Columns.

Column I	Column II
A. A domain of plant-like, heterotrophic organims that work primarily as decompose	1. Lichen
B. The slender, reproductive structures of fungi	2. Dikaryotic
C. Indicator of SO_2	3. Hyphae
D. Cells with two nuclei	4. Fungi

Codes

	A	B	C	D			A	B	C	D
(a)	4	3	1	2		(b)	1	2	3	4
(c)	4	3	2	1		(d)	3	2	1	4

23. Match the following Columns.

Column I	Column II
A. Morels	1. Deuteromycetes
B. Smut	2. Ascomycetes
C. Bread mould	3. Basidiomycetes
D. Imperfect fungi	4. Phycomycetes

Codes

	A	B	C	D			A	B	C	D
(a)	3	4	1	2		(b)	2	3	4	1
(c)	4	1	2	3		(d)	3	4	2	1
(e)	2	1	4	3						

24. Match the following Columns.

Column I	Column II
A. *Rizopus*	1. Eurotiomycetes
B. *Penicillium*	2. Ustilaginomycetes
C. *Ustilago*	3. Deuteromycetes
D. *Alternaria*	4. Zygomycetes

Codes

	A	B	C	D			A	B	C	D
(a)	4	3	1	2		(b)	2	3	4	1
(c)	4	1	2	3		(d)	3	4	2	1
(e)	2	1	4	3						

25. Match the following Columns.

Column I	Column II
A. Eubacteria	1. *Trichoderma*
B. Dinoflagellates	2. *Albugo*
C. Phycomycetes	3. *Gonyaulax*
D. Deuteromycetes	4. *Anabaena*

Codes

	A	B	C	D			A	B	C	D
(a)	1	2	3	4		(b)	2	3	4	1
(c)	4	3	2	1		(d)	4	3	1	2

26. Which one of the following is incorrectly matched?

(a) Puccinia — Smut
(b) Root — Exarch protoxylem
(c) Cassia — Imbricate aestivation
(d) Root pressure — Guttation

27. Study the figures given below.

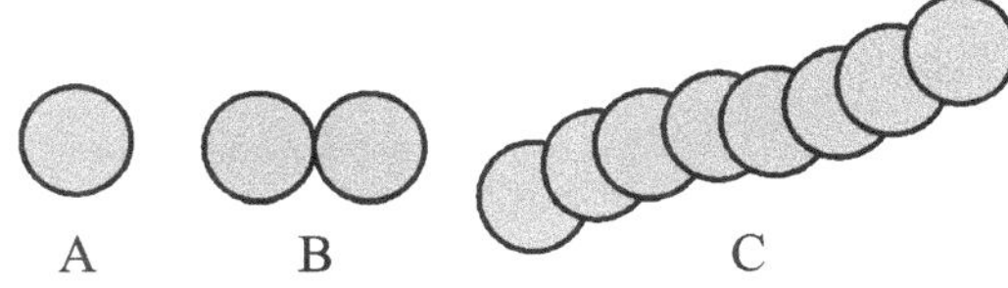

Choose the correct option.

	A	B	C
(a)	Monococcus	Diplococcus	Streptococcus
(b)	Bacillus	Diplococcus	Streptobacillus
(c)	Micrococcus	Bacillus	Streptobacillus
(d)	Streptococcus	Diplococcus	Bacillus

28. In Gram negative bacterial cell wall, the peptidoglycan chains are laterally linked by short chains of four amino acids which are constituted of

(a) L-Alanine; D-Glutamic acid; L-Lysine; D-alanine
(b) L-Alanine; D-Glutamic acid, diaminopimelic acid, D-Alanine
(c) L-Alanine; L-Lyisne; D-Alanine, diaminopimelic acid
(d) L-Alanine; D-Glutamic; L-Lyisne, diaminopimelic acid

29. Consider the following given bacteria and classify them as Gram positive (+) and Gram negative (–) bacteria.

Choose the correct option from the codes that follow.

I.	Acetobacter	II.	Escherichia
III.	Vibrio	IV.	Salmonella
V.	Streptococcus	VI.	Mycobacterium
VII.	Enterococcus	VIII.	Pneumococcus

	Gram positive	**Gram negative**
(a)	V, VI, VII, VIII	I, II, III, IV
(b)	I, II, III, IV	V, VI, VII, VIII
(c)	II, IV, VIII	I, III, V, VI, VII
(d)	I, VIII, III, II	IV, V, VI, VII

30. Select the correct pair(s).
    I.   Methanogens – *Methanogenium, Methanothrix*
    II.   Halophiles–*Halococcus, Haloarchaea*
    III.   Themoacidophiles–*Sulfolobus, Desulphurococcus*
    Choose the correct option.
    (a) I and II   (b) II and III
    (c) I and III   (d) All of these

31. Match the following Columns.

	Column I		Column II
A.	*Nitrobacter*	1.	Free-living aerobic nitrogen-fixer
B.	*Clostridium*	2.	Converts ammonia into nitrite
C.	*Nitrosococcus*	3.	Changes nitrite to nitrate
D.	*Azotobacter*	4.	Free-living anaerobic nitrogen-fixer

    Codes

	A	B	C	D
(a)	2	4	3	1
(b)	3	4	2	1
(c)	4	2	1	3
(d)	1	2	3	4

32. Match the following Columns.

	Column I		Column II
A.	Actinomycin-D	1.	Inhibits mRNA synthesis
B.	Tetracycline	2.	Inhibits 50S subunits of robosomes
C.	Streptomycin	3.	Inhibits binding of tRNA with ribosomes
D.	Chloramphenicol	4.	Alters 30S Subunits of ribosomes

    Codes

	A	B	C	D
(a)	1	2	3	4
(b)	3	4	2	1
(c)	1	3	2	4
(d)	1	3	4	2

33. **Column I :**
    A. Obligate aerobes
    B. Facultative anaerobes
    C. Obligate anaerobes
    D. Facultative aerobes
    Column II :
    1. Respire anaerobically under normal condition, but can respire aerobically when oxygen is available
    2. Respire only anaerobically
    3. Generally respire aerobically, but switch over to anaerobic mode of respiration if oxygen becomes deficient
    4. Respire only aerobically
    Column III :
    (i) *Bacillus subtilis*
    (ii) Halophiles
    (iii) *Clostridium botulinum*
    (iv) Rhodopseudomonas
    Codes

	A	B	C	D
(a)	4-(i)	3-(iii)	1-(iv)	3-(ii)
(b)	4-(i)	3-(ii)	2-(iii)	1-(iv)
(c)	1-(ii)	2-(i)	3-(iv)	4-(iii)
(d)	4-(iii)	3-(iv)	2-(i)	1-(ii)

34. Read the following statements and mark them as True(T)/False(F).
    I. The cell wall strengthening material in a bacterial cell is murein.
    II. The food reserve present in a bacterial cell is starch and maltose.
    III. The ribosomes present are of 70S type.
    IV. The mesosome helps in sexual reproduction.

	I	II	III	IV		I	II	III	IV
(a)	T	F	T	F	(b)	F	T	T	F
(c)	T	T	F	T	(d)	F	T	T	F

35. Match the following Columns.

	Column I		Column II
A.	Actinomycetes	1.	*Streptomyces*
B.	Enterobacteria	2.	*Salmonella*
C.	Spirochaetes	3.	*Treponema*
D.	Chemoautotroph	4.	*Nitrosomonas*

    Codes

	A	B	C	D
(a)	4	3	2	1
(b)	1	2	3	4
(c)	3	4	1	2
(d)	2	1	4	3

36. Match the following Columns.

Column I		Column II
A.	Archaebacteria	1. Do not possess photosynthetic pigments
B.	Mesosomes	2. Atrichous
C.	Pili	3. More prominent in Gram negative bacteria
D.	Cocci bacteria	4. One or two per cell
E.	Chemosynthetic	5. Lack peptidoglycan in cell wall bacteria

Codes

	A	B	C	D	E
(a)	5	3	4	2	1
(b)	1	2	3	4	5
(c)	4	2	1	3	5
(d)	5	4	3	2	1

37. Match the following Columns.

Column I		Column II
A.	Syphilis	1. *Acetobacter*
B.	Pathogen of Cattle	2. *Agrobacterium*
C.	Crown gall of apple	3. *Corynebacterium*
D.	Diphtheria	4. *Mycobacterium*
		5. *Treponema*

Codes

	A	B	C	D
(a)	3	1	4	2
(b)	5	4	2	3
(c)	5	3	2	1
(d)	2	4	5	3

38. Choose the incorrect match.
(a) Sarcomastigophora   – *Euglena*
(b) Sporozoa   – *Plasmodium*
(c) Cnidospora   – *Myxidium*
(d) Ciliophora   – *Monocystis*

39. Choose the correct option for the part labelled A-E of the given figure of *Trypanosoma*.

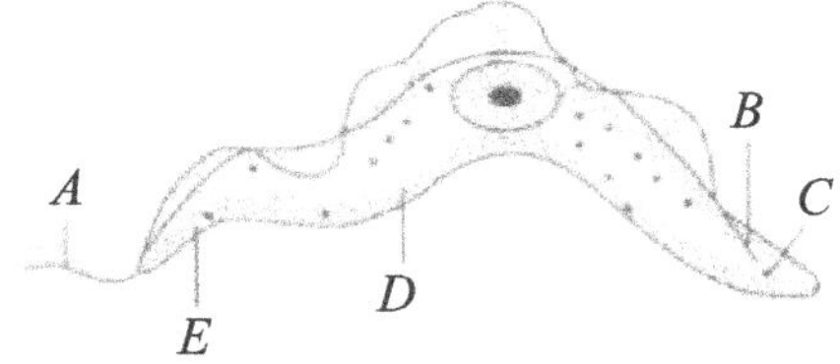

	A	B	C	D	E
(a)	Attached Flagella	Nucleus	Food granule	Endo-plasm	Endoplasm
(b)	Undulating membrane	Blepharoplast	Pellicle	Ecto-plasm	Kenetoplast
(c)	Free flagellum	Blepharoplast	Kinetoplast	Endo-plasm	Pellicle
(d)	Free flagellum	Nucleus	Kinetoplast	Pellicle	Food granule

40. Which is an incorrect combination?
(a) Haemocyanin – Prawn
(b) Haemocyanin – RBC
(c) Haemoglobin in plasma – *Pheretima*
(d) Haemozoin – *Plasmodium* cytoplasm

41. Choose the incorrect match
(a) *Trypanosoma rhodensia* – East African sleeping sickness
(b) *T. cruzi* – Chaga's disease
(c) *T. brucei* – South American sleeping sickness
(d) *T. evansi* – Surra disease

42. Match the following Columns.

Column I		Column II
A.	Protozoan	1. *Gonyaulax*
B.	Bacillariophyceae	2. Diatoms
C.	Euglenoid	3. *Paramecium*
D.	Dinoflagellates	4. *Euglena*

Codes:

	A	B	C	D			A	B	C	D
(a)	2	3	4	1		(b)	4	2	3	1
(c)	1	3	2	4		(d)	3	2	4	1

43. Match the following Columns.

Column I (Structures)		Column II (Features)
A.	Magna form	1. Precystic stage of Entamoeba.
B.	Minuta form	2. Most active form of Entamoeba.
C.	Trophozoite	3. Infective stage of *Entamoeba histolytica*.
D.	Tetranucleate cyst	4. The normal trophozoites in *Entamoeba histolytica*.

Codes

	A	B	C	D			A	B	C	D
(a)	1	2	3	4		(b)	4	1	3	2
(c)	4	1	2	3		(d)	3	4	1	2

44. Match the following Columns.

Column I	Column II
(Type of pseudopodia)	**(Protozoan species)**
A. Lobopodia	1. Euglypha
B. Filopodia	2. *Globigerina* (Forminiferans)
C. Reticulopodia	3. Amoeba
D. Axopodia	4. *Actinophyrus*

Codes

	A	B	C	D
(a)	3	1	2	4
(b)	4	3	2	1
(c)	1	2	3	4
(d)	2	4	1	3

45. Match the following Columns.

Column I	Column II
A. Dinoflagellate	1. *Dicyostelium*
B. *Plasmodium*	2. *Noctiluca*
C. Myxomycota	3. Slime mould
D. Acrasiomycota	4. *Fuligo*

Codes

	A	B	C	D
(a)	3	2	1	4
(b)	1	4	3	2
(c)	2	3	4	1
(d)	4	3	1	2

46. Match the following Columns.

Column I	Column II
A. *Entamoeba histolytic*	1. Cytozoic parasite
B. *Plamodium*	2. Coelozoic parasite
C. *Wuchereria*	3. Rhabditiform larva
D. Extraintestinal migration	4. Monogenic parasite
	5. Lymphadenitis

Codes

	A	B	C	D
(a)	4	2	1	3
(b)	4	1	5	3
(c)	5	1	2	3
(d)	4	2	5	1

47. Which of the following is not matched correctly?

(a)	*Anobaena*	–	Cyanobacteria
(b)	*Amoeba*	–	Protozoa
(c)	*Gonyaulax*	–	Dinoflagellated
(d)	*Thermoacidophiles*	–	Archaebacteria
(e)	*Albugo*	–	Chrysophytes

48. Match the following Columns.

Column I	Column II
A. *E. histolytica*	1. Kala-azar
B. *E. gingivalis*	2. Sleeping sickness
C. *P. vivax*	3. Amoebic dysentery
D. *T. gambiense*	4. Malaria
	5. Pyorrhoea

Codes

	A	B	C	D		A	B	C	D
(a)	4	3	2	1	(b)	3	4	5	1
(c)	3	5	4	2	(d)	3	5	2	1

49. Match the Columns I with coloumn II & choose the correct option.

Column I	Column II
A. Rhizopus	(i) Basidiomyates
B. Penicillium	(ii) Euarotimyates
C. Ustilago	(iii) Deuteromyates
D. Alternaria	(iv) Phyomycetes

(a) A – (i); B–(ii); C–(i); D–(iii)
(b) A – (ii); B–(i); C–(iv); D–(iii)
(c) A – (iv); B–(i); C–(iii); D–(ii)
(d) A – (iii); B–(ii); C–(iv); D–(i)

Solutions

1. (a)	**2.** (b)	**3.** (b)	**4.** (d)	**5.** (a)	**26.** (a)	**27.** (a)	**28.** (b)	**29.** (a)	**30.** (d)
6. (a)	**7.** (a)	**8.** (c)	**9.** (b)	**10.** (d)	**31.** (b)	**32.** (d)	**33.** (b)	**34.** (a)	**35.** (b)
11. (b)	**12.** (a)	**13.** (a)	**14.** (d)	**15.** (b)	**36.** (a)	**37.** (b)	**38.** (d)	**39.** (c)	**40.** (d)
16. (a)	**17.** (c)	**18.** (c)	**19.** (d)	**20.** (e)	**41.** (c)	**42.** (d)	**43.** (c)	**44.** (a)	**45.** (c)
21. (c)	**22.** (a)	**23.** (b)	**24.** (c)	**25.** (c)	**46.** (d)	**47.** (e)	**48.** (c)	**49.** (c)	

CHAPTER 3

Plant Kingdom

1. Match the following Columns.

Column I	Column II
A. Largest ovules	1. *Cannabis sativa*
B. *Cuscutta*	2. *Papaver sominiferum*
C. *Drosera*	3. *Cycas*
D. Morphine	4. Carnivorous plant
E. Opium	5. Parasitic plant

Codes

	A	B	C	D	E
(a)	3	5	4	1	2
(b)	1	3	2	4	5
(c)	3	2	1	5	4
(d)	4	2	1	3	5

2. Match the following Columns.

Column I	Column II
A. Cycadales	1. Vesseles present
B. Cycadofilicales	2. *Zamia*
C. Ginkgoals	3. Extinct genera
D. Gnetales	4. Single living species

Codes

	A	B	C	D			A	B	C	D
(a)	2	3	4	1	(b)		3	2	1	4
(c)	4	2	3	1	(d)		1	2	3	4

3. Match the following Columns.

Column I	Column II
A. Protonema	1. Numerous neck canal cell in the capsule
B. Columella	2. Bryophyte of economic importance
C. Sphagnum	3. Haploid structrue of Funaria
D. Funaria	4. Middle sterile region in moss capsul

Codes

	A	B	C	D
(a)	1	2	3	4
(b)	3	4	2	1
(c)	1	2	4	3
(d)	3	2	1	4

4. Match the following column with correct combination.

Column I	Column II
A. Anthoceros	1. Alga
B. *Adiantum*	2. Hornwort
C. *Sargassum*	3. Gametophyte
D. Prothallus	4. Inferae
E. Asthallus	5. Walking fern

Codes

	A	B	C	D	E
(a)	2	5	1	3	4
(b)	5	4	3	2	1
(c)	5	1	2	4	3
(d)	3	2	1	5	4

5. Match the following Columns.

Column I	Column II
A. Liverworts	1. *Funaria*
B. Hornworts	2. *Anthoceros*
C. Mosses	3. *Riccia*
D. Gnetales	4. *Ephedra*

Codes

	A	B	C	D
(a)	4	1	2	3
(b)	3	1	2	4
(c)	3	2	1	4
(d)	2	1	3	4

6. Match each term with its definition and choose your answer from the codes given:

I.	Isogamy	1.	The union of two gametes
II.	Syngamy	2.	Two gametes, one larger than the other
III.	Heterogamy	3.	Two kinds of gametes, one motile and other non motile
IV.	Anisogamy	4.	Two kinds of morphologically distinct gametes
V.	Oogamy	5.	Both gametes morphologically indistinguishable

Codes

	I	II	III	IV	V
(a)	1	2	3	4	5
(b)	4	1	2	3	4
(c)	5	1	2	4	3
(d)	3	1	2	4	5

7. Match Column-I with Column-II and select the correct option from the codes given below.

Column-I		Column-II
A. Psilopsida	(i)	***Psilotum***
B. Lycopsida	(ii)	***Equisetum***
C. Sphenopsida	(iii)	***Selaginella***
D. Pteropsida	(iv)	***Dryopteris***

(a) A-(i), B-(ii), C-(iii), D-(iv)
(b) A-(i), B-(iv), C-(iii), D-(ii)
(c) A-(i), B-(iii), C-(ii), D-(iv)
(d) A-(i), B-(iii), C-(iv), D-(ii)

8. Select the mismatched pair.

(a) Smallest angiosperm – *Rafflesia*
(b) Tallest angiosperm – *Eucalyptus regnans*
(c) Marine angiosperms – *Zostera, Thalassia*
(d) Angiosperm with smallest seed – Orchid

9. Which is the correct combination ?

Column-I		Column-II
(A) Agar	(I)	Single cell protein, use as food supplements by space travellers
(B) Algin	(II)	Red algae
(C) Carrageen	(III)	Brown algae
(D) *Chlorella and Spirullina*	(IV)	*Gelidium, Gracilaria*

(a) A → I; B → II; C → III; D → IV
(b) A → IV; B → III; C → II; D → I
(c) A → II; B → I; C → III; D → IV
(d) A → III; B → II; C → I; D → IV

10. Match the following

Column-I (Classes)		Column-II (Examples)
(A) Psilotopsida	(I)	*Dryopteris, Pteris, Adiantum*
(B) Lycopsida	(II)	*Equisetum*
(C) Sphenopsida	(III)	*Selaginella*
(D) Pteropsida	(IV)	*Lycopodium*
	(V)	*Psilotum*

(a) A → V; B → III; C → II; D → I
(b) A → I; B → II; C → III; D →! IV
(c) A → IV; B → III; C → II; D → I
(d) A → III; IV; B → V; C → I; D → II

11.

Column-I		Column-II
(A) Haplontic life cycle	(I)	Bryophytes, Pteridophytes, *Ectocarpus, Polysiphonia,* kelps
(B) Diplontic life cycle	(II)	Seed bearing plants (Gymnosperm and Angiosperm), *Fucus*
(C) Haplo-diplontic life cycle	(III)	Many algae (*Volvox, Spyrogyra,* and some species of *Chlamydomonas*)

Which is the correct combination ?

(a) A → III; B → II; C → I

(b) A → I; B → II; C → III

(c) A → II; B → I; C → III

(d) A → III; B → I; C → II

12. Match items in Column I with those in Column II :

Column -I		Column -II
(I)	Peritrichous flagellation	(J) *Ginkgo*
(II)	Living fossil	(K) *Macrocystis*
(III)	Rhizophore	(L) *Escherichia coli*
(IV)	Smallest flowering plant	(M) *Selaginella*
(V)	Largest perennial alga	(N) *Wolffia*

Select the correct answer from the following:

(a) I-L; II-J; III-M; IV-N; V-K;

(b) I-K; II-J; III-L; IV-M; V-N

(c) I-N; II-L; III-K; IV-N; V-J;

(d) I-J; II-K; III-N; IV-L; V-K

Solutions

1.	(a)	2.	(a)	3.	(b)	4.	(a)	5.	(c)
6.	(c)	7.	(c)	8.	(a)	9.	(b)	10.	(a)
11.	(a)	12.	(a)						

CHAPTER 4

Animal Kingdom

1. Match the following Columns.

Column I	Column II
(Phylum)	(Level of organisation)
A. Porifera	1. Cell tissue
B. Protozoa	2. Protoplasmic
C. Cnidaria	3. Organ system
D. Chordata	4. Cellular

Codes

	A	B	C	D
(a)	4	2	1	3
(b)	2	3	4	1
(c)	4	3	2	1
(d)	3	2	4	1

2. Match the follwoing Columns.

Column I	Column II
(Cells)	(Functions)
A. Epitheliomuscular cells	1. Totipotent
B. Glandular eclls	2. Unique cells of phylum-Coelenterata
C. Interstitial cells	3. Main cells of epidermis with the ability of contraction
D. Cnidoblats	4. Secretion
E. Sensory cells	5. Condition of stimulus

Codes

	A	B	C	D	E
(a)	3	4	1	2	5
(b)	1	2	3	4	5
(c)	5	4	3	2	1
(d)	4	3	2	1	5

3. Match the following Columns.

Column I	Column II
A. 10 hooked larva	1. Sponges
B. Acetabulum	2. *Hydra*
C. Stinging cells	3. *Planaria*
	4. *Ascaris*

Codes

	A	B	C			A	B	C
(a)	3	1	2	(b)	3	1	4
(c)	3	4	1	(d)	3	2	4

4. Match the following columns.

Column I	Column II
A. *Fasciola hepatica*	1. Sheep liver fluke
B. *Fasciola gigantica*	2. Cattle liver fluke
C. *Fasciolopsis buski*	3. Intestinal fluke
D. *Schistosoma mansoni*	4. Human blood fluke

Codes

	A	B	C	D			A	B	C	D
(a)	1	4	3	2	(b)	1	2	3	4
(c)	4	1	2	3	(d)	3	2	1	4

5. Match the following Columns.

Column I	Column II
(Symmetry)	(Phylum)
A. Asymmetry	1. Arthropoda
B. Radial symmetry	2. Ctenophora
C. Biradila symmetry	3. Cnidarai
D. Bilateral symmetry	4. Porifera

Codes

	A	B	C	D
(a)	4	2	3	1
(b)	2	3	4	1
(c)	3	2	4	1
(d)	4	3	2	1

6. Match the following Columns.

Column I (Phylum)	Column II (Body cavity)
A. Platyhelminthes	1. Enterocoel
B. Nematoda	2. No body cavity
C. Annelida	3. Pseudocoel
D. Echinodermata	4. Schizocoel

Codes

	A	B	C	D
(a)	4	2	3	1
(b)	2	3	4	1
(c)	4	3	2	1
(d)	3	2	4	1

7. Match the following Columns.

Column I	Column II
A. Mollusca	1. Prawn
B. Annelida	2. *Pila*
C. Arthropoda	3. Earthworm
D. Plathelminthes	4. *Fasciola*

Codes

	A	B	C	D			A	B	C	D
(a)	1	3	4	2		(b)	2	3	1	4
(c)	1	2	3	4		(d)	4	3	2	1

8. Match the following Columns.

Column I	Column II
A. Incomplete digetive system	1. Sponges
B. Cellular level of organisation	2. Coelentrates
C. Radial symmetry	3. Annelids
D. Pseudocoelomate	4. Platyhelminthes
E. Metamerism	5. Aschelminthes

Codes

	A	B	C	D	E
(a)	3	4	1	2	5
(b)	4	5	2	3	1
(c)	4	1	2	5	3
(d)	1	2	3	4	5
(e)	2	3	4	1	5

9. Match the Columns with reference to *Taenia*.

Column I	Column II
A. Mehlis' glands	1. Tegument formation
B. Vitelline gland	2. Osmoregulation and exceretion
C. Mesenchymal cells	3. Lubricate passage of capsules into uterus
D. Flame cells	4. Secretion of embryophore
	5. Capsule formation around zygote

Codes

	A	B	C	D			A	B	C	D
(a)	3	5	1	2		(b)	3	5	2	4
(c)	5	1	2	4		(d)	4	3	1	2

10. Match the following Columns.

Column I	Column II
A. Organ level	1. *Pheretima*
B. Cellular aggregate level	2. *Fasciola*
C. Tissue level	3. *Spongilla*
D. Organ system level	4. *Obelia*

Codes

	A	B	C	D			A	B	C	D
(a)	4	3	1	2		(b)	4	2	3	1
(c)	2	4	3	1		(d)	2	3	4	1

11. Match the following Columns.

Column I	Column II
A. *Physalia*	1. Sea anemone
B. *Meandrina*	2. Brain coral
C. *Gorgonia*	3. Sea fan
D. *Adamsia*	4. Portuguese man of war

Codes

	A	B	C	D			A	B	C	D
(a)	3	2	1	4		(b)	4	3	2	1
(c)	4	2	3	1		(d)	2	3	4	1
(e)	1	2	3	4						

12. Which one of the following phyla is correctly matched with its two general characteristics?

   (a) Chordata – Notochord at some stages and separate anal and urinary openings to the outside

   (b) Mollusca – Normally oviparous and development through a trochophore or veliger larva

   (c) Arthropoda – Body divided into head, thorax and abdomen; and respiration by tracheae

   (d) Echinodermata – Pentamerous radial symmetry and mostly internal fertilisation

13. Match the following Columns.

	Column I		Column II
A.	Nucleated RBCs	1.	Aves
B.	Sweat glands	2.	Mammary glands
C.	Carnivora	3.	Dogs, cats, tigers
D.	Cetacea	4.	Aquatic mammals

Codes

	A	B	C	D
(a)	1	2	3	4
(b)	4	3	2	1
(c)	3	2	1	4
(d)	1	2	4	3

14. Match the following Columns.

Column I	Column II	Column III
(Birds)	(Type of beak)	(Type of feet)
A. Duck	(i) Tearing and piercing	1. Raptorial
B. Sparrow	(ii) Water straining	2. Swimming
C. Owl	(iii) Seed eating	3. Perching
	(iv) Spatulate	4. Wading

Codes

	A	B	C
(a)	(iii), 3	(iv), 2	(ii), 4
(b)	(ii), 4	(iii), 3	(iv), 1
(c)	(i), 4	(iv), 1	(iii), 3
(d)	(ii), 2	(iii), 3	(i), 1

15. Identify and select the correct match in the Column I, II and III.

	Column I	Column II	Column III
(a)	Earthworm	Annelida	Superclass
(b)	Frog	Rana	Species
(c)	Lancelet	Vertebrata	Division
(d)	Walrus	Mammalia	Class

16. Match the following Columns.

	Column I		Column II
A.	Ostracodermi	1.	Lobe finned fishes
B.	Coelacanth	2.	*Exocoetus*
C.	Cyclostomes	3.	Extinct jawless fibres
D.	Osteichthyes	4.	Hagfish

Codes

	A	B	C	D
(a)	3	1	4	2
(b)	2	3	1	4
(c)	1	3	2	4
(d)	3	2	4	1

17. Match the following list of animals with their level of organisation and choose the correct sequence.

	Column I		Column II
A.	Organ level	(p)	*Pheretima*
B.	Cellular aggregate level	(q)	*Fasciola*
C.	Tissue level	(r)	*Spongilla*
D.	Organ system level	(t)	*Obleia*

(a) A-(s), B-(r), C-(p), D-(q)
(b) A-(s), B-(q), C-(r), D-(p)
(c) A-(q), B-(s), C-(r), D-(p)
(d) A-(q), B-(r), C-(s), D-(p)

18. Match the following and select the correct answer.

	Column I		Column II
A.	Choanocytes	1.	Platyhelminthes
B.	Cnidoblasts	2.	Ctenophora
C.	Flame cells	3.	Porifera
D.	Nephridia	4.	Coelenterata
E.	Comb plates	5.	Annelida

(a) A-2, B-1, C-4, D-5, E-3

(b) A-2, B-4, C-1, D-5, E-3

(c) A-5, B-1, C-3, D-2, E-4

(d) A-3, B-4, C-1, D-5, E-2

(e) A-3, B-1, C-4, D-5, E-2

19. Match the following and choose the correct option.

	Column I		Column II
(i)	*Physalia*	A.	Sea anemone
(ii)	*Meandrina*	B.	Brain coral
(iii)	*Gorgonia*	C.	Sea fan
(iv)	*Adamsia*	D.	Portuguese man-of-war

(a) (i)-C; (ii)-B; (iii)-A; (iv)-D

(b) (i)-D; (ii)-C; (iii)-B; (iv)-A

(c) (i)-D; (ii)-B; (iii)-C; (iv)-A

(d) (i)-B; (ii)-C; (iii)-A; (iv)-D

(e) (i)-A; (ii)-B; (iii)-C; (iv)-D

20. Match Column I with Column II and choose the correct answer.

	Column I		Column II
I.	Incomplete digestive system	A.	Sponges
II.	Cellular levle of organisation	B.	Coelenterates
III.	Radial symmetry	C.	Annelids
IV.	Pseudocoelomate	D.	Platyhelminthes
V.	Metamerism	E.	Aschelminthes

(a) I - C, II - D, III - A, IV - B, V - E

(b) I - D, II - E, III - B, IV - C, V - A

(c) I - D, II - A, III - B, IV - D, V - C

(d) I - A, II - B, III - C, IV - D, V - E

(e) I - B, II - C, III - D, IV - A, V - E

21. Which one of the following groups of 3 animals each is correctly matched with their one characteristic morphological features?

	Animals		Morphological features
(a)	Centipede, Prawn, Sea urchin	–	Jointed appendages
(b)	Cockroach, Locust, *Taenia*	–	Metameric segmentation
(c)	Scorpion, Spider, Cockroach	–	Ventral solid nerve cord
(d)	Liver fluke, Sea anemone, Sea cucumber	–	Bilateral symmetry

22. Choose the correct pair.

(a)	Radial symmetry	–	Coelenterates
(b)	Coelomates	–	Aschelminthes
(c)	Metamerism	–	Molluscs
(d)	Triploblastic	–	Sponges
(e)	Metagenesis	–	Echinoderms

23. Match Column I with Column II and Column III. Choose the correct option.

	Column I		Column II		Column III
1.	Cnidocytes	A.	*Ctenoplana*	(i)	Balancing
2.	Statocyst	B.	*Fasciola*	(ii)	Defence
3.	Radula	C.	*Pennatula*	(iii)	Feeding
4.	Flame cells	D.	*Locusta*	(iv)	Locomotion
5.	Comb plates	E.	*Pila*	(v)	Osmo-regulation

(a) 1-A-(ii), 2-B-(v), 3-E-(iii), 4-C-(i), 5-D-(iv)

(b) 1-A-(iii), 2-B-(iv), 3-E-(v), 4-C-(ii), 5-D-(i)

(c) 1-A-(ii), 2-B-(i), 3-E-(iii), 4-C-(v), 5-D-(iv)

(d) 1-A-(i), 2-B-(ii), 3-E-(iv), 4-C-(iii), 5-D-(v)

(e) 1-A-(ii), 2-B-(v), 3-E-(iv), 4-C-(i), 5-D-(iii)

24. Match the following organisms with respective characteristics.

(A) *Pila*   (i)   Flame cells

(B) *Bombyx*   (ii)   Comb plates

(C) *Pleurobrachia*   (iii) Radula

(D) *Taenia*   (iv) Malpighian tubules

Select the correct option from the following.

	(A)	(B)	(C)	(D)
(a)	(iii)	(ii)	(iv)	(i)
(b)	(iii)	(ii)	(i)	(iv)
(c)	(iii)	(iv)	(ii)	(i)
(d)	(ii)	(iv)	(iii)	(i)

25.

Organ	Phylum	Function
Parapodia	Annelida	A
B	Ctenophora	Locomotion
C	Mollusca	Rasping organ
Malpighian tubules	Arthropoda	D
Cnidoblasts	Coelenterata	E

From the above table find out the missing organ or function - A, B, C, D and E respectively.

(a) A-swimming, B-comb plates, C-radula, D-excretion, E-defence

(b) A-defence, B-radula, C-comb plates, D-excretion, E-swimming

(c) A-protection, B-parapodia, C-visceral mass, D-locomotion, E-excretion

(d) A-swimming, B-parapodis, C-comb plates, D-anchorag, E-digestion

26. In which one of the following the genus name, its two characters and its phylum are not correctly matched, whereas the remaining three are correct?

(a) *Pila*   (i) Body segmented   Mollusca

           (ii) Mouth with radula

(b) *Asterias*   (i) Spiny skinned   Echinodermata

           (ii) Water vascular system

(c) *Sycon*   (i) Pore bearing   Porifera

           (ii) Canal system

(d) *Periplaneta* (i) Jointed appendages   Arthropoda

           (ii) Chitinous exoskeleton

27. Match the following genera with their respective phylum.

(1) *Ophiura*   (i)   Mollusca

(2) *Physalia*   (ii)   Platyhelminthes

(3) *Pinctada*   (iii) Echinodermata

(4) *Planaria*   (iv) Coelenterata

Select the correct option.

(a) (1)-(iv), (2)-(i), (3)-(iii), (4)-(ii)

(b) (1)-(iii), (2)-(iv), (3)-(i), (4)-(ii)

(c) (1)-(i), (2)-(iii), (3)-(iv), (4)-(ii)

(d) (1)-(iii), (2)-(iv), (3)-(ii), (4)-(i)

28. Select the option that correctly matches characteristic features with the group of three animals.

(a) Skeleton of spicules - *Sycon, adamsia, spongilla*

(b) Excretion by flame - *Taenia, Fasciola, Ancylostoma*

(c) Mouth contains radula - *Dentalium, Octopus, Ophiura*

(d) Jointed appendages - *Limulus, Apis, Laccifer*

29. Some salient features and phyla of organisms are given below. Select the option which shows correct combination of organism, its phylum and salient features.

(a) *Hydra*   Coelen-terata   Bilateral symmetry   Cnidoblasts present

(b) *Planaria*   Platyhel-minthes   Bilateral symmetry   High regeneration capacity

(c) *Ancylo-stoma*   Annelida   Bilateral symmetry   Elongated and worm shape

(d) *Octopus*   Mollusca   Radial symmetry   External skeleton of shell present

30. Which one of the following matching pairs is wrong?

(a) Mollusca-Pseudocoel

(b) Cnidaria-Nematocyst

(c) Annelida-Chloragogan cells

(d) Echinodermata-Water vascular system

31. Column I contains larval stages and column II contains the groups to which they belong. Match them correctly and choose the right answer.

	Column I		Column II
A.	Planula	1.	Annelida
B.	Tornaria	2.	Mollusca
C.	Trochopore	3.	Arthropoda
D.	Bipinnaria	4.	Chordata
E.	Glochidium	5.	Echinodermata
		6.	Coelenterata

(a) A-6, B-4, C-1, D-5, E-2

(b) A-2, B-5, C-1, D-4, E-6

(c) A-5, B-4, C-3, D-2, E-1

(d) A-4, B-3, C-2, D-1, E-5

32. Find the wrongly matched pair.

	Animal	–	**Excretory organ/ structure**
(a)	*Balanoglossus*	–	Proboscis gland
(b)	Earthworm	–	Nephridia
(c)	Grasshopper	–	Malpighian tubules
(d)	Prawn	–	Flame cells
(e)	*Amphioxus*	–	Protonephridia

33. Match the name of the animal (column I), with one characteristic (column II), and the phylum/ class (column III) to which it belongs.

	Column I	Column II	Column II
(a)	*Limulus*	Body covered by chitinous exoskeleton	Pisces
(b)	*Adamsia*	Radially	Porifera
(c)	*Petromyzan*	Ectoparasite	Cyclostomata
(d)	*Ichthyophis*	Terrestrial	Reptilia

34. Match the following and select the correct option.

A.	Cyclostomes	(1)	Hemichordata
B.	Aves	(2)	Urochordata
C.	Tunicates	(3)	Agnatha
D.	*Balanoglossus*	(4)	Pisces
E.	Osteichtyes	(5)	Tetrapod

(a) A-1, B-2, C-3, D-4, E-5

(b) A-2, B-3, C-4, D-1, E-5

(c) A-3, B-5, C-2, D-1, E-4

(d) A-3, B-1, C-5, D-2, E-4

(e) A-5, B-3, C-2, D-1, E-4

35. Choose the correct option.

(a) Mammalia – *Ornithorynchus, Macropus, Betta*

(b) Aves – *Pteropus, Neophron, Aptenodytes*

(c) Amphibia – *Ichthyophis, Hyla, Salamandra*

(d) Reptilia – *Bangarus, Pristis, Crocodylus*

36. Identify the aquatic mammal(s) from the following.

(i) *Balaenoptera*

(ii) *Equus*

(iii) *Delphinus*

(iv) *Pteropus*

(v) *Felis*

(a) (i) and (iii) (b) (ii) and (iv)

(c) (v) only (d) (iv) and (v)

37. Which of the following is correct?

(a) *Macropus* – Ear pinna, body hari, 4 chambered heart

(b) *Pavo* – Long bones filled with bone marrow, forelimbs modified to wings

(c) *Ichtyophis* – Eyes lack eyelids, scales present on skin

(d) *Limulus* – Chitinous exoskeleton, respiration through coxal glands

38. Which one of the following animals is correctly matched with its one characteristic and the taxon?

	Animal	Characteristic	Taxon
(a)	Millipede	Ventral nerve cord	Arachnida
(b)	Sea Anemone	Triploblastic	Cnidaria
(c)	Silver fish	Pectoral and pelvic fins	Chordata
(d)	Duck-billed platypus	Oviparous	Mammalia

39. In which one of the following the genus name, its two characters and its class/phylum are correctly matched?

	Genus name		Two charcters Class/Phylum
(a)	*Ascaris*	(i)	Body segmented annelida
		(ii)	Males and females distince
(b)	*Salamandra*	(i)	A tympanum amphibia representes ear
		(ii)	Fertilisation is external
(c)	*Pteropus*	(i)	Skin possess Mammalia hair
		(ii)	Oviparous
(d)	*Aurelia*	(i)	Cnidoblasts
		(ii)	Organ level of organisation

40. Identify the Phylum X.

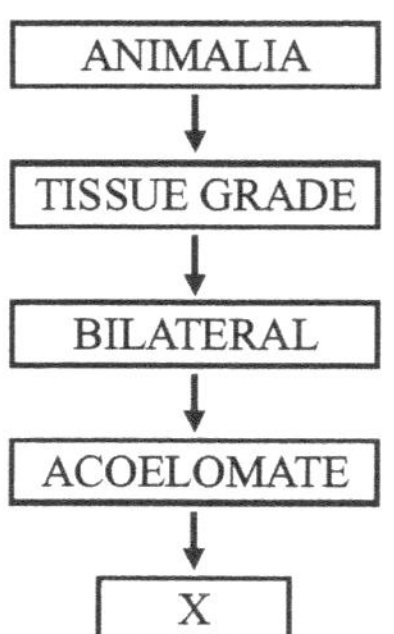

(a) Hemichordata

(b) Aschelminthes

(c) Platyhelminthes

(d) Ctenophora

41. Identify the correct sequence of classification of the following.

I.   Eutheria

II. Mammalia

III. Tuhulidentata

IV. Lagomorpha

V.   Hyracoidea

(a) II → IV → I → V → III

(b) II → I → IV → III → V

(c) II → I → IV → V → III

(d) I → V → III → II → IV

42. See the following figures and choose the correct option with their respective orders.

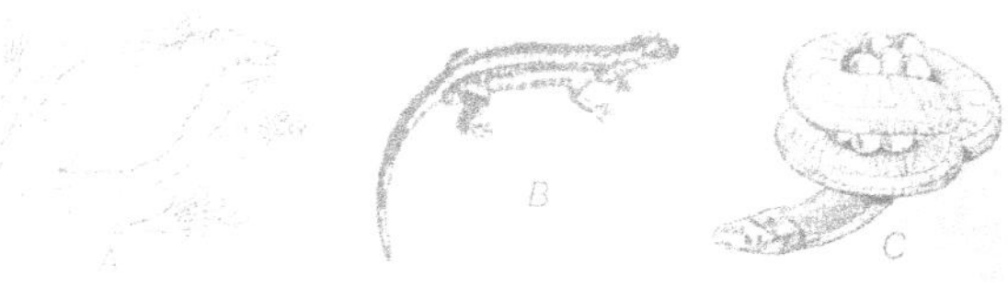

(a) A-Caecilians B-Caudata   C-Anura

(b) A-Caudata   B-Anura   C-Caecilians

(c) A-Anura   B-Caecilians C-Caudata

(d) A-Anura   B-Caudata   C-Caecilians

43. Choose the incorrect pair from the following.

(a) Emu-Flightless bird and confined to Australia

(b) Kiwi-National bird of New Zealand

(c) Ostrich-Wings modified into paddles (flippers)

(d) Dodo-Recently extinct bird

44. In most simple type of canal system of Porifera, water flows through which one of the following ways?

(a) Ostia → Spongocoel → Osculum → Exterior

(b) Spongocoel → Ostia → Osculum → Exterior

(c) Osculum → Spongocoel → Osita → Exterior

(d) Osculum → Ostia → Spongocoel → Exterior

Solutions

1. (a) 2. (a) 3. (a) 4. (b) 5. (a)

6. (b) 7. (b) 8. (c) 9. (a) 10. (d)

11. (c)

12. **(b)** Devil fish (*Octopus*) is a mollusc which can paralyse its prey by poisonous saliva. It feeds on prawns, crabs and small fishes.

13. (a) 14. (d)

15. **(d)** Out of the options given the correct one is walrus a large flippered marine mammal which belongs to class-Mammalia.

Correct matches for the three options are

Earthworm	Annelida	Phylum
Frog	Rana	Genus
Lancelet	Vertebrata	Subphylum

16. (a) 17. (d) 18. (d) 19. (c) 20. (c)

21. **(c)** Scorpion, spider and cockroach belonging to Phylum Arthropoda, have annelidan type of nervous system which constists of a nerve ring and a solid double ventral nerve cord with gangila.

22. (a) 23. (c)

24. **(c)** The buccal cavity of *Pila* (apple snail) possess rasping organ, radula, with transverse row of teeth for cutting grass. *Bombyx* (silk moth), an insect has Malpighian tubules, as excretory organ. *Pleurobrachia* is a ctenophore having eight ciliary plates called comb plates. *Taenia* is a platyhelminth having flame cells for excretion and osmoregulation.

25. (a)

26. **(a)** *Pila* belongs to phylum Mollusca. The body of molluscs (soft bodied animals) is unsegmented, with a distinct head, muscular foot and visceral hump. Buccal cavity of *Pila*, contains a brownish, curved, ribbon - like structure called radula. Radula acts as a rasping organ.

27. (b)

28. **(d)** In poriferans, the body is supported by a skeleton made up of spicules or spongin fibres. *Sycon* and *Spongilla* are examples of poriferans, whereas *Adamsia* is a coelenterate. In platyhelminths, specialised cells called flame cells help in excretion. *Taenia* and *Fasciola* are platyhelminths whereas *Ancylostoma* is an aschelminth. In molluscs, mouth contains a file-like rasping organ for feeding called radula. *Dentalium* and *Octopus* are molluscs whereas *Ophiura* is an echinoderm. Arthropods have jointed appendages. *Limulus*, *Apis* and *Laccifer* all three are arthropods.

29. **(b)** *Hydra* shows radial symmetry, *Ancylostoma* is an aschelminth. *Octopus* shows bilateral symmetry and also lacks an external skeleton of shell.

30. **(a)** Molluscs coelomates, i.e., possess true coelom. In molluscs, coelom, a body cavity develops as a split in the mesoderm sheet and is filled with coelomic fluid.

31. **None of the options is correct.**

Planula	–	Coelentrata
Tornaria	–	Hemichordata

(This was earlier considered as a sub-phylum under phylum chordata. But now it is placed as a separate phylum under non-chordata).

Trochophore	–	Annelida
Bipinnaria	–	Echinodermata
Glochidium	–	Mollusca

32. **(d)** Prawn is an Arthropod and have green glands or Malpighian tubules as excretory organs. Flame cells are excretory organs of Platyhelminthes.

33. **(c)** *Limulus* belongs to Phylum Arthropoda. *Adamsia* belongs to Phylum Coelenterata. *Petromyzon* (lamprey) (Cyclostomata) is a sanguivorous ectoparasite of larger fishes. *Ichthyophis* is a limbless amphibian and belongs to class Amphibia.

34. **(c)**

35. **(c)** *Betta* belongs to Class Osteichthyes, *Pteropus* belongs to class Mammalia, *Pristis* belongs to class chondrichthyes and Bangarus belongs to class *Reptilia*.

36. **(a)**   **37.** **(a)**

38. **(d)** Duck-billed platypus is oviparous and belongs to Class Mammalia. Millipede belongs to class Diplopoda. Sea anemone has two germ layers, *i.e.*, they are diploblastic. Silverfish (*Lepisma*) belongs to Non-chordata. It is an insect.

39. **None of the optios is correct**

Ascaris is member of Phylum Nemotoda, which are round worms. They do not have segmented body. In *Ascaris* female is longer than male.

Salamandra is member of amphibia. Salamanders do not have tympanum, although they have greatly reduced middle ears and fertilisation is usually internal in them.

Pteropus is member of Class Mammalia. They are viviparous a mantle of golden hair covers the head, neck and shoulders in *Pteropus*.

Aurelia is member of coelenterata, which has tissue level of organisation. Its epidermis contain cnidoblasts (stinging cells) for defence and offence purpose.

40. **None of the options is correct.**

Hemichordata, Aschelminthes and Platyhelminthes show organ system level of organisation, *i.e.*, organs get associated to form functional systems, each system concerned with a specific physiology function. Ctenophores have tissue grade level of organisation but are biradially symmetrical, *i.e.*, (radial + bilateral)

41. **(b)**   **42.** **(d)**   **43.** **(c)**   **44.** **(a)**

Morphology of Flowering Plants

1. Match the column A (type of root) with column B (example of plants)

	Column A		**Column B**
I.	Tap roots	1.	Maize
II.	Fibrous roots	2.	Mustard
		3.	Wheat
		4.	Sugarcane
		5.	Neem

(a) I-2, 4 and II-1, 3, 5
(b) I-2, 5 and II-1, 3, 4
(c) I-2, 5 and II-1, 3
(d) I-5 and II-1, 2, 3, 4

2. Match the column I with column II and choose the correct options

	Column I		**Column II**
A.	Storage roots	1.	*Taeniophyllum*
B.	Pneumatophores	2.	*Avicennia*
C.	Haustoria	3.	Carrot
D.	Prop roots	4.	Cuscuta
E.	Assimilatory roots	5.	Banyan

(a) A-3, B-2, C-4, D-5, E-1
(b) A-2, B-3, C-4, D-5, E-1
(c) A-3, B-4, C-5, D-1, E-2
(d) A-3, B-1, C-2, D-5, E-4

3. Match the column and find out the correct combination:

	A		
A.	Storage	1.	*Taeniophyllum*
B.	Pneumatophores	2.	*Avicennia*
C.	Haustoria	3.	Carrot
D.	Prop roots	4.	*Cuscuta*
E.	Assimilatory roots	5.	Banyan

(a) A-3, B-2, C-4, D-5, E-1
(b) A-2, B-3, C-4, D-5, E-1
(c) A-3, B-4, C-5, D-1, E-2
(d) A-3, B-1, C-2, D-5, E-4

4. Match the following columns and choose the correct options:

	Position of modified root	Genus	Function
A.	Underground	Turnip	Photosynthesis
B.	Aerial	*Taeniophyllum*	Liliaceae
C.	Aerial	*Vanda*	Respiration
D.	Underground	*Asparagus*	Storage

(a) A and B
(b) B and C
(c) B and D
(d) A and C

5. Which of the following pair is not correct?

	Column I		**Column II**
A.	Stem tendril	(1)	Grapes
B.	Leaf bladder	(2)	*Gloriosa*
C.	Leaf tendril	(3)	Pea
D.	Phyllode	(4)	*Australian acacia*

6. Match the columns and find out the correct combination:

A.	Opuntia	1.	Stem thorns
B.	Asparagus	2.	Phyllocaldes
C.	Citrus	3.	Cladodes

(a) A-1, B-2, C-3
(b) A-2, B-3, C-1
(c) A-3, B-2, C-1
(d) A-2, B-1, C-3

7. Match the columns and find out the correct combination:

A.	Horizontally growing underground stem	1.	*Amorphophallus*
B.	Obliquely growing underground stem	2.	*Curcuma*
C.	Reduced disc like stem	3.	*Allium cepa*
D.	Vertically growing underground stem with special adventitious roots americana	4.	*Chrysanthemum*
		5.	*Agave americana*

(a) A-2, B-4, C-3, D-5
(b) A-1, B-2, C-3, D-5
(c) A-2, B-4, C-3, D-1
(d) A-1, B-4, C-3, D-2

8. Match the columns and find out the correct combination:

A.	*Pistia*	Single internodal branch	Offset
B.	*Oxalis*	Many nodes and internodes	Runner
C.	*Pistia*	Bulged internode	Stem tuber
D.	Sweet potato	Nodes bear eyes	Tuberous stem

(a) A & B   (b) C & D

(c) B & C   (d) A & B

9. Match the column I with column II and choose the correct option:

	Column I		Column II
A.	Largest flower	1.	*Rafflesia*
B.	Zygomorphic flower	2.	*Brassica*
C.	Actinomorphic flower	3.	*Pisum*
D.	Asymmetric flower	4.	*Capsicum*
		5.	*Cana*

	A	B	C	D		A	B	C	D
(a)	1	3	2	5	(b)	5	3	2	1
(c)	2	3	1	5	(d)	3	1	2	4

10. Which of the following option is correct?

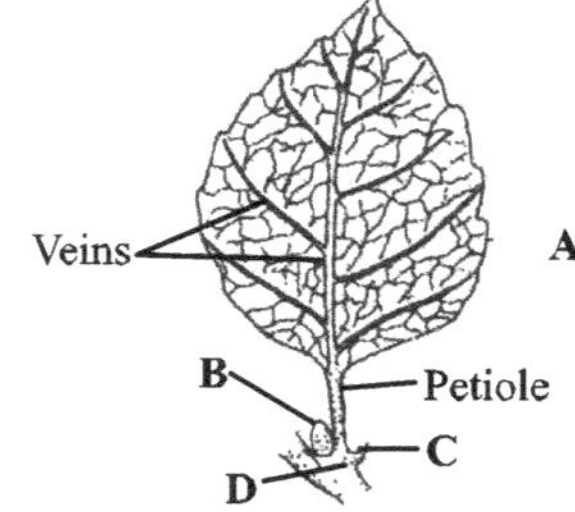

	A	B	C	D
(a)	Lamina	Axillary bud	Stipule	Leaf base
(b)	Lamina	Stipule	Axillary bud	Leaf base
(c)	Lamina	Axillary bud	Stipule	Pedicel
(d)	Leaflet	Axillary bud	Stipule	Leaf base

11. Chosse the correct combinations.

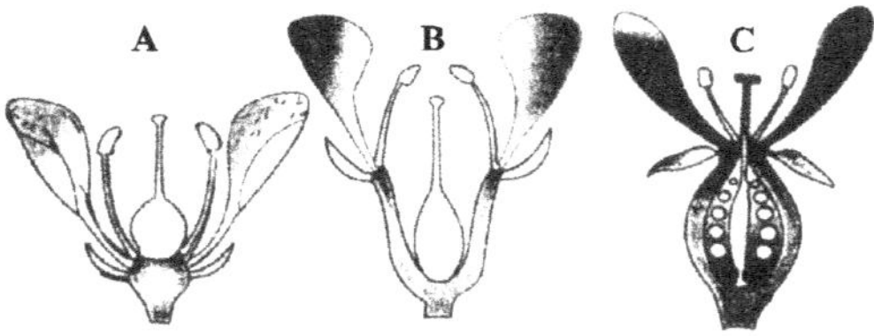

I. Hypogynous flower
II. Perigynous flower
III. Epigynous flower

(a) A-I, B-II, C-III
(b) A-I, B-III, C-II
(c) A-III, B-II, C-I
(d) A-III, B-I, C-II

12. Which is the correct combination?

	Column I		Column II		Column III
A.	Mariginal	I.		p.	Sunflower, Marigold
B.	Axile	II.		q.	Dianthus, Primrose
C.	Parietal	III.		r.	Musatrd, Argemone

D.   Free Central   IV.

s.   China rose, Tomato, Lemon

E.   Basal   V.

t.   Pea

(a)   A- V, t; B -II, s; C -I, r; D -III, q; E -IV, p
(b)   A - I, t; B - II, s; C - III, r; D - IV, p; E - V, q
(c)   A - V, p; B - II, s; C - I, q; D - III, r; E - IV, t
(d)   A - V, p; B - III, q; C - II, s; D - I, t; E - IV, r

13. Which one of the following option is correct?

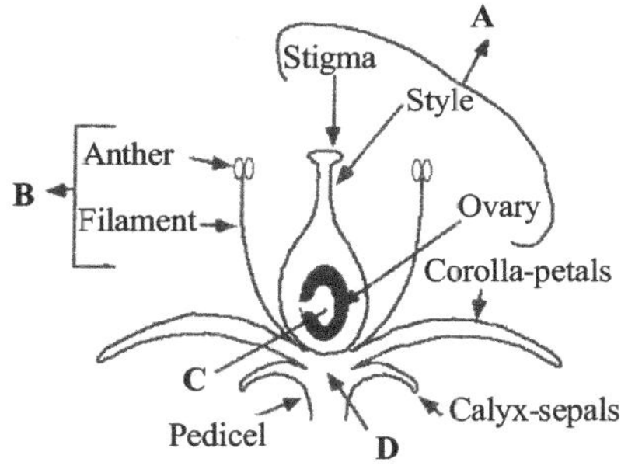

	A	**B**	**C**	**D**
(a)	Gynoecium	Megasporo-phyll	Ovule	Thalamus
(b)	Gynoecium	Stamen	Seed	Thalamus
(c)	Microsporo-phyll	Stamen	Ovule	Thalamus
(d)	Gynoecium	Stamen	Ovule	Thalamus

14. Matching the following and choose the correct option

	Column I		Column II
A.	Bud in the	I.	Pitcher plant axil of leaf and Venus fly trap
B.	Outer layer of	II.	Cacti seed coat
C.	Spines	III.	Testa (modified leaves)
D.	Leaves modiied	IV.	Simple leaf to catch insects
E.	Fleshy leaves	V.	Garlic and onion with stored food

	A	**B**	**C**	**D**	**E**
(a)	I	II	III	IV	V
(b)	V	IV	III	II	I
(c)	IV	III	II	I	V
(d)	IV	II	III	I	V

15. Choose the correct combinations.

	Column I		Column II
A.	Gamosepalous	I.	Flower of lily
B.	Polysepalous	II.	Sterile anther
C.	Gamopetalous	III.	Free petals
D.	Polypetalous	IV.	Free sepals
E.	Epiphyllous	V.	Fused petals
F.	Staminode	VI.	Fused sepals

	A	**B**	**C**	**D**	**E**	**F**
(a)	IV	V	III	I	VI	II
(b)	IV	V	III	I	II	VI
(c)	VI	IV	V	III	I	II
(d)	VI	IV	V	III	II	I

16. Matching the following and choose the correct option.

	Column I		Column II
A.	Coleorrhiza	I.	Grapes
B.	Food storing tissue	II.	Mango
C.	Parthenocarpic fruit	III.	Maize
D.	Single seeded fruit developing from monocarpellary superior ovary	IV.	Radicle
E.	Membranous seed coat	V.	Endosperm

(a)   A - III, B-I, C -IV, D - II, E - V
(b)   A - IV, B-II, C - V, D - I, E - III
(c)   A - V, B-I, C - III, D - IV, E - II
(d)   A - IV, B - V, C - I, D - II, E - III

17. Which is the correct combinations ?

	Column I (Members of Fabaceae)		Column II (Economic importance)
A.	Gram, sem, moong, soyabean	I.	Medicine
B.	Soyabean, groundnut	II.	Ornamental
C.	Indigofera	III.	Fodder
D.	Sunhemp	IV.	Fibres
E.	*Sesbania,* *Trifolium*	V.	Dye
F.	Lupin, Sweet potato	VI.	Edible oil
E.	*Mulaaithi*	VII.	Pulses

(a) A - I, B - II, C - III, D - IV, E - V, F - VI, G - VII
(b) A-VII, B - VI, C - V, D -IV, E - III, F - II, G-I
(c) A- II, B- IV, C - VI, D - I, E - III, F - V, G - VII
(d) A- I, B - III, C - V, D - VII, E - II, F - IV, G - VI

18. Match the following and choose the correct option

	List I		List II
I.	Acicular	(A)	Grass
II.	Linear	(B)	*Nerium*
III.	Lanceolate	(C)	Banana
IV.	Oblong	(D)	Pine

(a) I-D, II-A, III-B, IV-C
(b) I-D, II-A, III-C, IV-B
(c) I-D, II-B, III-C, IV-A
(d) I-D, II-C, III-B, IV-A

19. Match column I with II and choose the right option

	Column I		Column II
1.	*Artemisia*	A.	Fibre
2.	*Astragalus*	B.	Insecticide
3.	*Phormium*	C.	Rat poison
4.	*Chrysanthemum*	D.	Medicine
5.	*Withania*	E.	Vermifuge
		F.	Gum

(a) 1 - D, 2 - C, 3 - F, 4 - B, 5 - E
(b) 1 - B, 2 - E, 3 - D, 4 - C, 5 - A
(c) 1 - C, 2 - E, 3 - A, 4 - F, 5 - D
(d) 1 - E, 2 - F, 3 - A, 4 - B, 5 - D

20. Match the following and choose the correct combination from the options given below.

	Column I (Placentation in)		Column II (Represented Types)
A.	Basal	1	*Dianthus*
B.	Free central	2	Pea
C.	Parietal	3	Lemon
D.	Axile	4	Marigold
E.	Marginal	5	*Argemone*

(a) A – 1, B – 2, C – 3, D – 4, E – 5
(b) A – 2, B – 3, C – 4, D – 5, E – 1
(c) A – 4, B – 1, C – 5, D – 3, E – 2
(d) A – 4, B – 3, C – 5, D – 1, E – 2

21. Find out the pairs, which are correctly matched with respect to aestivation of petals.

I.	Valvate	-	*Calotropis*
II.	Twisted	-	Bean
III.	Imbricate	-	*Cassia*
IV.	Vexillary	-	China rose

(a) II and IV   (b) I and II
(c) I and III   (d) III and IV

22. Match the following and choose the correct combination from the options given.

	Column I (Family)		Column II (Androecium formula)
A.	Brassicaceae	1.	A_{3+3}
B.	Fabaceae	2.	$A_{(5)}$
C.	Solanaceae	3.	$A_{(9)+1}$
D.	Liliaceae	4.	A_{2+4}

(a) A – 4; B – 3; C – 2, D – 1
(b) A – 1; B – 2; C – 3, D – 4
(c) A – 2; B – 3; C – 4, D – 1
(d) A – 3; B – 4; C – 1, D – 2

23. Match the following and choose the correct combination from the options given.

	Column I (Position of floral parts on thalamus)		Column II (Represented in)
(A)	Hypogynous	(1)	Ray florets of sunflower
(B)	Perigynous	(2)	Brinjal
(C)	Epigynous	(3)	Peach

(a) A-2, B-1, C-3
(b) A-1, B-2, C-3
(c) A-3, B-2, C-1
(d) A-2, B-3, C-1

24. Matching the following and choose the correct option

Column – I		Column – II
A.	Tubercular storage roots	I. *Tinospora*
B.	Pneumatophores	II. *Heritiera*
C.	Haustoria	III. *Asparagus*
D.	Prop-roots	IV. *Viscum*
E.	Assimilatory roots	V. *Screwpine*

(a) A–II, B–III, C–IV, D–V, E–I
(b) A–III, B–IV, C–V, D–I, E–II
(c) A–III, B–I, C–II, D–V, E–IV
(d) A–III, B–II, C–IV, D–V, E–I

25. Chosse the correct combinations

List-I		List-II
(A)	Entire leaf modified into a spine	(i) *Clematis*
(B)	Leaf except stipules modified into a tendril	(ii) *Citrus*
(C)	Stipules modified into a tendril	(iii) *Euphorbia*
(D)	First leaf of axillary bud modified into a spine	(iv) *Lathyrus*

	A	B	C	D
(a)	(iii)	(iv)	(i)	(ii)
(b)	(iii)	(i)	(iv)	(ii)
(c)	(ii)	(iii)	(i)	(iv)
(d)	(iv)	(ii)	(i)	(iii)

26. Select the correct option

List I		List II
A.	Spike	I. *Bougainvillea*
B.	Capitulum	II. *Coleus*
C.	Dichasial cyme	III. *Adhatoda*
D.	Multiparous cyme	IV. *Zinnia*
E.	Verticillaster	V. *Asclepias*

(a) A – III, B – IV, C – I, D – V, E – II
(b) A – III, B – I, C – IV, D – V, E – II
(c) A – II, B – IV, C – I, D – V, E – III
(d) A – IV, B – II, C – V, D – I, E – III

27. Match the following and choose the correct combination.

Column I		Column II
A.	Pollen grains	I. Microsporangia
B.	Pollen sacs	II. Microspores
C.	Stamens	III. Microsporophylls

	A	B	C
(a)	I	II	III
(b)	II	I	III
(c)	III	I	II
(d)	I	III	II

28. Choose the correct option-

Column I		Column II
A.	Apple	I. Outer portion of receptacle
B.	Coconut	II. Fleshy thalamus
C.	Jack fruit	III. Thalamus & pericarp
D.	Guava	IV. Endosperm
E.	Pineapple	V. Bract, perianth & seeds

(a) A – II, B – III, C – IV, D – V, E – I
(b) A – V, B – III, C – I, D – IV, E – II
(c) A – II, B – III, C – I, D – V, E – IV
(d) A – II, B – IV, C – V, D – III, E – I
(e) A – V, B – IV, C – III, D – II, E – I

29. Match the following

List-I		List-II
(1)	Spongy aril	(I) *Jussiaea*
(2)	Multiple epidermis	(II) *Pistia*
(3)	Respiratory roots	(III) *Nerium*
(4)	Root pockets	(IV) *Sagittaria*
		(V) *Nymphaea*

	A	B	C	D
(a)	I	III	II	V
(b)	II	I	IV	III
(c)	IV	II	III	I
(d)	V	III	I	II

30. Match the following-

List-I		List-II
(A)	Coleorhiza	(I) Development of sporophyte directly from gametophyte without intervention of gametes

(B) Apogamy	(II) Development of gametophyte directly from sporophyte without the involvement of reduction division.	(D) Caudex	(IV) Protective covering of radicle
(C) Indusium	(III) An unbranched columnar stem with a crown of leaves.		(V) Protective structure of a sorus.

	A	B	C	D
(a)	V	II	IV	I
(b)	IV	I	V	III
(c)	III	V	II	IV
(d)	II	III	I	V

Solutions

1. (b)	2. (a)	3. (a)	4. (c)	5. (b)	16. (d)	17. (b)	18. (a)	19. (d)	20. (c)
6. (b)	7. (c)	8. (b)	9. (a)	10. (a)	21. (c)	22. (a)	23. (d)	24. (d)	25. (a)
11. (a)	12. (a)	13. (d)	14. (c)	15. (c)	26. (a)	27. (b)	28. (d)	29. (d)	30. (b)

Anatomy of Flowering Plants

1. Pair the species with the type of wood.

Species		Type of wood
A. *Tectona grandis*	I	Softwood
B. *Cedrus deodara*	II	Hardwood
C. *Shorea robusta*		
D. *Dalbergia sissoo*		

	A	B	C	D
(a)	I	II	II	I
(b)	I	I	II	II
(c)	II	I	II	II
(d)	II	I	I	II

2. Match the names of the structures listed under column-I with the functions given under column-II, choose the answer which gives the correct combination of the alphabets of the two columns :

Column-I (Structure)	Column-II (Function)
A. Stomata	(i) Protection of stem
B. Bark	(ii) Plant movement
C. Cambium	(iii) Secondary growth
D. Hydathode	(iv) Transpiration
	(v) Guttation

(a) A – (v), B – (iii), C – (i), D – (iv)
(b) A – (i), B – (iv), C – (v), D – (iii)
(c) A – (ii), B – (iv), C – (i), D – (iii)
(d) A – (iv), B – (i), C – (iii), D – (v)

3. Match the following and choose the correct option

A.	Cuticle	i.	guard cells
B.	Bulliform cells	ii.	outer layer
C.	Stomata	iii.	waxy layer
D.	Epidermis	iv.	empty colourless cell

(a) A–iii, B–iv, C–i, D–ii
(b) A–i, B–ii, C–iii, D–iv
(c) A–iii, B–ii, C–iv, D–i
(d) A–iii, B–ii, C–i, D–iv

4. Match the Column I with Column II and choose the correct combination

A.	Radial vascular bundle	i.	*Cucurbita pepo*
B.	Collateral vascular bundle	ii.	*Dracaena*
C.	Bicollateral vascular	iii.	Root of angiosperms
D.	Bundle	iv.	Sunflower stem
E.	Amphivasal vascular bundle	v.	Fern

(a) A–iii, B–iv, C–i, D–v, E–ii
(b) A–ii, B–iii, C–i, D–v, E–iv
(c) A–iii, B–iv, C–v, D–i, E–ii
(d) A–iv, B–v, C–i, D–ii, E–iii
(e) A–iii, B–i, C–ii, D–iv, E–v

5. Match the following and choose the correct combination

A.	Xylem vessels	i.	Store food materials
B.	Xylem tracheids	ii.	Obliterated lumen

C. Xylem fibre   iii. Perforated plates

D. Xylem parenchyma   iv. Chisel-like ends

(a) A–iv, B–iii, C–ii, D–i

(b) A–iii, B–ii, C–i, D–iv

(c) A–iii, B–iv, C–ii, D–i

(d) A–i, B–ii, C–iii, D–iv

6. Match the followings and choose the correct option.

A. Meristem   i. Photosynthesis, storage

B. Parenchyma   ii. Mechanical support

C. Collenchyma   iii. Actively dividing cells

D. Sclerenchyma   iv. Stomata

E. Epidermal tissue   v. Sclereids

(a) A–i, B–iii, C–v, D–ii, E–iv

(b) A–iii, B–i, C–ii, D–v, E–iv

(c) A–ii, B–iv, C–v, D–i, E–iii

(d) A–v, B–iv, C–iii, D–ii, E–i

7. Match the followings and choose the right combination

A. Endodermis   i. Companion cells

B. Stomata   ii. Lenticels

C. Sieve tube   iii. Palisade cells

D. Periderm   iv. Passage cells

E. Mesophyll   v. Accessory cells

(a) A–iv, B–v, C–ii, D–i, E–iii

(b) A–v, B–iii, C–i, D–ii, E–iv

(c) A–iv, B–v, C–i, D–ii, E–iii

(d) A–ii, B–v, C–iii, D–iv, E–i

8. Match Column I with Column II and choose the correct option.

Column I		Column II
(A) Bulliform cells	1.	Initiation of lateral roots
(B) Pericycle	2.	Root

(C) Endarch xylem   3. Grasses

(D) Exarch xylem   4. Dicot leaf

(E) Bundle sheath cells   5. Stem

(a) A-3, B-5, C-4, D-1, E-2

(b) A-2, B-5, C-1, D-3, E-4

(c) A-2, B-4, C-1, D-3, E-5

(d) A-3, B-1, C-5, D-2, E-4

(e) A-5, B-4, C-2, D-1, E-3

9.

Column-I		Column-II
A. Spring wood or early wood	I.	Lighter in colour
B. Autumn wood or late wood	II.	Density high
	III.	Density low
	IV.	Darker in colour
	V.	Larger number of xylem elements
	VI.	Vessels with wider cavity
	VII.	Lesser number of xylem elements
	VIII.	Vessels with small cavity

Which of the following combination is correct?

(a) A – II, IV, VII, VIII; B – I, III, V, VI

(b) A – I, II, VII, VIII; B – III, IV, V, VI

(c) A – I, III, V, VI; B – II, IV, VII, VIII

(d) A – I, III, VII, VIII; B – II, IV, V, VI

10. Select the option with correct identification of type of tissue from which the given structure is formed:

	Hypodermis in dicot stem	Medullary rays
(a)	Parenchyma	Parenchyma
(b)	Parenchyma	Parenchyma

(c)   Parenchyma   Sclerenchyma

(d)   Sclerenchyma   Collenchyma

11. During secondary growth in stellar region of a dicot stem, many changes come in the various tissues. Select the option in which is the particular tissue is incorrectly matched with its fate:

	Tissue	**Fate during secondary growth**
(a)	Secondary xylem	Produced in high amount
(b)	Primary phloem	Produced in low amount
(c)	Cambial ring	Cut off secondary permanent tissue on both side
(d)	Secondary phloem	Synthesized on outer side

12. Match the following columns:

	Column I		**Column II**
A.	Cuticle	1.	Guard cells
B.	Bulliform cells	2.	Single layer
C.	Stomata	3.	Waxy layer
D.	Epidermis	4.	Empty colourless cell

(a)   A-3, B-4, C-1, D-2   (b)   A-1, B-2, C-3, D-4

(c)   A-3, B-2, C-4, D-1   (d)   A-3, B-2, C-1, D-4

13. Match the columns and find out the correct combination:

	Column I		**Column II**
A.	Xylem vessels	1.	Store food material
B.	Xylem trachieds	2.	Obliterated lumen
C.	Xylem fibre	3.	Perforated plates
D.	Xylem parenchyma	4.	Chisel-like ends

(a)   A-4, B-3, C-2, D-2

(b)   A-3, B-2, C-1, D-4

(c)   A-2, B-1, C-4, D-3

(d)   A-3, B-2, C-3, D-4

(e)   A-3, A-4, C-2, D-1

14. Which of the following permanent tissue is incorrectly matched with its cell wall component and function?

(a)	Collenchyma	Cellulose, hemicelluloses and pectin	Mechanical support
(b)	Sclerenchyma	Lignin	Mechanical support
(c)	Xylem vessel	Suberin	Mechanical support and condition of water
(d)	Parenchyma	Cellulose	Photosynthesis and storage

15. Which of the following meristem is correctly

(a)	Apical meristem	Shoot and root apex	Elongation of stem and root
(b)	Intercalary meristem	In between the apical meristem	Growth in grasses
(c)	Intrafasicular cambium	In the vascular bundles	Increases the girth of stem/root
(d)	Interfascicular cambium	In between vascular bundles	Increases the girth of stem/root

Solutions

1. (c) 2. (d) 3. (a) 4. (a) 5. (c)
6. (b) 7. (c) 8. (d) 9. (c) 10. (a)
11. (b) 12. (a) 13. (a) 14. (c) 15. (a)

Structural Organisation in Animals

1. Match the following cell structure with its characteristic feature.

   (A) Tight junctions (i) Cement neighbouring cells toghether to form sheet

   (B) Adhering Junctions (ii) Transmit information through chemical to another cells

   (C) Gap junctions (iii) Establish a barrier to prevent leakage of fluid across epithelial cells

   (D) Synaptic junctions (iv) Cytoplasmic channels to facilitate communication between adjacent cells

   Select correct option from the following.

	(A)	(B)	(C)	(D)
(a)	(ii)	(iv)	(i)	(iii)
(b)	(iv)	(ii)	(i)	(iii)
(c)	(iii)	(i)	(iv)	(iii)
(d)	(iv)	(iii)	(i)	(iii)

2. Match the following.

List I		List II	
(i)	Squamous epithelium	A.	Bone
(ii)	Dense regular connective tissue	B.	skin
(iii)	Glandular epithelium	C.	Air sacs of lungs
(iv)	Specialised connective tissue	D.	Tendon
(v)	Dense irregular Connective tissue	E.	Goblet cells

   (a) (i)-B, (ii)-E, (iii)-C, (iv)-D, (v)-A
   (b) (i)-C, (ii)-E, (iii)-A, (iv)-B, (v)-D
   (c) (i)-C, (ii)-D, (iii)-E, (iv)-A, (v)-B
   (d) (i)-E, (ii)-A, (iii)-B, (iv)-D, (v)-C
   (e) (i)-D, (ii)-C, (iii)-E, (iv)-B, (v)-A

3. Choose the correctly matched pair.

   (a) Inner lining of salivary ducts - Ciliated epithelium
   (b) Moist surface of buccal cavity - Glandular epithelium
   (c) Tubular parts of nephrons - Cuboidal epithelium
   (d) Inner surface of bronchioles - Squamous epithelium

4. Choose the wrongly matched pair regarding the position of reproductive structure in earthworm.

   (a) Testes - 10th and 11th segments
   (b) Spermathecae - 6th to 9th segments
   (c) Male genital pore - 9th segments
   (d) Ovaries - Inter segmental septum of 12th and 13th segments
   (e) Female genital pore - 14th segment

5. Match the following regarding the morphology of cockroach and choose the correct option.

List-I		List-II	
(i)	Tergites	A.	Forewings
(ii)	Tegmina	B.	Upper lip
(iii)	Hypopharynx	C.	Dorsal sclerite
(iv)	Labium	D.	Tongue
(v)	Labrum	E.	Lower lip

   (a) (i)-D, (ii)-E, (iii)-C, (iv)-B, (v)-A
   (b) (i)-B, (ii)-C, (iii)-E, (iv)-D, (v)-A
   (c) (i)-E, (ii)-A, (iii)-C, (iv)-D, (v)-B
   (d) (i)-C, (ii)-A, (iii)-D, (iv)-E, (v)-B
   (e) (i)-C, (ii)-B, (iii)-E, (iv)-A, (v)-D

6. Match the columns.

Column I	Column II
A. Squamus	1. Intestinal glands
B. Cuboidal	2. Trachea
C. Columnar	3. Ovary
D. Ciliated	4. Blood vessels
E. Pseudostratified	5. Bronchioles

   (a) A - 5, B - 4, C - 2, D - 1, E - 3
   (b) A - 4, B - 3, C - 1, D - 5, E - 2
   (c) A - 4, B - 3, C - 1, D - 2, E - 5
   (d) A - 4, B - 5, C - 1, D - 2, E - 3

7. Match the following and select the correct option.

Glands		Mode of secretion
A. Merocrine	(i)	Entire cell disintegrates and is discharged as secretion.
B. Apocrine	(ii)	Secretion is discharged by simple diffusion.
C. Holocrine	(iii)	Apical part breaks off and is discharged as secretion.

   (a) A-(i), B-(iii), C-(ii)
   (b) A-(ii), B-(i), C-(iii)
   (c) A-(ii), B-(iii), C-(i)
   (d) A-(i), B-(ii), C-(iii)

8. Match the types of animal tissues listed under column I with the location given under column II. Choose the answer which gives the correct combination of the alphabets of the two columns.

Column I (Tissues)	Column II (Location)
A. Simple columnar epithelium	p. Wall of heart
B. Cardiac muscle	q. Bone joint
C. Adipose tissue	r. Inner lining of stomach and intestince
D. Hyaline cartilage	s. Below the skin in the abdomen, buttocks, thighs and breasts
	t. Diaphragm

   (a) A - r, B - p, C - t, D - s
   (b) A - r, B - t, C - q, D - s
   (c) A - p, B - r, C - s, D - t
   (d) A - r, B - p, C - s, D - q

9. Match the following Columns.

Column I	Column II
A. Neutrophil	1. Single large nucleus
B. Eosinophil	2. Usually trilobed nucleus
C. Basophil	3. Kidney-shaped nucleus
D. Lymphocyte	4. Multilobed nucleus
E. Monocyte	5. Bilobed nucleus

Codes

	A	B	C	D	E
(a)	4	1	3	5	2
(b)	2	5	1	4	3
(c)	4	5	2	1	3
(d)	2	4	5	3	1

10. Identify the pair that does not match.

   (a) Sarcomere — Ultrastructural unit of striated muscle
   (b) Copper containing respiratory pigment of Arachnida — Haemocyanim
   (c) Osteoclast — Bone destroying cells
   (d) Volkmann's canal — Which drain blood from bones

11. Match the following Columns.

Column I	Column II
A. Pseudostratified ciliated columner epithelium	1. Trachea and large bronchi
B. Stratified squamous epithelium	2. Lining the oral cavity
C. Transitional epithelium	3. Wall of urinary bladder
D. Simple ciliated columnar epithelium	4. Lining the respiratory tract

Codes

	A	B	C	D
(a)	1	2	3	4
(b)	3	1	2	4
(c)	4	3	1	2
(d)	2	4	1	3

12. Match the following Columns.

Column I	Column II
A. Simple acinar gland	1. Parotid gland
B. Compound tubular glnad	2. Seminal vesicle
C. Compound tubulo-acinar gland	3. Intestinal gland
D. Simple tubular gland	4. Liver
E. Compound acinar gland	5. Mammary gland

Codes

	A	B	C	D	E
(a)	2	3	4	1	5
(b)	4	2	1	3	5
(c)	3	1	2	4	5
(d)	5	4	3	2	1

13. Match the following Columns.

Column I	Column II
A. Adipose tissue	1. Nose
B. Stratified epithelium	2. Blood
C. Hyaline cartilage	3. Skin
D. Fluid connective tissue	4. Fat storage

Codes

	A	B	C	D
(a)	1	2	3	4
(b)	4	3	1	2
(c)	3	1	4	2
(d)	2	1	4	3

14. Select the correctly matched pair.

(a) Chondroblast – Form chondrocyte in cartilage

(b) Elastic cartilage – Pubic symphysis

(c) Fibrous cartilage – Pinna of ear

(d) Hyaline cartilage – Intervertebral disc

15. Which word combination applies to stratified squamous epithelium?

(a) Mesoderm – Calcification

(b) Ectoderm – Keratinisation

(c) Mesoderm – Ossification

(d) Endoderm – Cornification

16. Select the option having all the correct characteristcs.

Structure	Percentage of WBCs	Function
(a) 	0.3 – 0.5	Phagocytic
(b) 	0.5 – 1.0	Secrete histamine and serotonin
(c) 	30 – 40	Defence against parasites
(d) 	30 – 40	Allargic reactions

17. Match the following Columns.

	Column I		Column II
A.	Hermaphrodite	1.	Produces blood cells and haemoglobin
B.	Direct development	2.	Testis and ovary in the same animal
C.	Chemoreceptor	3.	Larval form absent
D.	Blood gland in earthworm	4.	Sense of chemical substanes

Codes

	A	B	C	D
(a)	2	3	4	1
(b)	3	2	4	1
(c)	1	3	2	4
(d)	2	4	3	1

18. Match the following Columns.

Column I (Parts of reproductive system or earthworm)		Column II (Respective segments)
A. Testes	1.	10th-11th
B. Seminal vesicles	2.	11th-12th
C. Accessory gland	3.	17th-19th
D. Spermathecae	4.	6th-9th

Codes

	A	B	C	D
(a)	1	2	3	4
(b)	4	3	2	1
(c)	3	1	4	2
(d)	2	4	1	3

19. Match the following Columns.

	Column I		Column II
A.	Phallomere	1.	Chain of developing ova
B.	Gonopore	2.	Bundls of sperm
C.	Spermatophore	3.	Opening of the ejaculatory duct
D.	Ovarioles	4.	The external genitalia

20. Choose the correctly matched pair.
    (a) Adipose tissue – Dense connective tissue
    (b) Areolar tissue – Loose connective tissue
    (c) Cartilage – Loose connective tissue
    (d) Tendon – Specialised connective tissue

21. Match the column I with column II and choose the correct option:

	Column I		Column II
A.	Anal Cerci	(i)	4th and 6th segments
B.	Tegmina	(ii)	10th segment
C.	Testes	(iii)	Forewings
D.	Ommatidia	(iv)	Sclerites
E.	Exoskeleton	(v)	Visual unit

	A	B	C	D	E
(a)	(ii)	(iii)	(i)	(v)	(iv)
(b)	(iv)	(iii)	(ii)	(v)	(i)
(c)	(iii)	(iv)	(v)	(ii)	(i)
(d)	(v)	(iv)	(iii)	(ii)	(i)

22. Match the column I with column II and choose the correct option:

	Column I		Column II
A.	Hermaphrodite	(i)	Produces blood cells and haemoglobin
B.	Direct development	(ii)	Testis and ovary in the same animal
C.	Chemoreceptor	(iii)	Larval form absent
D.	Blood gland in earthworm	(iv)	Sense of chemical substances

	A	B	C	D
(a)	(ii)	(iii)	(iv)	(i)
(b)	(iii)	(ii)	(iv)	(i)
(c)	(i)	(iii)	(ii)	(iv)
(d)	(ii)	(iv)	(iii)	(i)

23. Match the following cell structure with its characteristic feature :

Column-I		Column-II
(a) Tight junctions	(i)	Cement neighbouring cells together to form sheet.
(b) Adhering junctions	(ii)	Transmit information through chemical to another cells.
(c) Gap junctions	(iii)	Establish a barrier to prevent leakage of fluid across epithelial cells.
(d) Synaptic junctions	(iv)	Cytoplasmic channels to facilitate communication between adjacent cells.

Select correct option from the following :

(a) (a)-(iv), (B)-(iii), (C)-(i), (D)-(ii)
(b) (a)-(ii), (B)-(iv), (C)-(i), (D)-(iii)
(c) (a)-(iv), (B)-(ii), (C)-(i), (D)-(iii)
(d) (a)-(iii), (B)-(i), (C)-(iv), (D)-(ii)

24. Which type of tissue correctly matches with its location ?

	Tissue	Location
(a)	Smooth muscle	Wall of intestine
(b)	Areolar tissue	Tendons
(c)	Transitional epithelium	Tip nose
(d)	Cuboidal epithelium	Lining of stomach

25. Given below is the diagrammatic sketch of a certain type of connective tissue. Identify the parts labeled A, B, C and D, and select the correct answer from the given option.

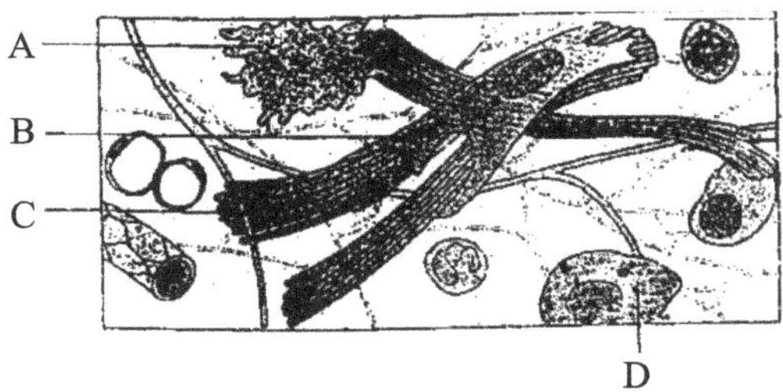

	Part-A	Part-B	Part-C	Part - D
(a)	Macro-phage	Fibro-blast	Collagenfibres	Mast cells
(b)	Mastcell	Macro-phage	Fibroblast	Collagenfibres
(c)	Macro-phage	Collagenfibres	Fibroblast	Mast cell
(d)	Mast cell	Collagenfibres	Fibroblast	Macrophage

26. The four sketches (1, 2, 3 and 4) given below, represent four different types of animal tissues. Which one of these is correctly identified in the options given, along with its correct location and function?

(1) 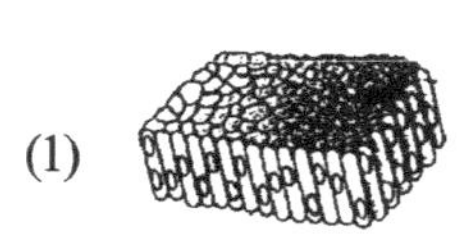   (2) 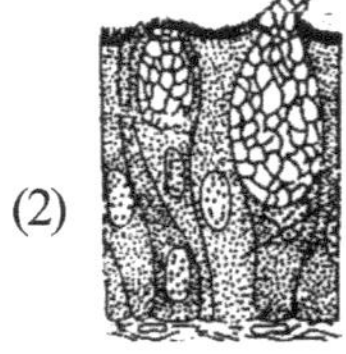   (3)    (4) 

		Tissue	Location	Function
(a)	(2)	Glandular epithelium	Intestine	Secretion
(b)	(3)	Collagen fibres	Cartilage	Attach skeletal muscles to bones
(c)	(4)	Smooth muscle tissue	Heart	Heart contraction
(d)	(1)	Columnar epithelium	Nephron	Secretion and absorption

27. Which one of the following is correct pairing of a body part and the kind of muscle tissue that moves it?

(a) Biceps of upper arm–Smooth muscle fibres

(b) Abdominal wall–Smooth muscle

(c) Iris–Involuntary smooth muscle

(d) Heart wall–Involuntary unstriated muscle

Solutions

1. (c) 2. (c) 3. (c)
4. (c) Male genital pore is present in 18th segment.
5. (d) 6. (b) 7. (a) 8. (d) 9. (c)
10. (d) 11. (a) 12. (a) 13. (b) 14. (a)
15. (b) 16. (b) 17. (a) 18. (a) 19. (b)
20. (b) 21. (a) 22. (a)
23. (d) *Tight junctions* provide a barrier which prevents leakage of fluid across epithelial cells.

    Adherens junctions aid to cement adjacent cells to form a sheet.

    Gap junctions provide cytoplasmic channels to facilitate communication between adjacent cells.

    Synaptic junctions help in transmission of information through chemicals.
24. (a) Wall of intestine is made of smooth muscle. Tendons consist of dense regular connective tissue fascicles encased in dense irregular connective tissue sheaths. Tip of nose consists of squamous epithelium. Lining of epithelium is made of columnar epithelium.
25. (a) Connective tissue is the most diverse of the four tissue types with a wide variety of functions. Connective tissue is made up of cells and fibers in a "jelly-like" ground substance.
26. (a) Glandular epithelium invaginates epithelia into connective tissue which differentiate into secretory units. Examples include sebaceous glands of the skin and glands in the intestinal lining (exocrine glands), and many endocrine glands releasing hormones, such as the thyroid follicle.
27. (b) The structure of the abdominal wall is similar in principle to the thoracic wall. There are three layers, an external, internal and innermost layer. The vessels and nerves lie between the internal and innermost layers. The abdomen can be divided into quadrants or nine abdominal regions.

Cell: The Unit of Life

1. Match the column I with column II.

Column I		Column II
A. Golgi appartus	(i)	Synthesis of protein
B. Lysosomes	(ii)	Trap waste and excretory products
C. Vacuoles	(iii)	Formation of glycoproteins and glycolipids
D. Ribosomes	(iv)	Digesting biomolecules

   Choose the right match from options given below.
   (a) A-(iii), B-(iv), C-(ii), D-(i)
   (b) A-(iv), B-(iii), C-(i), D-(ii)
   (c) A-(iii), B-(ii), C-(iv), D-(i)
   (d) A-(i), B-(ii), C-(iv), D-(iii)

2. Match the following.

Column I		Column II
A. Protein	(i)	SER
B. Lipid	(ii)	Golgi body
C. Glycoprotein	(iii)	Lysosome
D. Hydrolytic enzyme	(iv)	RER

   (a) A-(i), B-(ii), C-(iii), D-(iv)
   (b) A-(iv), B-(ii), C-(i), D-(iii)
   (c) A-(iv), B-(i), C-(ii), D-(iii)
   (d) A-(i), B-(iii), C-(ii), D-(iv)

3. Match the columns and identify the correct option.

Column I		Column II
A. Thylakoids	(i)	Disc-shaped sacs in Golgi appartus
B. Cristae	(ii)	Condensed structure of DNA
C. Cisternae	(iii)	Flat membranous sacs in stroma
D. Chromation	(iv)	Infoldings in mitochondria

   (a) A-(iii), B-(i), C-(iv), D-(ii)
   (b) A-(iii), B-(iv), C-(ii), D-(i)
   (c) A-(iv), B-(iii), C-(i), D-(ii)
   (d) A-(iii), B-(iv), C-(i), D-(ii)

4. Which of these is wrongly matched?
   (a) 70S ribosomes – Prokaryotes
   (b) 80S ribosomes – Eukaryotes
   (c) Axoneme – Cilia
   (d) Centromere – Centrosome
   (e) Thylakoids – Chloroplast

5. Given below are cell organelles and their functions. Select the incorrect match.
   (a) Lysosome – Phagocytosis
   (b) Centriole – Spindle formation
   (c) Sphaerosomes – Storage and synthesis of fats
   (d) Leucoplast – Photosynthesis

6. Match the column I with that of column II and choose the correct combination from the options given.

Column I		Column II
Organelle		Site for
A. Rough ER	(i)	Synthesis of glycoproteins
B. Smooth ER	(ii)	Aerobic respiration

C. Mitochondria   (iii) Synthesis of lipid

D. Golgi appartus   (iv) Protein synthesis

(a) A - (i), B - (ii), C - (iii), D - (iv)

(b) A - (ii), B - (iii), C - (iv), D - (i)

(c) A - (iii), B - (iv), C - (ii), D - (i)

(d) A - (iv), B - (iii), C - (ii), D - (i)

(e) A - (iv), B - (iii), C - (i), D - (ii)

7. Match the following and select the correct answer.

(A) Centriole   (i) Infoldings in mitochondria

(B) Chlorophyll   (ii) Thylakoids

(C) Cristae   (iii) Nucleic acids

(D) Ribozymes   (iv) Basal body of cilia or flagella

	A	B	C	D
(a)	(iv)	(ii)	(i)	(iii)
(b)	(i)	(ii)	(iv)	(iii)
(c)	(i)	(iii)	(ii)	(iv)
(d)	(iv)	(iii)	(i)	(ii)

8. Choose the matched ones.

(A) Vibrio - Rod like bacteria

(B) Mesosome - Helps in cell wall formation

(C) Smooth endoplasmic - synthesis of lipid reticulum

(D) Vacuoles - Rich in hydrolytic enzymes

(a) (B) and (C) only

(b) (A) and (D) only

(c) (A), (B) and (C) only

(d) (B) and (D) only

(e) (B), (C) and (D) only

9. Which of these is wrongly matched?

(a) Chloroplasts – Chlorophyll

(b) Elaioplasts – Starch

(c) Chromoplasts – Carotenoids

(d) Amyloplasts – Carbohydrates

(e) Aleuroplasts – Proteins

10. Match the following Columns.

Column I		Column II
A. Dictyosomes	1.	Osmoregulation
B. Mitochondria	2.	Photosynthesis
C. Vacuoles	3.	Transort
D. Grana	4.	Secretion
	5.	Respiration

Codes

	A	B	C	D
(a)	4	5	1	2
(b)	3	4	2	1
(c)	4	5	3	2
(d)	4	3	1	2

11. Match the following Columns.

Column I		Column II
A. Karyolymph	1.	Nucleolus
B. Ribonucleoprotein	2.	Nucleus
C. Spindle fibre	3.	DNA
D. Genes	4.	Centrioles
E. Rough endoplasmic reticulum	5.	Protein synthesis

Codes

	A	B	C	D	E
(a)	1	3	2	4	5
(b)	4	2	3	5	1
(c)	2	1	4	3	5
(d)	1	2	3	4	5

12. Analyse the following pairs and identify the correct options given

A. Chromoplasts - Contains pigments other than chlorophyll

B. Leucoplasts - Devoid of any pigments

C. Amyloplasts - Store proteins

D. Alueroplasts - Store oils and fats

E. Elaioplasts - Store carbohydrates

(a) B and C are correct

(b) C and D are correct

(c) D and E are correct

(d) A and B are correct

13. Match the following and choose the correct combination from the options given.

Column I		Column II
Cell type		Size
A. Viruses	(1)	1-2 mm
B. PPLO	(2)	10-20 mm
C. Eukaryotic cell	(3)	About 0.1 mm
D. Bacterium	(4)	0.02 - 0.2 mm

(a) A-1, B-2, C-3, D-4

(b) A-4, B-3, C-2, D-1

(c) A-1, B-3, C-2, D-4

(d) A-4, B-2, C-3, D-1

14. Match the following and select the correct answer:

A. Centriole	(i)	Infoldings in mitochondria
B. Chlorophyll	(ii)	Thylakoids
C. Cristae	(iii)	Nucleic acids
D. Ribozymes	(iv)	Basal body cilia or fiagella

	A	B	C	D
(a)	(iv)	(ii)	(i)	(iii)
(b)	(i)	(ii)	(iv)	(iii)
(c)	(i)	(iii)	(ii)	(iv)
(d)	(iv)	(iii)	(i)	(ii)

15. Match the following and select the correct answer:

A. Centriole	(i)	Infoldings in mitochondria
B. Chlorophyll	(ii)	Thylakoids
C. Cristae	(iii)	Nucleic acids
D. Ribozymes	(iv)	Basal body cilia or fiagella

	A	B	C	D
(a)	(iv)	(ii)	(i)	(iii)
(b)	(i)	(ii)	(iv)	(iii)
(c)	(i)	(iii)	(ii)	(iv)
(d)	(iv)	(iii)	(i)	(ii)

16. Match the columns and identify the correct option.

Column-I		**Column-II**
A. Thylakoids	(i)	Disc-shaped sacs in Golgi apparatus
B. Cristae	(ii)	Condensed structure of DNA
C. Cisternae	(iii)	Flat membranous sacs in stroma
D. Chromatin	(iv)	Infoldings in mitochondria

	A	B	C	D
(a)	(iii)	(iv)	(i)	(ii)
(b)	(iii)	(i)	(iv)	(ii)
(c)	(iii)	(iv)	(ii)	(i)
(d)	(iv)	(iii)	(i)	(ii)

17. Match the items in column I with column II and choose the correct option.

	Column I		**Column II**
A.	Sap vacuole	1.	Contain digestive enzyme
B.	Contractile vacuole	2.	Store metabolic gases
C.	Food vacuole	3.	Osmoregulation
D.	Air vacuole	4.	Store lipids
E.	Spherosomes	5.	Store and concentrate mineral salts and nutrients

	A	B	C	D	E
(a)	5	3	1	2	4
(b)	2	3	4	5	1
(c)	5	3	2	4	1
(d)	4	1	3	5	2

18. Which of the following four cell structures is correctly matched with the accompanying description ?

(a) Plasma membrane   —   Outer layer of cellulose or chitin

(b) Mitochondria — Bacteria like elements with inner membrane forming sacs containing chlorophyll, found in plant cell and algae

(c) Chloroplasts — Bacteria like elements with inner membrane highly folded

(d) Golgi apparatus — Stacks of flattened vesicles

19. Match column I and column II and select the correct option.

Column I		Column II
A.	Endoplasmic recticulum	1. Stack of cisternae
B.	Spherosome	2. Store oils or fats
C.	Dictyosome	3. Synthesis and storage of lipids
D.	Peroxisome	4. Photorespiration
E.	Elaioplasts	5. Detoxification of drugs

	A	B	C	D	E
(a)	5	3	1	4	2
(b)	2	3	2	4	1
(c)	2	3	1	4	5
(d)	3	5	1	4	2

20. Match List I and List II and select the correct answer

List I	List II
(i) Lysosome	A. Bacteria without walls
(ii) Mycoplasma	B. A virus that infects bacterial cells
(iii) Thylakoid	C. Flattened sacs in a chloroplast
(iv) Bacteriophage	D. A vesicle in which hydrolytic enzymes are stored

(a) (i) – C, (ii) – A, (iii) – B, (iv) – D

(b) (i) – D, (ii) – A, (iii) – C, (iv) – B

(c) (i) – B, (ii) – C, (iii) – D, (iv) – A

(d) (i) – A, (ii) – D, (iii) – B, (iv) – C

Solutions

1. (a)   2. (c)   3. (d)

4. (d) The two chromatids are attached to each other by a narrow area called centromere or primary constriction.

   The complex formed from centrioles and centrosphere is called centrosome.

5. (d) Leucoplasts take part in storage of various substances like starch (amyloplasts), fat(elaioplasts) and protein(aleuroplasts). These are colourless plastids that lack grana and photosynthetic pigments.

6. (d)   7. (a)

8. (a) Vibrio are comma shaped bacteria. Vacuolar sap contains mineral salts, sugars, amino acids, esters, proteins, waste products and water soluble pigments called anthocyanin. Lysosomes are rich in hydrolytic enzymes.

9. (b) Elaioplasts are colourless plastids which store lipids *e.g.*, tube rose.

10. (a)   11. (c)   12. (d)   13. (b)   14. (a)

15. (a)   16. (a)   17. (a)   18. (b)   19. (a)

20. (b)

Biomolecules

9

1. Match the following Columns.

	Column I		Column II
A.	Cellulose	1.	Insulin
B.	Peptide	2.	Alkaline phosphatase
C.	Steroid	3.	Cotton fibres
D.	Phospholipid	4.	Diosgenin
E.	Enzymes	5.	Lecithin

   Codes

	A	B	C	D	E
(a)	3	4	5	1	2
(b)	2	1	4	5	3
(c)	3	1	4	5	2
(d)	1	4	3	5	2

2. Match the following Columns.

	Column I		Column II
A.	Abrin	1.	Lectin
B.	GLUT-4	2.	Intercellular ground substcne
C.	Collagen	3.	Hormone
D.	Concanavalin	4.	Enables glucose transport into cells
		5.	Toxin

   Codes

	A	B	C	D
(a)	3	4	2	1
(b)	5	4	2	1
(c)	3	4	2	5
(d)	3	5	2	1

3. Match the following Columns.

	Column I		Column II
A.	Oxidoreductase	1.	Linking of two copounds
B.	Isomerases	2.	Removal of group from sustrates
C.	Ligases	3.	Interconversion of isomers
D.	Lyases	4.	Dehydrogenases
		5.	Hydrolysis

   Codes

	A	B	C	D
(a)	4	1	3	2
(b)	4	3	1	2
(c)	3	4	2	5
(d)	2	5	3	1

4. Identify the incorrect match between protein and its role.

   (a) Keratin - Structural component of hair

   (b) Immunoglobulins - Protection of body against diseases

   (c) Haemoglobin - Transport of oxygen in muscles

   (d) Thrombin - Blood clotting

5. Match the follwing Columns.

	Column I		Column II
A.	Nitrogen bae	1.	RNA
B.	Nucleoside	2.	Thymidylic acid
C.	Nucleotide	3.	Cytidine
D.	Nucleic acid	4.	Uracil

Codes

	A	B	C	D
(a)	1	2	3	4
(b)	1	3	2	4
(c)	4	3	2	1
(d)	4	1	2	3
(e)	4	2	3	1

6. Find out the wrongly matched pair.

  (a) Primary metabolite   – Ribose

  (b) Secondary metabolite – Anthocyanin

  (c) Protein   – Insulin

  (d) Chitin   – Polysccharide

  (e) Cellulose   – Heteropolymer

7. Match the following Columns.

	Column I		**Column II**
A.	Triglycerides	1.	Galactose
B.	Lactose	2.	Glycerol
C.	RNA	3.	Palmitic acid
D.	b-pleats	4.	Uracil
E.	Bee-wax	5.	Secondary structure

Codes

	A	B	C	D	E
(a)	4	1	5	2	3
(b)	5	1	4	2	3
(c)	3	1	4	5	2
(d)	2	1	4	5	3

8. Which one of the following biomolecules is correctley characterised?

  (a) Lecithin - a phophorylated glyceride found in cell membrane.

  (b) Palmitic acid - an unsaturated fatty acid wiht 18 carbon atoms.

  (c) Adenylic acide - adenosine with a glucose phosphate molecule.

  (d) Alanine amino acid - contains an amino group and an acidic group anywhere in the molecule.

9. Match the following and choose the correct combination from the options given.

	Column I		**Column II**
	(Organic Compound)		**(Example)**
A.	Fattyacid	1.	Glutamic acid
B.	Phospholipid	2.	Tryptophan
C.	Aromatic amino acid	3.	Lecithin
D.	Acidic amino acid	4.	Palmitic acid

  (a) A-1, B-2, C-3, D-4   (b) A-4, B-3, C-2, D-1

  (c) A-2, B-3, C-4, D-1   (d) A-3, B-4, C-1, D-2

  (e) A-4, B-3, C-1, D-2

10. Match the following and choose the correct combination from the options given.

	Column I		**Column II**
	(Chemical compounds)		**(Examples)**
A.	Nitrogen base	I.	RNA
B.	Nucleoside	II.	Thymidylic acid
C.	Nucleotide	III.	Cytidine
D.	Nucleic acid	IV.	Uracil

  (a) A-I, B-II, C-III, D-IV

  (b) A-I, B-III, C-II, D-IV

  (c) A-IV, B-III, C-II, D-I

  (d) A-IV, B-I, C-II, D-III

  (e) A-IV, B-II, C-III, D-I

11. Match the itemes in colum I with those in colum II and choose the correct answer.

	Column I		**Column II**
	(Biomolecules)		**(Examples)**
A.	Carbohydrates	1.	Trypsin
B.	Protein	2.	Cholestrol
C.	Nucleic acid	3.	Insulin
D.	Lipid	4.	Adenylic acid

  (a) A-3; B-1: C-4; D-2

  (b) A-2; B-3 C-4; D-1

  (c) A-3; B-4 C-1; D-2

  (d) A-4; B-1; C-2; D-3

  (e) A-1; B-2; C-3; D-4

12. Match column I with column II and select the correct option from codes given below.

	Column I		Column II
A.	Pigments	(i)	Abrin, ricin
B.	Toxins	(ii)	Concanavalin A
C.	Alkaloids	(iii)	Carotenoids
D.	Lectins	(iv)	Morphine, codeine

(a) A-(iv), B-(iii), C-(i), D-(ii)

(b) A-(ii), B-(iv), C-(i), D-(iii)

(c) A-(ii), B-(i), C-(iv), D-(ii)

(d) A-(i), B-(ii), C-(iii), D-(iv)

13. Which of the following secondary metabolites belong to the group drugs?

I.	Morphine	II.	Curcumin
III.	Codeine	IV.	Vinblastin
V.	Abrin		

(a) I and II only

(b) I and V only

(c) II and III only

(d) II and IV only

(e) III and IV only

14. Which of these is/are wrongly matched?

I.	Alkaloid	-	Codeine
II.	Lectin	-	Morphine
III.	Toxic	-	Abrin
IV.	Terpene	-	Curcumin

(a) I and II only

(b) II and III only

(c) II and IV only

(d) III and IV only

(e) I and IV only

15. Find out the wrongly matched pair.

(a) Primary metabolite - Ribose

(b) Secondary metabolite - Anthocyanins

(c) Protein - Insulin

(d) Chitin - Polysaccharide

(e) Cellulose - Heteropolymer

16. Match the following nutritional vitamin deficiencies in column I with the causes/deficiencies in column II and choose the correct option from the answer key. **[Kerala '05]**

	Column I		Column II
A.	Kwashiorkar	p.	Iron
B.	General anaemia	q.	Menadione
C.	Dermatitis	r.	Protein
D.	Marasmus	s.	Pyridoxine
E.	Bleeding	t.	Biotin

(1) A = p, B = t, C = q, D = r, E = s

(2) A = t, B = q, C = r, D = s, E = p

(3) A = t, B = r, C = s, D = p, E = q

(4) A = r, B = s, C = p, D = t, E = q

17. Match the items in column I with items in column II and choose the correct answer **[Kerala'06]**

	Column I		Column II
a.	triglyceride	1.	animal hormones
b.	membrane lipid	2.	feathers and leaves
c.	steroid	3.	phospholipids
d.	wax	4.	fat stored in form of droplets

(1) a–4, b–3, c–1, d–2

(2) a–2, b–3, c–4, d–1

(3) a–3, b–4, c–1, d–2

(4) a–4, b–1, c–2, d–3

18. Match the column I and II and choose the correct combination from the options given.

	Column I		Column II
A.	Acidic amino acid	(i)	Valine
B.	Basic amino acid	(ii)	Glutamic acid
C.	Neutral amino acid	(iii)	Phenylalanine
D.	Aromatic amino acid	(iv)	Lysine

(a) A-(ii), B-(iv), C-(i), D-(iii)

(b) A-(ii), B-(i), C-(iv), D-(iii)

(c) A-(iii), B-(ii), C-(i), D-(iv)

(d) A-(i), B-(iv), C-(iii), D-(ii)

19. Match the columns and find out the correct combination

Proteinaceous amino acids	R-group
A. Serine	1. Hydrogen
B. Glycine	2. Hydroxyl methyl
C. Alanine	3. Methyl group

(a) A-3, B-1, C-2   (b) A-2, B-2, C-1

(c) A-2, B-2, C-3   (d) A-2, B-1, C-3

20. Correctly match the column-I with column-II

Column I	Column II
A. Drugs	I. Gums, cellulose
B. Polymeric substances	II. Morphine, codeine
C. Alkaloids	III. Carotenoids, Anthocyanins
D. Pigments	IV. Vinblastin, curcumin

(a) A-c, B-a, C-b, D-d

(b) A-d, B-b, C-a, D-c

(c) A-d, B-a, C-b, D-c

(d) A-a, B-d, C-b, D-c

21. Which of the following polysaccharide is wrongly matched with its monomer?

(a) Starch — Glucose

(b) Chitin — N-acetyl glucosamine (NAG)

(c) Inulin — Mannose

(d) Mucopolysaccharide — Amino sugars and other chemically modified sugars

Solutions

1. (c) 2. (b) 3. (b) 4. (c) 5. (c)

6. (e) Cellulose is the most important structural component of the cell wall of plants. It is a linear polymer of β-D glucose units connected through β-1, 4-glycosidic linkage. The linear chains form microfibrillae or bundles of parallel chains held together by hydrogen bonds.

7. (d)

8. (a) Lecithin is a triglyceride lipid where one fatty acid is replaced by phosphoric acid which is linked to additional nitrogenous group called choline. It is a common membrane lipid. It is an amphipathic phospholipid having both hydrophilic polar and hydrophobic nonpolar groups.

9. (b) 10. (c) 11. (a) 12. (c)

13. (d) secondary metabolites are derivatives of primary metabolites. These metabolites are generally found in plant, fungal and microbial cells. These are organic compounds which are not involved in primary metabolism and seen to have no direct function in growth and development of plants. Curcumin and vinblastin are drugs, morphine and codeine are alkaloids and abrin is toxin.

14. (c) Morphine is an alkaloid and curcumin is a drug.

15. (e) Cellulose is a polysaccharide and a homopolymer that consists of a long unbranched chain of glucose units. It is the main constituent of the cell walls of all plants, many algae, and some fungi and is responsible for providing the rigidity of the cell wall.

16. (d) 17. (a) 18. (a) 19. (d) 20. (c)

21. (c)

Cell Cycle and Cell Division

10

1. Identify the stage of mitosis with its characteristics.

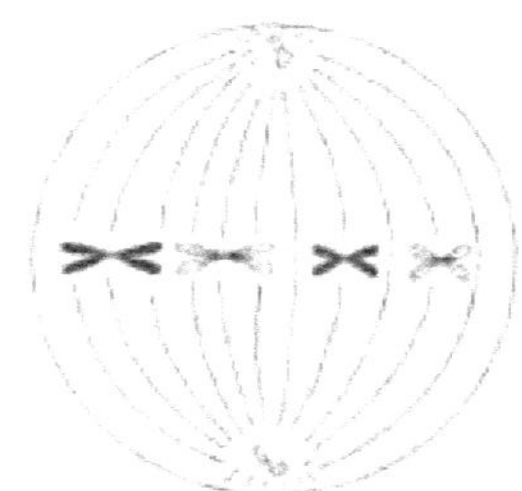

(a) Metaphase – Chromosomes move to spindle equator, chromosomes made up of two chromatids

(b) Anaphase – Centromeres split, chromatids separate and start moving away

(c) Late prophase – Chromosomes move to spindle equator

(d) Metaphase – Spindle fibres attached move to kinetochores, centromeres split and chromatids separate

2. Identify the pair which is a mismatch for plant cell division.

(a) Spindle – amphiaster

(b) Centrioles – absent

(c) Cytokinesis – by cell plate formation which grows centrigugally

(d) New cell membrane – endoplasmic reticulum

3. At which stage of mitosis, do these events occur?

	Spiralisation and condensation of DNA	Nuclear envelope breakdown	centromeres split
(a)	Interphase	Interphase	Metaphase
(b)	Interphase	Prophase	Metaphase
(c)	Prophase	Metaphase	Anaphase
(d)	Prophase	Prophase	Anaphase

4. Beads on string of A are seen in B which condense to form chromosomes in C-stage of cell division

	A	B	C
(a)	Chromonema	Chromatin	Metaphase
(b)	Chromation	Chromatid	Metaphase
(c)	Chromonema	Chromosome	Anaphase
(d)	Chromonema	Chromatid	Anaphase

5. Match the following Columns.

Column I	Column II
A. Interkinesis	1. S-phase
B. Histone synthesis	2. Cytokinesis
C. Colchicine	3. Chromosome fibre
D. Terminalisation	4. Spindle

Codes

	A	B	C	D
(a)	4	1	2	3
(b)	2	1	4	3
(c)	1	2	3	4
(d)	3	2	1	4

6. Match the following Columns.

	Column I		Column II
A.	Synapsis aligns homologous chromosomes	1.	Anaphase-II
B.	Synthesis of RNA and protein	2.	Zygotene
C.	Action of enzyme recombinase	3.	G_2 - phase
D.	Centromeres do not separate, but chromatids move towards opposite poles	4.	Anaphase-I
		5.	Pachytene

Codes

	A	B	C	D
(a)	2	1	3	4
(b)	2	3	5	4
(c)	1	2	5	4
(d)	2	3	4	5

7. Match of the item in Column I with those in Column II and the choose the correct answer.

	Column I		Column II
A.	Mitosis	1.	Occurs in diploid cells only
B.	Meiosis	2.	Occurs in both haploid and diploid cells
		3.	Daughter and parent cells have same chromosome numbers
		4.	Synapsis of homologous chromosomes

Codes

	A	B			A	B
(a)	1	2		(b)	2	3
(c)	3	4		(d)	4	1

8. Match the following Columns.

	Column I		Column II
A.	G_1-phase	1.	Replication of DNA
B.	S-phase	2.	Quiescent stage
C.	G_2-phase	3.	Condensation of chromatin
D.	G_0-phase	4.	Protein synthesis
		5.	Interval between mitosis and initiation of DNA replication

Codes

	A	B	C	D
(a)	3	5	1	2
(b)	5	4	1	3
(c)	5	1	4	2
(d)	5	2	3	4

9. Match the following Columns.

	Column I		Column II
A.	Leptotene	1.	Terminalisation of chiasms
B.	Zygotene	2.	Crossing over and recombination
C.	Pachytene	3.	Synapsis
D.	Diakinesis	4.	Visibility of chromosomes

Codes

	A	B	C	D
(a)	1	2	3	4
(b)	1	3	2	4
(c)	4	3	2	1
(d)	4	1	2	3
(e)	4	2	3	1

10. Match the stages of meiosis in column I to their characteristics features in column II and select the correct option using the codes given below.

	Column I		Column II
A.	Pachytene	(i)	Pairing of homologous chromosomes
B.	Metaphase I	(ii)	Terminalisation of chiasmata
C.	Diakinesis	(iii)	Crossing-over takes place
D.	Zygotene	(iv)	Chromosomes aligh at equatorial plate

(a) A-(iii), B-(iv), C-(ii), D-(i)

(b) A-(i), B-(iv), C-(ii), D-(iii)

(c) A-(ii), B-(iv), C-(iii), D-(i)

(d) A-(iv), B-(iii), C-(ii), D-(i)

11. Match the items in column I with those in column II, and choose the correct answer.

Column I		**Column II**
P. Mitosis	(i)	Occurs in diploid cells only
Q. Meiosis	(ii)	Occurs in both haploid and diploid cells.
	(iii)	Daughter and parent cells have same chromosome numbers
	(iv)	Synapsis of homologous chromosomes

(a) P-(i), Q-(ii)   (b) P-(ii), Q-(iii)

(c) P-(iii), Q-(iv)   (d) P-(iv), Q-(i)

12. Match the sub-stage of prophase I of meiosis in column I and the events in column II and choose the right option.

Column I		**Column II**
A. Leptotene	I.	Terminalisation of chiasma
B. Zygotene	II.	Crossing over and recombination
C. Pachytene	III.	Synapsis
D. Diakinesis	IV.	Visibility of chromosomes

(a) A-I, B-II, C-III, D-IV

(b) A-I, B-III, C-II, D-IV

(c) A-IV, B-III, C-II, D-I

(d) A-IV, B-I, C-II, D-III

(e) A-IV, B-II, C-III, D-I

13. Find the correctly matched pairs and choose the correct option.

    A. Leptotene – The chromosomes become invisible

    B. Zygotene – Pairing of homlogous chromosomes

    C. Pachytene – Dissolution of the synaptonemal complex takes place

    D. Diplotene – Bivalent chromosomes appear as tetrads

    E. Diakinesis – Terminalisation of chiasmata takes place.

(a) A and B are correct.

(b) B and D are correct.

(c) B and E are correct.

(d) B and C are correct.

(e) C and D are correct.

14. Select the correct match.

    (A) S phase – DNA replication

    (B) Zygotene – Synapsis

    (C) Diplotene – Crossing over

    (D) Meiosis – Both haploid and diploid cells

    (E) Gap 2 phase – Quiescent stage

(a) nuclease

(b) RNA polymerase

(c) recombinase

(d) DNA polymerase.

15. Identify the correct stage in cell division with its characteristics.

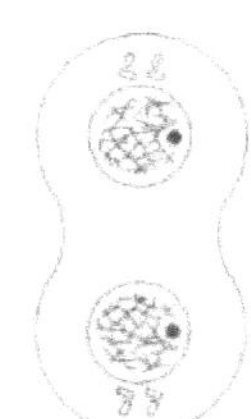

(a) Telophase – Endoplasmic reticulum and nucleolus not reformed yet

(b) Telophase – Nuclear envelop reforms, Golgi complex reforms

(c) Late anaphase – Chromosomes move away from equatorial plate, Golgi complex not present

(d) Cytokinesis – Cell plate formed, mitochondria distributed between two daughter cells

16. Match the following and choose the correct option.

	Column I		**Column II**
I.	Chromosomes are moved to spindle equator	(A)	Pachytene
II.	Centromere splits and chromatids apart	(B)	Zygotene
III.	Pairing between homologous chromosomes takes place	(C)	Anaphase
IV.	Crossing between homologous chromosomes	(D)	Metaphase

	I	II	III	IV
(a)	A	B	C	D
(b)	B	C	D	A
(c)	D	C	B	A
(d)	C	A	D	B

17. Match the following and choose the correct option.

	Column I		**Column II**
I.	Terminalization of chiasmata	A.	Zygotene
II.	Synapsis	B.	Diplotene
III.	Crossing over	C.	Metaphase I
IV.	Dissolution of Synaptonemal complex	D.	Diakinesis
V.	Best stage for the study of chiasmata	E.	Pachytene
VI.	Nuclear membrane and nucleolus disappear		
VII.	Tetrads are arranged on equatorial line		

(a) A - II, B - V, C - VII, D - I, IV, VI, E - III

(b) A - II, B - III, C - VII, D - I, IV, VI, E - V

(c) A - II, B - VII, C - III, D - I, IV, V, E - VI

(d) A - II, B - I, C - IV, D - V, III, E - VI

18. Find the correctly matched pairs and choose the correct option.

A.	Leptotene	-	The chromosomes become invisible
B.	Zygotene	-	Pairing of homologous chromosomes
C.	Pachytene	-	Dissolution of the complex synaptonemal takes place
D.	Diplotene	-	Bivalent chromosomes appear as tetrads
E.	Diakinesis	-	Terminalization of chiasmata takes place

(a) A and B are correct

(b) B and D are correct

(c) B and E are correct

(d) B and C are correct

19. A stage in cell division is shown in the figure. Select the answer which gives correct identification of the stage with its characteristics.

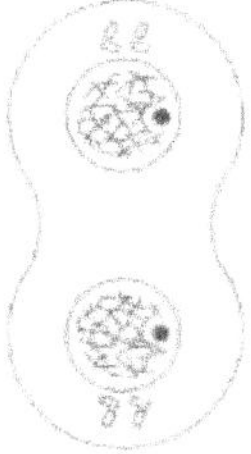

(a)	Late anaphase	Chromosomes move away from equatorial plate, Golgi complex not present
(b)	Cytokinesis	Cell plate formed, mitochondria distributed between two daughter cells
(c)	Telophase	Endoplasmic reticulum and nucleolus not reformed yet
(d)	Telophase	Nuclear envelop reforms, golgi complex reforms

20. Select the correct option :

	I		II
A	"Synapsis aligns homologous chromosomes"	(i)	Anaphase-II
B	"Synthesis of RNA and protein"	(ii)	Zygotene
C	"Action of enzyme recombinase"	(iii)	G2-phase
D	"Centromeres do not separate but chromatids move towards opposite poles"	(iv)	Anaphase-I
		(v)	Pachytene

	A	B	C	D
(a)	(ii)	(iii)	(v)	(iv)
(b)	(i)	(ii)	(v)	(iv)
(c)	(ii)	(iii)	(iv)	(v)
(d)	(ii)	(i)	(iii)	(iv)

Solutions

1. (a)   **2.** (a)   **3.** (d)   **4.** (d)   **5.** (b)

6. (b)   **7.** (c)   **8.** (c)   **9.** (c)   **10.** (a)

11. (c)   **12.** (c)

13. **(c)** Prophase I of meiosis consists of 5 stages: leptotene, zygotene, pachytene, diplotene and diakinesis. Leptotene is the initial stage of prophase. During this, chromosomes become gradually visible under the light microscope due to condensation. In zygotene, pairing of homologous chromosomes occur by formation of synaptonemal complexes. Next, pachytene is characterised by occurrence of crossing over. Bivalent chromosomes now clearly appears as tetrads. Diplotene follows pachytene and involves dissolution of synaptonemal complex. Terminalisation of chaiasmata is observed in diakinesis.

14. **(a)** During S phase DNA replication takes place. During zygotense synapsis occurs. The process of attachment of the homologous chromosomes is called synapsis.

15. (b)   **16.** (c)   **17.** (a)   **18.** (c)   **19.** (d)

20. (a)

Transport in Plants

1. The table below shows the comparison of different transport process. Identify the correct comparison.

	Property	Simple Diffusion	Facilitated Diffusion	Active Transport
(a)	Needs carrier protein	Yes	Yes	Yes
(b)	Uphill transport	No	Yes	Yes
(c)	Transport saturates	No	No	No
(d)	Needs ATP energy	No	No	Yes

2. During osmosis, water moves through a membrane

	From	To
(a)	Low water potential	High water potential
(b)	High solute concentration	Low solute concentration
(c)	High osmotic potential	Low osmotic potential
(d)	A hypotonic solution (less solute)	A hypertonic solution (more solute)

3. Match the name of the activities listed under column I with the description of activity given under column II.

	Column I		Column II
A.	Transpiration	I.	Anaerobic respiration in yeast
B.	Guttation	II.	Active absorption of water
C.	Exudation	III.	Loss of water vapour from plant parts
D.	Fermentation	IV.	Loss of liquid water from leaves.
		V.	Loss of water from injured plant parts.

(a) A-I; B-II; C-III; D-V
(b) A-II; B-I; C-IV; D-III
(c) A-III; B-IV; C-V; D-I
(d) A-IV; B-V; C-II; D-III

4. Match the theories given in column I with the name of scientists listed in column II. Choose the answer which gives the correct combination of the alphabet.

	Column I		Column II
(A)	Relay Pump Theory	(I)	Stocking
(B)	Transpiration Cohesion Theory	(II)	Sir J. C. Bose
(C)	Mass Flow Theory	(III)	Godlewski
(D)	Pulsation Theory	(IV)	Dixon and Jolly
		(V)	Ernest Munch

(a) A–III, B–II, C–V, D–I
(b) A–II, B–I, C–V, D–III
(c) A–III, B–IV, C–V, D–II
(d) A–IV, B–III, C–I, D–II

5. Match the following

	Column I		Column II
(A)	Hypotonic	(I)	Water
(B)	Hypertonic	(II)	Sucrose
(C)	Solute	(III)	Lower tonicity
(D)	Solvent	(IV)	Higher tonicity

(a) A–I, B–II, C–III, D–IV
(b) A–III, B–II, C–I, D–IV
(c) A–III, B–IV, C–II, D–I
(d) A–III, B–II, C–IV, D–I

6. The value of osmotic potential (π) and pressure potential (p) of cells a, b, c, d are given below Cells

Cells	π	P
A	– 1.0	0.5
B	– 0.6	0.3
C	– 1.2	0.6
D	– 0.8	0.4

Identify the correct sequence that shows the path of movement of water from the following

(a) $D \to C \to A \to B$

(b) $B \to D \to A \to C$

(c) $B \to C \to D \to A$

(d) $C \to B \to A \to D$

7. Match List – I with List – II and find out the correct answer from the code given below.

List – I	List – II
(A) Diffusion	(i) hydrophoilic substances
(B) Osmosis	(ii) shrinkage of protoplasm
(C) Imbibition	(iii) semipermeable membrane
(D) Plasmolysis	(iv) free movement of ions and gases

(a) A – (II), B – (I), C –(IV), D – (III)

(b) A – (IV), B – (III). C – (I), D – (II)

(c) A – (III), B – (I), C – (IV), D – (II)

(d) A – (II), B – (III), C – (IV), D – (I)

8. The osmotic potential and pressure potential of three cells (A, B, C) located in different parts of an actively transpiring plant are given below.

Cell	Osmotic Potential (Mpa)	Pressure Potential (MPa)
A	–0.87	0.44
B	–0.92	0.34
C	–0.68	0.27

Identify these three cells as root hair, root cortical and leaf mesophyll cells respectively.

(a) A, B, C

(b) A, C, B

(c) C, A, B

(d) B, C, A

9. Match the terms of column I with the appropriate terms of column II.

Column I	Column II
(i) K^+ pump theory	(A) Semi-permeable membrane
(ii) Plasmolysis	(B) Hydathodes
(iii) Imbibition	(C) Stomatal movement
(iv) Guttation	(D) Exosmosis
(v) Osmosis	(E) Hydrophilic colloids

(a) (I)-(C); (II)-(D); (III)-(E); (IV)-(B); (V)-(A)

(b) (I)-(A); (II)-(B); (III)-(C); (IV)-(D); (V)-(E)

(c) (I)-(B); (II)-(C); (III)-(E); (IV)-(A); (V)-(D)

(d) (I)-(D); (II)-(E); (III)-(B); (IV)-(C); (V)-(A)

10. The graph shows the relationship between ψ (water potential), ψ_s (solute potential) and ψ_p (pressure potential) for a plant cell placed in pure water.

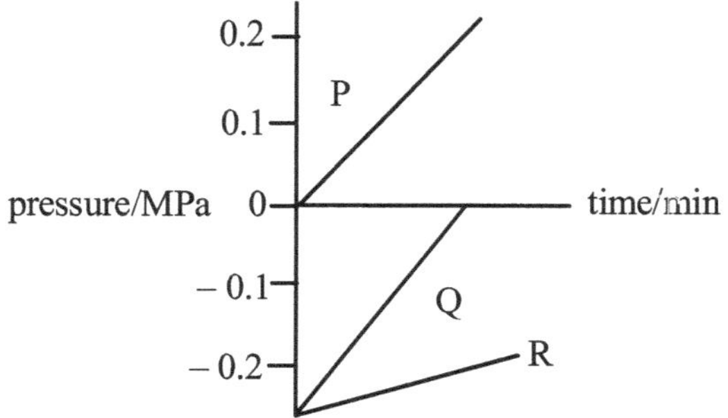

What are the correct labels for the graph?

	P	Q	R
(a)	ψ	ψ_p	ψ_s
(b)	ψ	ψ_s	ψ_p
(c)	ψ_p	ψ	ψ_s
(d)	ψ_p	ψ_s	ψ

11. In cells A, B, C, D potentials are as given below.

Cell	Solute potential	Pressure potential
A	– 15.0 bars	5.0 bars
B	– 25.0 bars	15.0 bars
C	– 30.0 bars	20.0 bars
D	– 35.0 bars	25.0 bars

Water will move from
   (a) A to B
   (b) B to A
   (c) A to B to C to D
   (d) Remain stationary

12. Match the columns and find out the correct combination:

   A. Simultaneous transport of two types of molecules   1. Uniport
   B. Co-transport of two molecules across the membrane in same direction   2. Co-transport
   C. Co-transport of two molecules across the membrane in opposite directions   3. Symport
   D. Transport of a molecule across a membrane, independent of other molecules   4. Antiport
      5. Passive transport

   (a) A-5, B-2, C-1, D-3
   (b) A-2, B-3, C-1, D-4
   (c) A-2, B-3, C-4, D-1
   (d) A-5, B-1, C-2, D-4

13. Find the wrongly match pair:
   (a) Guttation — Loss of impure water
   (b) Transpiration — Account for the majority of water transport
   (c) Girdling — Pholem is responsible for translocation of food
   (d) Unloading of minerals at the fine vein endings — Through active transport

14. Match the columns and find out the correct combinations:

   A. Potential gradient between root and leaf   1. Helps in gaseous exchange
   B. Organic solute gradient between source and sink   2. Helps in ascent of sap
   C. Positive hydrostatic pressure near roots   3. Helps in guttation
   D. Negative hydrostatic pressure near leaf   4. Helps in bulk flow of photosynthates
      5. Helps in transpiration pull (tension)

   (a) A-5, B-4, C-3, D-2
   (b) A-5, B-3, C-4, D-1
   (c) A-3, B-2, C-1, D-4
   (d) A-3, B-2, C-4, D-5

Solutions

1. (b)   2. (a)   3. (c)   4. (c)   5. (c)

6. (b)   7. (b)

8. (c)   Water potentials of the given cells are

$\Psi w = \Psi s + \Psi p$

$A = -0.87 + 0.44 = -0.43$

$B = -0.92 + 0.34 = -0.58$

$C = -0.68 + 0.27 = -0.41$

As water moves from greater water potential to less, root hair, root cortical and leaf mesophyll cells are C, A, B respectively.

9. (a)

10. (c)   Pure water has the highest water potential as zero. As water enters the cells, solute potential becomes less negative and the pressure potential is usually positive. As water enters the cell, the volume of protoplast increases, causing the pressure potential to rise from zero MPa.

11. (d)   Water potentials of all the four cells are equal.

12. (c)   13. (d)   14. (a)

Mineral Nutrition 

1. Select incorrect match with respect to mineral and the function:
   - (a) Zinc — Synthesis of auxin
   - (b) Chlorine — Photolysis of water
   - (c) Copper — Activator of alcohol dehydrogenase
   - (d) Molybednum — Nitrogen metabolism

2. Find out correctly matched pair:

Nutrients	Functions
(a) Zinc	Helps to maintain ribosome structure
(b) Magnesium	Needed during formation of mitotic spindle
(c) Potassium	Plays a role in opening and closing of stomata
(d) Calcium	Needed in splitting of water to liberate oxygen during photosynthesis.

3. Match the columns and choose the correct combination:

A.	Phosphorus	1.	Cell wall formation
B.	Potassium	2.	Activation of RuBisCo
C.	Calcium	3.	Phosphorylation
D.	Magnesium	4.	Take part in electron transport
		5.	Closing and opening of stomata

   - (a) A-1, B-5, C-3, D-2
   - (b) A-3, B-5, C-1, D-2
   - (c) A-2, B-5, C-1, D-3
   - (d) A-3, B-5, C-2, D-1

4. Match the columns and choose the correct options:

Disease	Deficiency of Minerals
(A) Khaira Disease	(i) Mn
(B) Marsh spot of Pea	(ii) Zn
(C) Brown rot disease	(iii) Mo
(D) Whip tail of cauliflower	(iv) B

   - (a) A-ii , B-i, C-iii, D-iv
   - (b) A-ii, B-i, C-iv, D-iii
   - (c) A-i, B-ii, C-iii, D-iv
   - (d) A-i, B-ii, C-iv, D-iii

5. Match the columns-I and column-II and choose the correct option:

Column I	Column II
1. Micronutrients	A. Fe, Mn
2. Macronutrients	B. *Nitrosomonas*
3. Nitrification	C. K, S
4. Denitrification	D. *Thiobacillus*

   - (a) 1-C, 2-A, 3-D, 4-B
   - (b) 1-C, 2-A, 3-B, 4-D
   - (c) 1-A, 2-C, 3-D, 4-B
   - (d) 1-A, 2-C, 3-B, 4-D

6. Match the columns:

Column I	Column II
A. Hydroponics	1. Zinc
B. Trace elements	2. Fe
C. Activation of catalase	3. Julius von sachs
D. Dark reaction	4. Calvin

   - (a) A-3, B-2, C-1, D-4
   - (b) A-4, B-3, C-2, D-1

7. Match the column-I with column-II

Column-I		Column-II
(A) Mg	p.	Found in some amino acids
(B) S	q.	Structural component of chlorophyll
(C) I	r.	Not important for plants
(D) Mn	s.	Required for photolysis of water

(a) A-q, B-p, C-r, D-s   (b) A-p, B-q, C-r, D-s
(c) A-p, B-r, C-s, D-q   (d) A-q, B-r, C-p, D-s

8. Match the Column-I containing minerals with the functions given in Column-II.

Column-I		Column-II
I. K	A.	Stomatal opening
II. Mo	B.	Constituent of cell membrane
III. P	C.	Photolysis of water
IV. Mn	D.	Free ion
	E.	Component of nitrogenase and nitrate reductase

	I	II	III	IV
(a)	A, D	E	B	C
(b)	A, E	D	C	B
(c)	A ,E	D	B	C
(d)	D	A	C	B, E

9. Refer the figure given below and select the option which gives correct words for all the four blanks A, B, C and D.

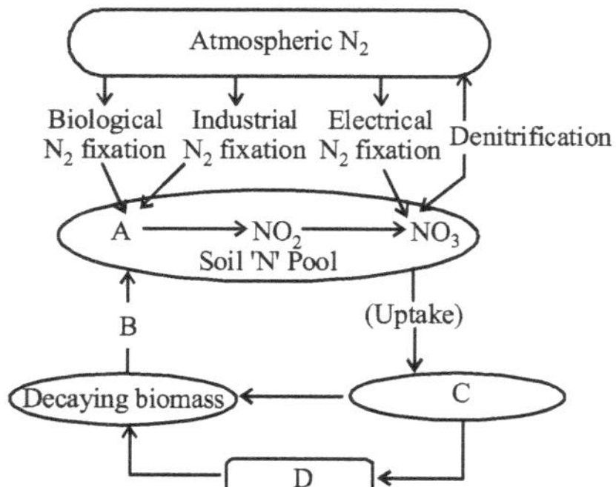

	A	B	C	D
(a)	K	Ammonification	Animal biomass	Plant biomass
(b)	NH₃	Ammonification	Plant biomass	Animal biomass
(c)	CO₂	Denitrification	Animal biomass	Plant biomass
(d)	CHO	Nitrification	Plant biomass	Animal biomass

10. A small aquatic plant was put in each of the petridishes -X, Y & Z, containing different culture solutions. After six weeks the plant in dish X had the same number of leaves as it had previously & were all small and yellowish. Plant in dish Y had more leaves of normal size and dark green colour. Plants in dish Z had more leaves of normal size but very pale. Which of the following show the element missing in the culture?

	X	Y	Z
(a)	Magnesium	Phosphorus	Nitrogen
(b)	Phosphorus	Magnesium	Nitrogen
(c)	Phosphorus	Nitrogen	Magnesium
(d)	Magnesium	Nitrogen	Phosphorus

11. Match the words of column I with the phrases in column II. Choose the answer which gives the correct combination.

Column I		Column II
(1) Magnesium	(p)	Found in some amino acids
(2) Sulphur	(q)	Not important for plants
(3) Iodine	(r)	Structural component of chlorophyll
(4) Manganese	(s)	Component of sugar
	(t)	Required for enzyme activity

(a) (1) – (r), (2) – (s), (3) – (q), (4) – (p)
(b) (1) – (r), (2) – (p), (3) – (q), (4) – (s)
(c) (1) – (r), (2) – (p), (3) – (q), (4) – (t)
(d) (1) – (s), (2) – (r), (3) – (p), (4) – (t)

12. Match the following and choose the correct combination from the options given.

	Column I		Column II
A.	Potassium	I.	Constituent of ferredoxin
B.	Sulphur	II.	Involved in stomatal movement
C.	Molybdenum	III.	Needed in the synthesis of auxin
D.	Zinc	IV.	Component of nitrogenase

(a) A-II, B-I, C-IV, D-III
(b) A-I, B-II, C-III, C-IV
(c) A-IV, B-III, C-II, D-I
(d) A-I, B-III, C-IV, D-II

13. Which of the following option shows correct co-relation between Column-I, II and III.

	Calumn-I		Column-II		Column-III
(A)	Calcium	(I)	Required for ionic-balance.	(i)	Grey blot on leaves.
(B)	Boron	(II)	Essential for constitution of nucleic acid	(ii)	Fruit-yield decreases.
(C)	Phosphorus	(III)	Required for absorption of calcium.	(iii)	Red blots on leaves.
(D)	Chlorine	(IV)	Required to activate respiratory enzyme.	(iv)	Fruit-size diminishes.
(E)	Manganese	(V)	Required for synthesis of bipolar spindle.	(v)	Young root tip begin to die.

(a) (A-I-iv), (B-II-v), (C-III-iii), (D-IV-i), (E-V-ii)
(b) (A-V-v), (B-IV-iv), (C-III-i), (D-III-iii), (E-I-ii)
(c) (A-IV-iii), (B-I-iv), (C-V-v), (D-III-ii), (E-II-i)
(d) (A-V-v), (B-III-iv), (C-II-iii), (D-I-ii), (E-IV-i)

14. Study the following lists.

	List I		List II
(A)	Photolysis of water	(i)	Zinc
(B)	Diazotrophy	(ii)	Copper
(C)	Cytochrome 'c' oxidase	(iii)	Manganese
(D)	Biosynthesis of IAA	(iv)	Molybdenum
		(v)	Boron

Identify the correct match.

(a) A – iii, B – iv, C – ii, D – i
(b) A – v, B – ii, C – iii, D – iv
(c) A – iii, B – ii, C – i, D – iv
(d) A – iv, B – i, C – iii, D – ii

15. Match the following and choose the correct combination from the options given.

	Column I		Column II
(A)	Sulphur	I.	Chlorophyll
(B)	Zinc	II.	Nitrogenase
(C)	Magnesium	III.	Methionine
(D)	Molybdenum	IV.	Auxin

(1) A – I, B – II, C – III, D – IV
(2) A – III, B – IV, C – I, D – II
(3) A – III, B – I, C – II, D – IV
(4) A – II, B – IV, C – I, D – III

19. Match column-I and Column-II and choose the correct option given below the columns.

Column-I (Element)	Column-II (Function)
A. Calcium	1. Required for ionic-balance.
B. Boron	2. Essential for constitution of nucleic acid
C. Phosphorus	3. Required for absorption of calcium.
D. Chlorine	4. Required to activate respiratory enzyme.
E. Manganese	5. Required for synthesis of mitotic spindle.

(a) A → 1; B → 2; C → 3; D → 4; E → 5
(b) A → 5; B → 4; C → 3; D → 2; E → 1
(c) A → 4; B → 1; C → 5; D → 3; E → 2
(d) A → 5; B → 3; C → 2; D → 1; E → 4

20. The given diagram shows a typical setup for hydroponic technique. Select the option which gives correct labelling for A, B and C.

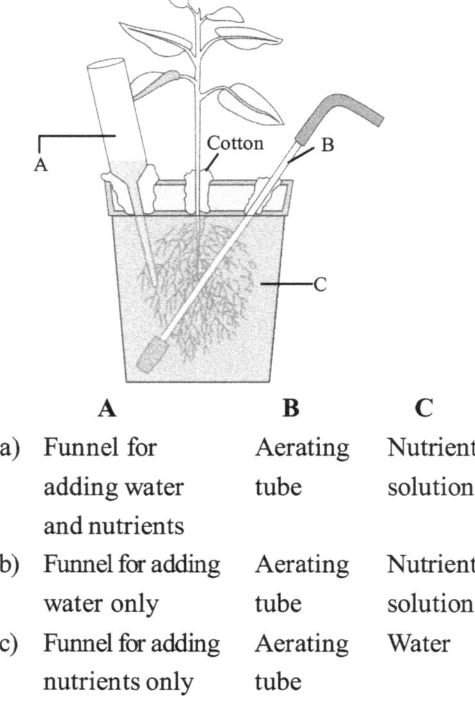

	A	B	C
(a)	Funnel for adding water and nutrients	Aerating tube	Nutrient solution
(b)	Funnel for adding water only	Aerating tube	Nutrient solution
(c)	Funnel for adding nutrients only	Aerating tube	Water
(d)	Funnel for adding water and nutrients	Aerating tube	Water

Solutions

1. (c)	2. (c)	3. (b)	4. (b)	5. (d)
6. (c)	7. (a)	8. (a)	9. (b)	10. (a)
11. (c)	12. (a)	13. (d)	14. (a)	15. (b)
19. (a)	20. (a)			

Photosynthesis

1. The rate of photosynthesis of a freshwater plant is measured using five spectral colours. Which sequence of colours would give an increasing photosynthetic response?

   Smallest → Largest response

   (a) Blue   Green   Yellow   Orange Red
   (b) Green   Yellow   Orange   Red   Blue
   (c) Red   Orange   Yellow   Green   Blue
   (d) Yellow   Green   Orange   Blue   Red

2. Which one of the following correctly identifies X and Y and shows their functions?

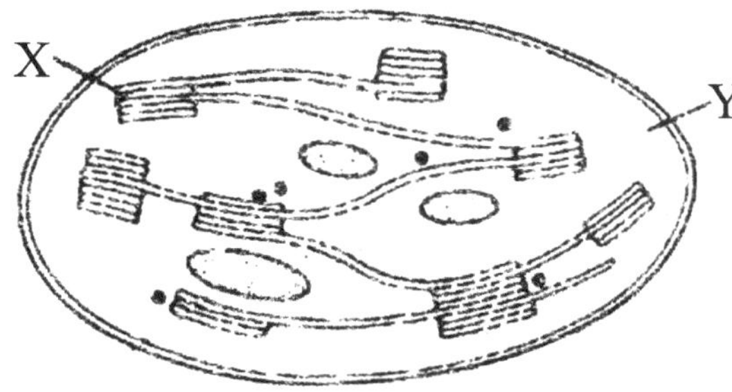

	X		Y	
	Structure	Function	Structure	Function
(a)	Grana	Photolysis of water	Stroma	CO_2 fixation
(b)	Grana	CO_2 fixation	Stroma	Photolysis of water
(c)	Stroma	Photolysis	Grana	CO_2 fixation
(d)	Grana	CO_2 fixation	Lamellae	Photolysis of water

3. Which of the following changes in concentration of chemicals (RuBP & GP) would occur if an illuminated green plant cell's source of carbon dioxide were removed?

	Ribulose bisphosphate	Glycerate phosphate
(a)	increase	increase
(b)	decrease	decrease
(c)	increase	decrease
(d)	decrease	increase

4. Which of the following with respect to early experiments of photosynthesis is wrongly matched?

   (a) Joseph Priestley   - Showed that plants release O_2

   (b) Jan Ingenhousz   - Showed that sunlight is essential for photosynthesis

   (c) Julius von Sachs   - Proved that plants produce glucose when they grow.

   (d) T. W. Engelmann   - Showed that the green substance is located within special bodies in plants

5. Which of following ratio is correct for the production of one molecule of glucose through 6 round of Calvin cycle?

	CO_2	:	ATP	:	$NADPH_2$
(a)	1	:	2	:	2
(b)	6	:	18	:	12
(c)	6	:	12	:	18
(d)	5	:	6	:	9

6. Which one is correct for C_4-plants?

	Mesophyll		Bundle Sheath	
(a)	PEPcase	C₄-Cycle	RuBisCO	C₃-Cycle
(b)	PEPcase	Calvin Cycle	RuBisCO	C₄-Cycle
(c)	RuBisCO	C₄-Cycle	PEPcase	C₃-Cycle
(d)	RuBisCO	C₂-Cycle	PEPcase	C₃-Cycle

7. The given diagram shows the ultrastructure of a chloroplast as seen in section. What are the functions of A, B and C?

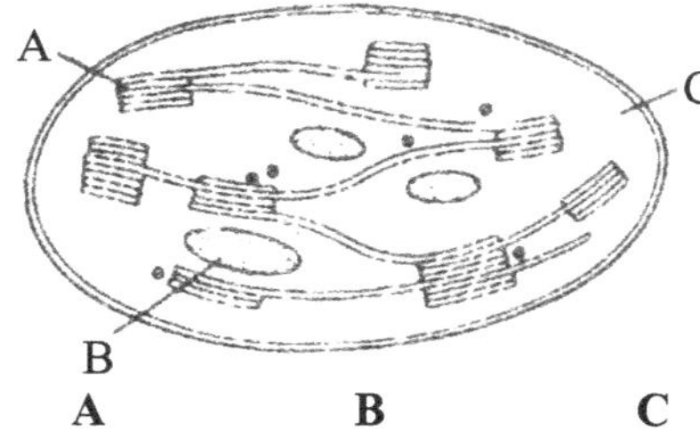

	A	**B**	**C**
(a)	Carbohydrate storage	Carbohydrate synthesis	Light reaction
(b)	Light reaction	Carbohydrate synthesis	Carbohydrate storage
(c)	Light reaction	Carbohydrate storage	Carbohydrate synthesis
(d)	Light absorption	Carbohydrate synthesis	Carbohydrate storage

8. The diagram below shows the movement of substances into in and out of a chloroplast with labelling A, B, C & D.

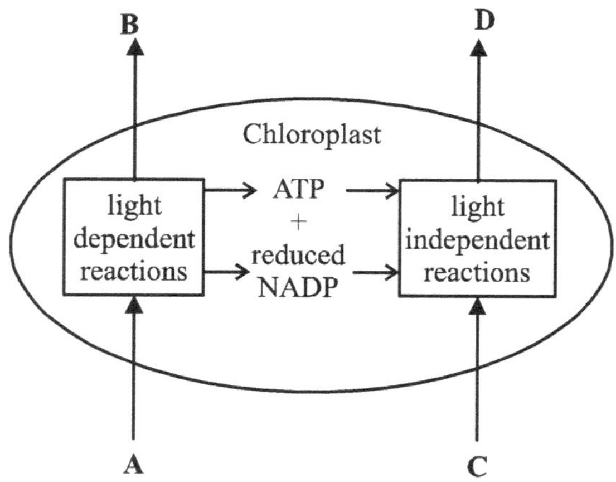

What do labels A to D represent ?

	A	**B**	**C**	**D**
(a)	CO_2	ATP	H_2O	Starch
(b)	CO_2	H_2O	Sugars	O_2
(c)	H_2O	O_2	CO_2	Sugar
(d)	Sugar	H_2O	ATP	O_2

9. Study the figure showing graph of light intensity on the rate of photosynthesis. Choose the correct option by matching the column I with column II

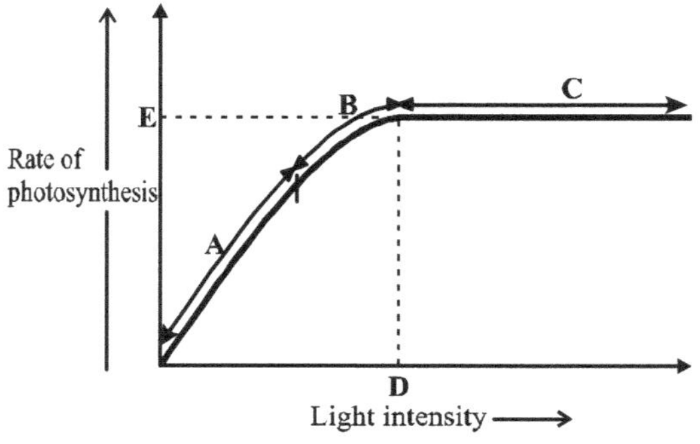

Column - I		**Column - II**
I.	Limiting factor in region A	A. Some factor other than light intensity is becoming the limiting factor
II.	B represents to	B. Light is no longer limiting factor
III.	C represents to	C. Light intensity
IV.	D represents to	D. Maximum rate of photosynthesis
V.	E represents to	E. Saturation point for light intensity

The correct option is -

(a) I - A, II - B, III - C, IV - D, V - E
(b) I - C, II - A, III - B, IV - E, V - D
(c) I - D, II - B, III - E, IV - C, V - A
(d) I - E, II - D, III - C, IV - B, V - A

10. The diagram below shows the Calvin cycle.

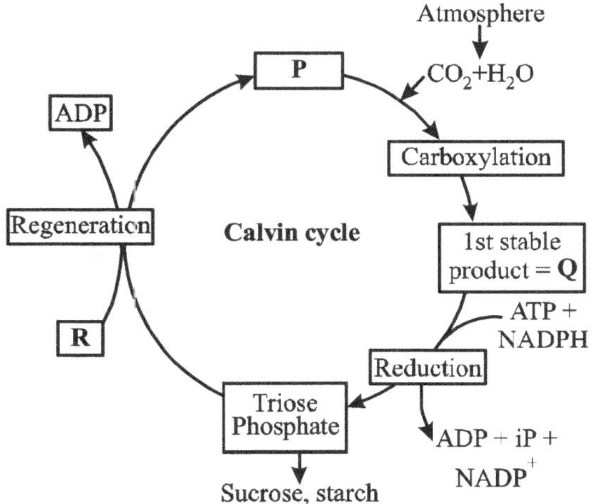

Identify P, Q and R

	P	**Q**	**R**
(a)	ATP	3PGA	RuBP
(c)	3PGA	ATP	Sugar
(b)	RuBP	3-PGA	ATP
(d)	Sugar	RuDP	NADPH

11. Two groups of isolated thylakoids are placed in an acidic bathing solution so that H^+ diffuses into the thylakoids. They are then transferred to a basic bathing solution, and one group is placed in the light, while the other group is kept in the dark. Select the choice given below that describes what you expect each group of thylakoids to produce.

	In Light	**In Dark**
(a)	ATP only	Nothing
(b)	ATP, O_2	ATP only
(c)	ATP, O_2, glucose	ATP, O_2
(d)	ATP, O_2	O_2

12. Make column I with column II.

Column-I	**Column-II**
(A) Emerson effect	(I) C_4 cycle
(B) Hill reaction	(II) Photolysis
(C) Calvin's cycle	(III) C_3 cycle
(D) Hatch and Slack cycle	(IV) Photosystem-I and II

(a) AI, BII, CIII, DIV

(b) AI, BIII, CIV, DI

(c) AIII, BIV, CI, DII

(d) AIV, BII, CIV, DI

Solutions

1.	(b)	2.	(a)	3.	(c)	4.	(d)	5.	(b)	11.	(b)	12.	(d)
6.	(a)	7.	(c)	8.	(c)	9.	(b)	10.	(c)				

Respiration in Plants  14

1. Choose the correct combination between respiratory substrates and their respective RQs.

	Carbohydrate	Fat	Protein
(a)	2	1	1
(b)	0	1	1
(c)	1	0.7	0.9
(d)	0.5	0.5	0.5

2. Refer the figure showing major pathway of anaerobic respiration.

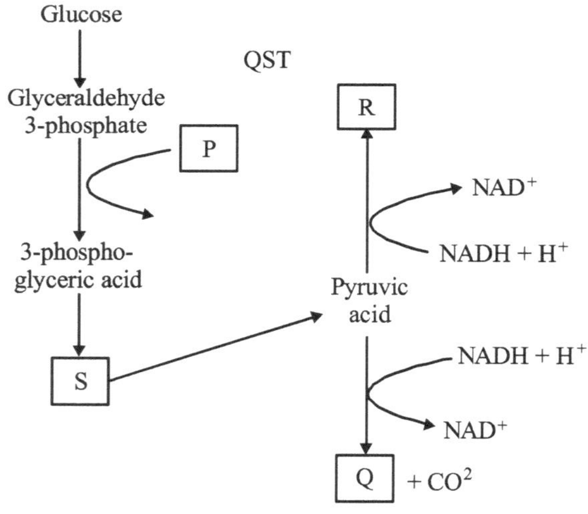

Identify P, Q, R and S in the above.

	P	Q	R	S
(a)	NAD^+	Ethanol	Lactic acid	PEP
(b)	Ethanol	NAD^+	Lactic acid	ATP
(c)	Lactic acid	Ethanol	Glucose	ADP
(d)	NAD	Lactic acid	Ethanol	DHAP

3. Refer the figure and answer the question.

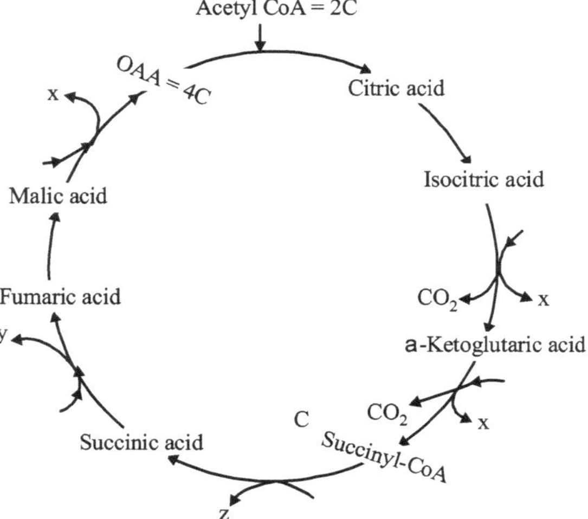

Identify X, Y and Z.

	X	Y	Z
(a)	GTP	$NADH_2$	CO_2
(b)	$FADH_2$	$NADH_2$	GTP
(c)	$NADH_2$	$FADH_2$	GTP
(d)	CO_2	$NADH_2$	ADP

4. The expressions given below shows the summary equations.

(i) Pyruvate $\xrightarrow{\quad NADH + H^+ \quad\quad NAD^+\quad}$

$C_2H_5OH + CO_2$

(i) $C_6H_{12}O_6 + NAD^+ + 2ADP + 2\,iP \rightarrow 2C_3H_4O_3 + 2ATP + 2NADH + 2H^+$

(iii) Pyruvic acid $+ 4NAD^+ + FAD^+ + 2H_2O + ADP + Pi \rightarrow 3CO_2 + 4NADH + 4H^+ + ATP + FADH_2$

Categorise the summary equations under respective phases.

	I	II	III
(a)	Krebs' cycle	Glycolysis	Fermentation
(b)	Glycolysis	Krebs' cycle	Fermentation
(c)	Fermentation	Krebs' cycle	Glycolysis
(d)	Fermentation	Glycolysis	Krebs' cycle

5. Match the number of carbon atoms given in List - I with that of the compounds given in List - II and select the correct option.

List - I	List - II
A. 4C Compound	I. Acetyl CoA
B. 2C Compound	II. Pyruvate
C. 5C Compound	III. Citric acid
D. 3C Compound	IV. α-ketoglutaric acid
	V. Malic acid

(a) A-II, B-V, C-III, D-I
(b) A-V, B-I, C-IV, D-II
(c) A-III, B-I, C-IV, D-II
(d) A-V, B-III, C-I, D-II

6. Match the column I with column II

Column I	Column II
(A) EMP pathway	I. Mitochondrial matrix
(B) TCA cycle	II. Cytoplasm
(C) ETC	III. Inner mitochondrial membrane

	A	B	C
(a)	I	II	III
(b)	II	I	III
(c)	II	III	I
(d)	III	II	I

7. Match the sites in column I with processes in column II and choose the correct combination from the options.

Column I	Column II
(A) Grana of chloroplast	(i) Krebs cycle
(B) Stroma of chloroplast	(ii) Light reaction
(C) Cytoplasm	(iii) Dark reaction
(D) Mitochondrial matrix	(iv) Glycolysis

(a) A – (iv), B – (iii), C – (ii), D – (i)
(b) A – (i), B – (ii), C – (iv), D – (iii)
(c) A – (ii), B – (i), C – (iii), D – (iv)
(d) A – (ii), B – (iii), C – (iv), D – (i)

8. Choose the correct combination of labelling the number of carbon compounds in the substrate molecules, involved in the citric acid cycle.

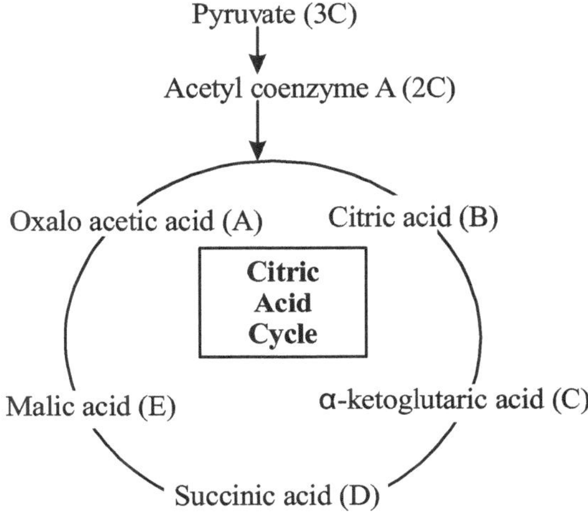

(a) (A) 4C, (B) 6C, (C) 5C, (D) 4C, (E) 4C
(b) (A) 6C, (B) 5C, (C) 4C, (D) 3C, (E) 2C
(c) (A) 2C, (B) 5C, (C) 6C, (D) 4C, (E) 4C
(d) (A) 4C, (B) 6C, (C) 4C, (D) 4C, (E) 5C

9. Match the compounds given in Column I with the number of carbon atoms present in them which are listed under Column II. Choose the answer which gives the correct combination of alphabets of the two column.

Column-I	Column-II
A. Oxaloacetate	p. 6-C compound
B. Phosphoglycrealdehyde	q. 5-C compound
C. Isocitrate	r. 4-C compound
D. α-ketoglutarate	s. 3-C compound
	t. 2-C compound

	A	B	C	D
(a)	s	t	q	r
(b)	r	s	p	q
(c)	r	t	p	q
(d)	q	s	p	t

10. At the end of glycolysis X is the net energy gain from one molecule of glucose *via* Y, but there is also energy stored in the form of Z. Identify X, Y and Z from the given options.

	X	**Y**	**Z**
(a)	1ATP	Oxidative phosphorylation	$NADH + H^+$
(b)	2ATPs	Oxidative phosphorylation	$NADH + H^+$
(c)	2ATPs	Substrate level phosphorylation	$NADPH + H^+$
(d)	2ATPs	Substrate level phosphorylation	$NADH + H^+$

11. The figure indicates the interrelationship among metabolic pathways. Now identify A to D.

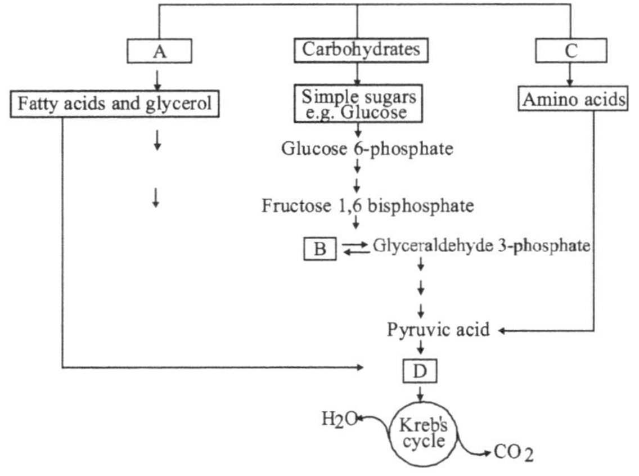

	A	**B**	**C**	**D**
(a)	Protein	Acetyl CoA	Fat	DHAP
(b)	Fat	DHAP	Protein	Acetyl CoA
(c)	Acetyl CoA	Fat	DHAP	Protein
(d)	Fat	DHAP	Acetyl CoA	Protein

12. The diagram shows stalked particles on part of a crista membrane in a mitochondrion.

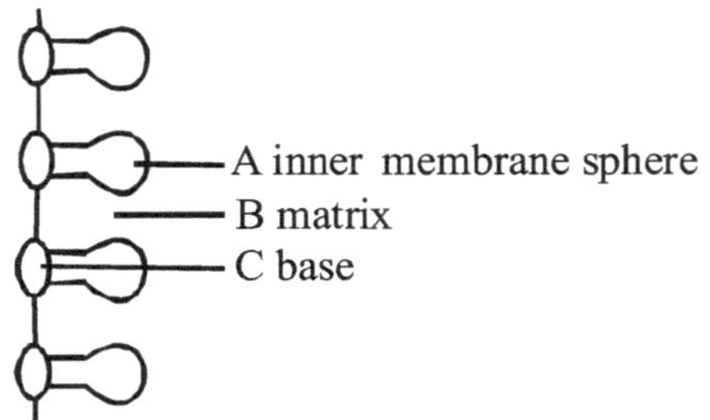

What occurs in each of the numbered regions?

	A	**B**	**C**
(a)	ADP synthesis	Electron transport	Krebs cycle
(b)	ADP synthesis	Glycolysis	Krebs cycle
(c)	ATP synthesis	Krebs cycle	Electron transport
(d)	ATP synthesis	Krebs cycle	Glycolysis

Solutions

1. (c) 2. (a) 3. (c) 4. (d) 5. (b)
6. (b) 7. (d) 8. (a) 9. (b) 10. (d)
11. (b)
12. (c) The electron transport system occurs in 3, and is coupled to proton transport across the inner membrane (1), generating the proton-motive force, powering ATP synthesis. Krebs cycle occurs in the matrix, where two molecules of acetyl CoA are oxidized.

Plant Growth and Development

CHAPTER 15

1. Refer the functions of the growth hormones given below.

   I. Cell division
   II. Cell enlargement
   III. Pattern formation
   IV. Tropic growth
   V Flowering
   VI. Fruiting
   VII. Seed germination
   VIII. Response to wound
   IX. Response to stresses of biotic and abiotic origin

   Identify the functions of growth promoters and growth inhibitors from the above.

	Functions of growth promoters	Functions of growth inhibitor
(a)	I, II, VII, IX	III, IV, V, VI, VII
(b)	VIII, IX	I, II, III, IV, V, VI, VII
(c)	I, II, III, IV, V, VI, VII	VIII, IX
(d)	I, II, III, IV, V, VI, VII, IX	VIII

2. Match the column A (Scientists) with column B (Discovery).

	Column-A		Column-B
I.	C. Darwin and F. Darwin	A.	Cytokinin
II.	Miller and Skoog	B.	ABA
III.	F.W. Went	C.	C_2H_4
IV.	Kurosawa	D.	Auxin
		E.	GA

	I	II	III	IV
(a)	D	A	C	E
(b)	D	A	E	B
(c)	C	A	B	D
(d)	E	D	A	C

3. Refer the statements given below.

   Statement-I :
   Confirmation of the release of volatile substance from ripened oranges that hastened the ripening of stored unripe bananas.

   Statement-II :
   Callus formation takes place from internodal segments of tobacco stem with the auxin and the nutrient medium containing extracts of vascular tissues/yeast/coconut milk/ DNA. Later, cytokinesis promoting substance was identified, crystallized and named as Kinetin.

   Statement-III :
   Reporting of appearance of symptoms of bakane/foolish seedling disease caused by fungus, Gibberella fujikuroi, in uninfected seedling when they were treated with sterile filtrates of the fungus. The active substances were later identified as GA.

   Choose the correct option.

	I	II	III
(a)	Miller + Skoog	Cousins	Kurosawa
(b)	Kurosawa	Cousins	Miller + Skoog
(c)	Cousins	Kurosawa	Miller + Skoog
(d)	Cousins	Miller + Skoog	Kurosawa

4. The picture below shows three different types of plants (marked as P-I, P-II and P-III) which flower on the basis of their critical photoperiod. Now identify these plants (P-I, II and III)."

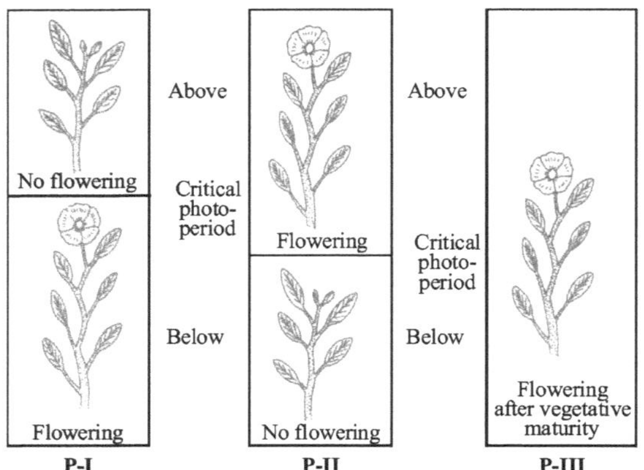

(a) P-I = Long day plant; P-II = Short day plant; P-III = Day neutral plant

(b) P-I = Short day plant; P-II = Long day plant; P-III = Day neutral plant

(c) P-I = Short day plant; P-II = Short day plant; P-III = Day neutral plant

(d) P-I = Long day plant; P-II = Long day plant; P-III = Day neutral plant

5. The picture below shows a graph drawn on the parameters of growth versus time. A, B, C respectively represent

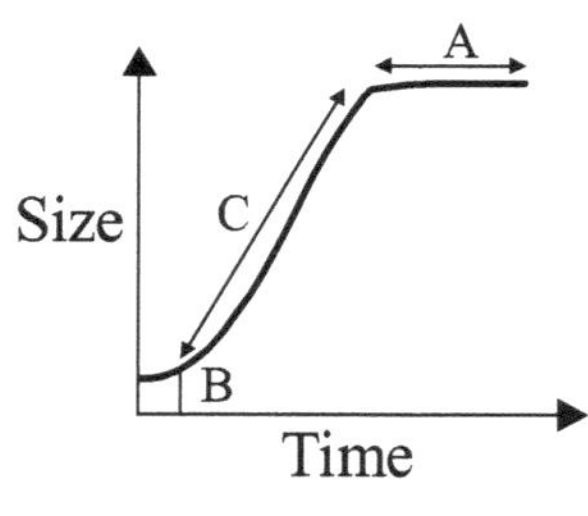

	A	B	C
(a)	Exponential phase	Log phase	Steady state phase
(b)	Steady state phase	Lag phase	Log phase
(c)	Log phase	Steady state phase	Logarithmic phase
(d)	Log phase	Lag phase	Steady state phase

6. Refer the diagram which shows the stages of seed germination.

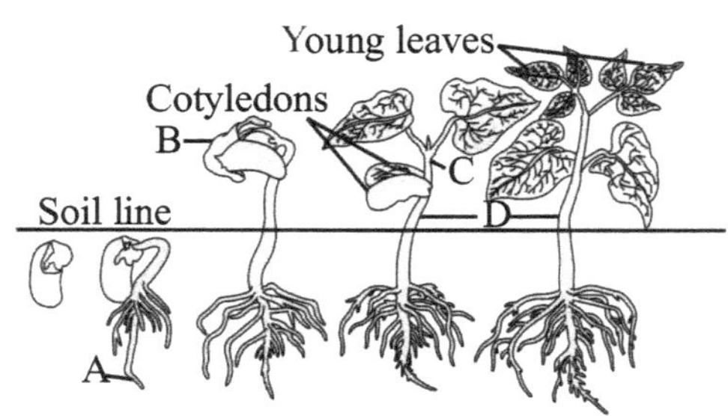

Identify A, B, C and D.

	A	B	C	D
(a)	Plumule	Cotyledons	Hypocotyl	Epicotyl
(b)	Radicle	Seed coat	Epicotyl	Hypocotyl
(c)	Hypocotyl	Cotyledons	Epicotyl	Root hair
(d)	Root hair	Cotyledons	Plumule	Hypocotyl

7. Match the plant hormones listed in column-I with their major role listed in column-II. Select the correct option from the codes given below.

Column-A	Column-B
(A) Auxin	(I) Fruit ripening
(B) Cytokinins	(II) Phototropism
(C) Abscisic acid	(III) Antagonist to GAs
(D) Ethylene	(IV) Stomatal opening and closing
	(V) Growth of lateral buds

(a) A-IV; B-V; C-III; D-I

(b) A-II; B-IV; C-III, IV; D-I

(c) A-I; B-V; C-III, IV; D-I

(d) A-III, IV; B-V; C-II; D-I

8. Match the growth regulators in column-I with the processes in column-II and choose the correct combination.

Column-I	Column-II
(A) Auxin	(i) Colouring test in lemon
(B) Gibberellin	(ii) Cell division test in plants
(C) Cytokinin	(iii) Avena curvature test
(D) Ethylene	(iv) Dwarf corn test

(a) (A) – (iii), (B) – (iv), (C) – (ii), (D) – (i)
(b) (A) – (i), (B) – (iv), (C) – (ii), (D) – (iii)
(c) (A) – (iv), (B) – (iii), (C) – (i), (D) – (ii)
(d) (A) – (ii), (B) – (i), (C) – (iv), (D) – (iii)

9. Which of the following is **incorrectly** matched?

(a) Explant   – Excised plant part used for callus formation
(b) Cytokinins   – Root initiation in callus
(c) Somatic embryo   – Embryo produced from a vegetative cell
(d) Anther culture   – Haploid plants

10. Match list I and list II and select the correct option.

List-I	List-II
(A) Auxin	(I) Herring sperm DNA
(B) Cytokinin	(II) Inhibitor of growth
(C) Gibberellin	(III) Apical dominance
(D) Ethylene	(IV) Epinasty
(E) Abscisic acid	(V) Induces amylase synthesis

(a) A-III, B-I, C-V, D-IV, E-II
(b) A-IV, B-V, C-I, D-III, E-II
(c) A-II, B-I, C-V, D-III, E-IV
(d) A-III, B-I, C-V, D-II, E-IV

11. Match the following and choose the correct combination

Column I	Column II
(1) Zeatin	1. Flowering hormone
(2) Florigen	2. Synthetic auxin
(3) IBA	3. Cytokinin
(4) NAA	4. Natural auxin

(a) A – 3, B – 4, C – 1, D – 2
(b) A – 2, B – 1, C – 4, D – 3
(c) A – 1, B – 2, C – 3, D – 4
(d) A – 3, B – 1, C – 4, D – 2

12. Which one of the following pairs, is not correctly matched?

(a) Abscisic acid   — Stomatal closure
(b) Gibberellic acid — Leaf fall
(3) Cytokinin   — Cell division
(4) IAA   — Cell wall elongation

13. Which one of the following pairs is incorrectly matched?

(a) Adenine derivative   - kinetin
(b) Carotenoid derivative - ABA
(c) Terpenes   - IAA
(d) Indole compounds   - IBA

14. Match the following and choose the correct combination from the options given.

Column I (Growth Regulator)	Column II (Action)
(A) Abscisic acid	1. Delays leaf senescence
(B) Ethylene	2. Inhibits seed germination
(C) Cytokinin	3. Herbicide
(D) Auxin	4. Hastens fruit ripening

(a) A-2, B-4, C-1, D-3
(b) A-1, B-2, C-3, D-4
(c) A-2, B-3, C-4, D-1
(d) A-2, B-1, C-3, D-4

15. Match the following columns and choose the correct combination

Column A	Column B
(A) Zeatin	(i) Flowering hormone
(B) Florigen	(ii) Natural auxin
(C) IBA	(iii) Cytokinin
(D) NAA	(iv) Synthetic auxin

	A	B	C	D
(a)	iii	i	iv	ii
(b)	iii	iv	i	ii
(c)	ii	i	iv	iii
(d)	i	ii	iii	iv

Solutions

1. (c) 2. (a) 3. (d) 4. (b) 5. (b)
6. (b) 7. (c) 8. (a) 9. (b) 10. (a)
11. (d) 12. (b) 13. (c) 14. (a) 15. (a)

Digestion and Absorption

1. Match the entities of Column I with Column II and choose the right option from the codes given below.

	Column I		Column II
A.	Cardiac sphincter	1.	Hepatopancreatic duct
B.	Pyloric sphincter	2.	Join gall bladder to common bile duct
C.	Sphincter of Oddi	3.	Opening of stomach into duodenum
D.	Cystic ducts	4.	Opening of oesophagus into stomach

Codes

	A	B	C	D
(a)	4	3	1	2
(b)	4	3	2	1
(c)	3	4	1	2
(d)	2	1	3	4

2. Match the following Columns.

	Column I		Column II
A.	Kupffer's cells	1.	Islets of Langerhans
B.	β - cells	2.	Liver sinusoids
C.	Bruch border cells	3.	Thyroid gland
D.	Paneth cells	4.	Proximal convoluted tubule
		5.	Small intestine

Codes

	A	B	C	D
(a)	3	1	4	2
(b)	4	5	1	2
(c)	2	1	4	5
(d)	3	5	4	1

3. Match the following Column.

	Column I		Column II
A.	Vitamin - B_1	1.	Thiamin
B.	Vitamin - B_3	2.	Niacin
C.	Vitamin - A	3.	Retinol
D.	Vitamin - B_2	4.	Riboflavin

Codes

	A	B	C	D
(a)	1	2	3	4
(b)	1	3	4	2
(c)	3	4	2	1
(d)	4	3	2	1

4. Match the following Column.

	Column I		Column II
A.	Retinol	1.	Inhibits oxidation of unsaturated fatty acids
B.	Tocoferol	2.	Absorption of calcium ions
C.	Calciferol	3.	Essential for maintenance of epithelial tissue
D.	Ascorbic acid	4.	Required for amino acid metabolism

Codes

	A	B	C	D
(a)	3	2	4	1
(b)	2	3	1	4
(c)	3	1	2	4
(d)	4	1	2	3

5. Match the enzyme with their rrespective substrates and choose the right one among options given.

Column I	Column II
A. Lipase	1. Dipeptides
B. Nuclease	2. Fats
C. Carboxypeptidase	3. Nucleic acids
D. Dipeptidases	4. Proteins, peptones and proteoses

Codes

	A	B	C	D
(a)	2	3	1	4
(b)	3	4	2	1
(c)	3	1	4	2
(d)	2	3	4	1

6. Match column I with column II and select the correct option frorm the given codes.

Column I (Types of cell)	Column II (Secretions)
A. Peptic cells	(i) Mucus
B. Oxyntic cells	(ii) Alkaline fluid
C. Goblet cells	(iii) Pro-enzymes
	(iv) HCl

(a) A-(ii),   B-(iii),   C-(i)
(b) A-(iii),   B-(ii),   C-(i)
(c) A-(i),   B-(ii),   C-(iii)
(d) A-(ii),   B-(i),   C-(iii)

7. Match column I with column II and select the correct option frorm the given codes.

Column I	Column II
A. Van Kupffer cells	(i) Islets of Langerhans
B. β-cells	(ii) Liver sinusoids
C. Oxyntic cells	(iii) Thyroid gland
D. Crypts of Lieberkuhn	(iv) Stomach
	(v) Small intestine

(a) A-(iv),   B-(v),   C-(i),   D-(ii)
(b) A-(iii),   B-(i),   C-(iv),   D-(ii)
(c) A-(iv),   B-(v),   C-(iii),   D-(i)
(d) A-(ii),   B-(i),   C-(iv),   D-(v)

8. Column I contains names of the sphincter muscles of the alimentary canal and Column II contains their locations. Match them properly and choose the correct answer.

Column I	Column II
A. Sphincter of ani internus	1. Opening of hepato-pancreatic duct into duodenum
B. Cardiac sphincter	2. Between duodenum and posterior stomach
C. Sphincter of Oddi	3. Guarding the terminal part of alimentary canal
D. Ileocaecal	4. Between oesophagus sphincter and anterior stomach
E. Pyloric sphincter	5. Between small intestine and bowel

(a) A – 3,   B – 2,   C – 4,   D – 1,   E – 5
(b) A – 2,   B – 5,   C – 1,   D – 4,   E – 3
(c) A – 3,   B – 4,   C – 1,   D – 5,   E – 2
(d) A – 4,   B – 3,   C – 1,   D – 2,   E – 5

9. Match the column I with column II and column III. Choose the correct option.

Column I (Substrate)	Column II (Enzyme)	Column III (Product)
1. Lactose	A. Lipase	I. Galactose
2. Monoglycerides	B. Trypsin	II. Maltose
3. Starch	C. Lactase	III. Fatty acid
4. Peptones	D. Amylase	IV. Dipeptides

(a) 1-A-I; 2-C-II; 3-B-III; 4-D-IV
(b) 1-D-I; 2-A-II; 3-B-III; 4-C-IV
(c) 1-C-I; 2-A-III; 3-D-II; 4-B-IV
(d) 1-C-I; 2-A-II; 3-D-III; 4-B-IV
(e) 1-D-I; 2-D-II; 3-C-III; 4-A-IV

10. Match column I with column II and choose the correct option.

	Column I		Column II
A.	Goblet cells	1.	Antibacterial agent
B.	Lysozyme	2.	Mucus
C.	Saliva	3.	HCl
D.	Oxyntic cells	4.	Sublingual gland

(a) A-3, B-1, C-4, D-2
(b) A-1, B-3, C-4, D-2
(c) A-2, B-3, C-1, D-4
(d) A-4, B-1, C-2, D-3
(e) A-2, B-1, C-4, D-3

11. Match the items given in column I with those in column II and choose the correct option.

	Column I		Column II
A.	Rennin	(i)	Vitamin B_{12}
B.	Enterokinase	(ii)	Facilitated transport
C.	Oxyntic cells	(iii)	Milk proteins
D.	Fructose	(iv)	Trypsinogen

(a) A-iii, B-iv, C-ii, D-i
(b) A-iv, B-iii, C-i, D-ii
(c) A-iv, B-iii, C-ii, D-i
(d) A-iii, B-iv, C-i, D-ii

12. Select the correct match of the digested products in humans given in column I with their absorption site and mechanism in column II.

	Column I	Column II
(a)	Glycerol, fatty acids	Duodenum, move as chylomicrons
(b)	Cholesterol, maltose	Large intestine, active absorption
(c)	Glycine, glucose	Small intestine, active absorption
(d)	Fructose, Na^+	Small intestine, passive absorption

13. Match column I with column II.

	Column I		Column II
A.	Vitamin B1	1.	Accumulation of fat
B.	Gastric juice	2.	Loss of fat
C.	Starvation	3.	Pepsin
D.	Obesity	4.	Beri-beri

(a) P-(iii), Q-(iv), R-(ii), S-(i)
(b) P-(iii), Q-(iv), R-(i), S-(ii)
(c) P-(iv), Q-(iii), R-(ii), S-(i)
(d) P-(iv), Q-(ii), R-(iii), S-(i)

14. Which one of the following four secretions is correctly matched with its source, target and nature of action ?

	Secretion	Source	Target	Action
(1)	Gastrin	Stomach lining	Oxyntic cells	Production of HCl
(2)	Inhibin	Sertoli cells	Hypotha-lamus	inhibition of secretion of ganadotropin releasing hormone
(3)	Entero-kinase	Duode-num	Gall bladder	Release of bile juice
(4)	Atrial Natriuretic factor (ANF)	Sinu atrial node(SAN) M-cells of Atria	Juxta-glomerular apparatus (JGA)	Inhibition of release of renin

15. Find out the correct matching between the cells of gastric gland and their respective secretory products:

	Column I		Column II
A.	Neck cells	I.	HCl, Intrinsic factor
B.	Peptic/ Chief cells	II.	Mucus
C.	Parietal/ Oxyntic cells	III.	Pepsinogen

(a) A-II, B-III, C-I
(b) A-III, B-II, C-I
(c) A-I, B-II, C-III
(d) A-I, B-III, C-II

16. Match the following structures with their respective location in organs

	Column I		Column II
A.	Crypts of Lieberkuhn	i.	Pancreas
B.	Glisson's Capsule	ii.	Duodenum
C.	Islets of Langerhans	iii.	Small intestine
D.	Brunner' glands	iv.	Liver

Select the correct option from the following

	(A)	(B)	(C)	(D)
(a)	(iii)	(i)	(ii)	(iv)
(b)	(ii)	(iv)	(i)	(iii)
(c)	(iii)	(iv)	(i)	(ii)
(d)	(iii)	(ii)	(i)	(iv)

17. Read the following table carefully and choose the incorrectly matched option

	Enzyme	State of Function	Substrate	Products
(a)	Ptyalin	Mouth	Starch	Disaccharides
(b)	Pepsin	Stomach	Protein	Large peptides
(c)	Lipase	Small Intestine	Triglycerides	Fatty acids
(d)	Nucleotidase	Large Intestine	Nucleotidase	Nucleosides phosphoric acid

18. Match the following

	Column I		Column II
A.	Mucosa	(i)	Bases of villi
B.	Villi	(ii)	Small intestine
C.	Submucosa	(iii)	Villi and rugae
D.	Crypts	(iv)	Nerves, blood and lymphatic vessels

(a) A-(ii), B-(iii), C-(i), D-(iv)
(b) A-(i), B-(iv), C-(ii), D-(iii)
(c) A-(iii), B-(ii), C-(iv), D-(i)
(d) A-(ii), B-(iii), C-(iv), D-(i)

Solutions

1. (a)   **2.** (c)   **3.** (a)   **4.** (c)   **5.** (d)

6. (d) Gastic glands are numerous, microscopic, simple tubular glands present in the wall of the stomach. They have three common types of gland cell : (i) Peptic (= chief or zymogen) cells that are usually basal in location and secrete digestive enzymes pepsinogen and proprennin (proenzymes) and small amounts of gastric amylase and gastric lipase. (ii) Parietal (= oxyntic) cells secrete HCl and Castle's intrinsic factor. (iii) Mucous (= Goblet) cells secrete mucus.

7. (d)   **8.** (c)   **9.** (a)   **10.** (e)   **11.** (d)

12. (c) Glycerol and fatty acids are absorbed in jejunum by diffusion into intestinal cells where thy are converted into chylomicrons. Cholesterol is also absorbed by simple diffusion in small intestine. Maltose is broken into glucose and galactose which are absorbed by active transport into small intestine. Fructose is absorbed by facilitated diffusion. Amino acids are also absorbed in small intestine, some by active transport and some by facilitated diffusion.

13. (c)   **14.** (d)   **15.** (a)   **16.** (c)   **17.** (d)

18. (c)

CHAPTER 17

Breathing and Exchange of Gases

1. Match the items listed under column I with those given under column II. Choose the appropriate option from the given choices.

Column I		Column II
(a)	Residual volume (RV)	p. 4000mL - 4600 mL
(b)	Inspiratory Reserve Volume (IRV)	q. 1100mL-1200 mL
(c)	Vital capacity (VC)	r. 1000mL - 1100 mL
(d)	Expiratory Reserve Volume (ERV)	s. 3000mL - 3500 mL
(e)	Inspiratory capacity (IC)	t. 2500mL - 3000 mL

	A	B	C	D	E
(a)	t	q	s	r	p
(b)	q	r	s	t	p
(c)	q	t	p	r	s
(d)	r	t	p	q	s

2. Listed below are four respiratory capacities (i-iv) and four jumbled respiratory volumes of a normal human adult.

Respiratory capacities	Respiratory volumes
(i) Residual volume	2500 mL
(ii) Vital capacity	3500 mL
(iii) Inspiratory reserve volume	1200 mL
(iv) Inspiratory capacity	4500 mL

Which one oif the following is the correct matching of two capacities and volumes?

(a) (ii) 2500 mL,   (iii) 4500 mL
(b) (iii) 1200 mL,   (iv) 2500 mL
(c) (iv) 3500 mL,   (i) 1200 mL
(d) (i) 4500 mL,   (ii) 3500 mL

3. Match the columns and select the corect option from the codes given below.

A. TV + ERV   1. Expiratory capacity
B. RV + ERV + TV + IRV   2. Total lung capacity
C. ERV + RV   3. Functional residual capacity

(a) A-(i),   B-(ii)   C-(iii)
(b) A-(iii),   B-(i)   C-(ii)
(c) A-(iii),   B-(ii)   C-(i)
(d) A-(ii),   B-(iii)   C-(i)

4. Read the following statements with regard to oxyhaemoglobin dissociation curve.

I. The curve is ___A___ shaped under normal conditions.

II. ___B___ has an affinity to bind with deoxygenated haemoglobin by producing conformational changes in it.

III. The Curve is ___C___ in the presence of weak electrolytes. Identify A, B and C.

	A	B	C
(a)	sigmoid,	Carbon monoxide,	sigmoid
(b)	sigmoid,	2, 3-DPG,	hyperbolic
(c)	sigmoid,	Oxygen	hyperbolic
(d)	sigmoid,	Carbon monoxide,	straight

6. Match the following Columns.

	Column I		Column II
A.	Tiny air sacs in the lungs	1.	Internal respiration
B.	Gas diffusion between alveoli and blood in lungs	2.	Haemoglobin
C.	Gas exchange between blood and interstitial fluid	3.	Alveoli
D.	Molecule specialised for oxygen transprot	4.	External respiration

Codes

	A	B	C	D
(a)	3	4	1	2
(b)	1	2	3	4
(c)	4	3	2	1
(d)	2	1	4	3

7. Match the following Columns.

	Column I		Column II
A.	Bronchial tree	1.	Passage way for air from nasal cavity to larynx and food from mouth cavity to oesophagus
B.	Larynx	2.	Conducts air from trachea to the alveoli to its mucous lining continues to filter air
C.	Trachea	3.	Passage way for air, prevents foreign objects from entering trachea and houses vocal cords
D.	Pharynx	4.	Flexible tube, which connects larynx with bronchial tree

8. Match the following Columns.

	Column I		Column II
A.	pO_2 of alveoli lungs	1.	40 mm Hg
B.	pO_2 of atmospheric air	2.	95 mm Hg
C.	pO_2 of deoxygenated blood	3.	104 mm Hg
D.	pO_2 of oxygenated blood	4.	159 mm Hg

Codes

	A	B	C	D
(a)	2	4	1	3
(b)	3	4	1	2
(c)	3	2	1	4
(d)	2	4	3	1

9. The correct match for kind of respiration is

	Animal		*Respiration*
A.	Earthworm	1.	Pulmonary
B.	Human	2.	Branchial
C.	Prawn	3.	Tracheal
D.	Insects	4.	Cutaneous

(a) 1-A, 2-B, 3-C, 4-D
(b) 4-A, 2-B, 1-C, 3-D
(c) 4-A, 1-B, 2-C, 3-D
(d) 3-A, 2-B, 4-C, 1-D

10. Match the disorders given in column I with symptoms under column II. Choose the answer which gives the correct combination of alphabets with numbers.

	Column I		Column II
A.	Asthma	1.	Inflammation of nasal tract

B. Bronchitis 2. Spasm of bronchial muscles

C. Rhinitis 3. Fully blown out alveoli

D. Amphysema 4. Inflammation of bronchi

5. Cough with blood strained sputum

(a) A = 4, B = 2, C = 5, D = 1

(b) A = 5, B = 3, C = 2, D = 1

(c) A = 3, B = 1, C = 5, D = 4

(d) A = 2, B = 4, C = 1, D = 3

11. Listed below are four respiratory capacities (a-d) and four jumbled respiratory volume of a normal human adult:

Respiratory capacities	*Respiratory volumes*
(a) Residual volume	2500 mL
(b) Vital capacity	3500 mL
(c) Inspiratory reserve volume	1200 mL
(d) Inspiratory capacity	4500 mL

12. Identify the wrong differences between inspiration and expiration:

Inspiration	Expiration
(A) EICM	Contract Relax
(B) Size of thoracic cavity	Increases Decreases
(C) Shape of diaphragm	Flat Dome shaped
(D) Movement of air	Atmosphere to lungs Lungs to atmosphere

(a) A, B   (b) B,C

(c) B,D   (d) C,D

13. Match the items given in column I with column II and choose the correct option:

Column I		Column II
A. Hypocapnia	(i)	Destroy the alveolar wall
B. Anoxia	(ii)	Difficulty in breathing
C. Tachypnoea	(iii)	Decrease CO_2 concentration in blood
D. Asthma	(iv)	To stop O_2 supply in tissue
E. Emphysema	(v)	To increase breathing rate
F. Dyspnoea	(vi)	Spasm in respiratory tubules

	A	B	C	D	E	F
(a)	(v)	(i)	(iii)	(ii)	(vi)	(iv)
(b)	(iii)	(iv)	(v)	(vi)	(i)	(ii)
(c)	(iii)	(iv)	(v)	(i)	(vi)	(ii)
(d)	(iv)	(v)	(vi)	(ii)	(iii)	(i)

Solutions

1. (c)

2. (c)

Respiratory capacities	Respiratory volumes
Residual volume	1200 mL
Vital capacity	4500 mL
Inspiratory reserve volume	2500 mL
Inspiratory capacity	3500 mL

3. (a)   4. (b)   6. (a)   7. (b)   8. (b)

9. (c)   10. (d)   11. (d)   12. (b)   13. (b)

Body Fluids and Circulation

1. A red blood cell, entering the right side of the heart passes by or through the following structures.
   1. Atrioventricular valves
   2. Semilunar valves
   3. Right atrium
   4. Right ventricle
   5. SAN

   Which of the following options represents the correct sequence?
   (a) $2 \rightarrow 3 \rightarrow 1 \rightarrow 4 \rightarrow 5$
   (b) $3 \rightarrow 1 \rightarrow 5 \rightarrow 2 \rightarrow 4$
   (c) $3 \rightarrow 5 \rightarrow 1 \rightarrow 2 \rightarrow 4$
   (d) $5 \rightarrow 3 \rightarrow 1 \rightarrow 4 \rightarrow 2$

2. Identify the components labelled (A-D) in the given flow chart of the blood clotting process.

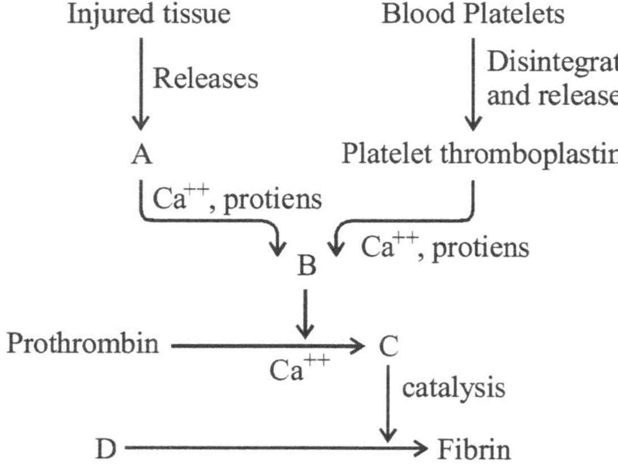

	A	B	C	D
(a)	Thrombo-plastin	Prothrom-binase	Thrombin	Fibrinogen
(b)	Fibrinogen	Thrombin	Prothrom-binase	Thrombo-plastin
(c)	Prothrom-binase	Fibrinogen	Thrombo-plastin	Thrombin
(d)	Thrombin	Thrombo-plastin	Fibrinogen	Prothrom-binase

3. Match the column I and column II and select the appropriate option with the given code.

	Column I		Column II
(a)	Coronary sinus	(i)	Mitral valve
(b)	Base of systemic aorta	(ii)	Eustachian valve
(c)	Left atrioventricular valve	(iii)	Semilunar valves
(d)	Opening of inferior vena cava	(iv)	Thebesian valve

   (a) P-(iv); Q-(iii), R-(i), S-(ii)
   (b) P-(iii); Q-(iv), R-(ii), S-(i)
   (c) P-(ii); Q-(i), R-(iv), S-(iii)
   (d) P-(i); Q-(ii), R-(iii), S-(iv)

4. Match the items given in column I with those in column II and select the correct option given below.

	Column-I		Column-II
A.	Tricuspid valve	(i)	Between left atrium and left ventricle
B.	Bicuspid valve	(ii)	Between right ventricle and pulmonary artery
C.	Semilunar valve	(iii)	Between right atrium and right ventricle

	A	B	C
(a)	(iii)	(i)	(ii)
(b)	(i)	(iii)	(ii)
(c)	(i)	(ii)	(iii)
(d)	(ii)	(i)	(iii)

5. Choose the correctly matched pair.

(a) CAD - Atherosclerosis

(b) Tetany - Disorder of neuromuscular junction

(c) Gout - Rapid spasms in muscles

(d) Goitre - Hyperthyroidism

(e) Asthma - Alveolar wall are damaged

6. The given diagram shows the human heart.

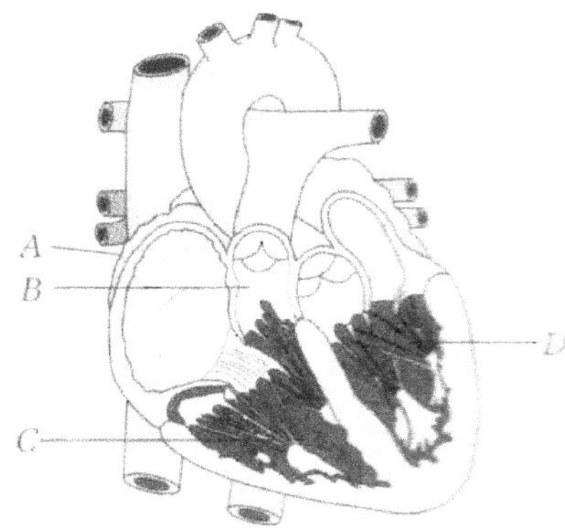

Which site represents the generation of action potential in human heart?

(a) D   (b) C

(c) B   (d) A

7. In diagram of the vertical section of human heart given here, certain parts have been indicated by alphabets. Choose the answer in which these alphabets have been correctly matched with the parts they indicate.

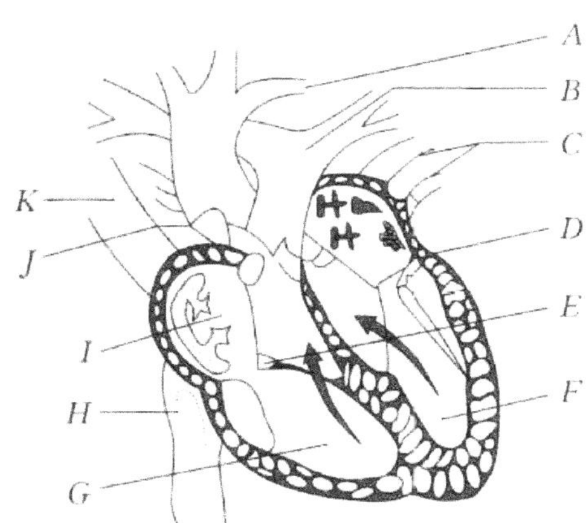

(a) *A-Aorta, B*-Pulmonary vein, *C*-Pulmonaryarteries, *D*-Left ventricle, *E*-Semilunar valves, *F-Left* auricle, *G*-Right auricle, *H*-Superior vena cava, *I-Right* ventricle, *J*-Tricuspid valves, *K*-Inferior vena cava

(b) *A-Aorta, B*-Pulmonary artery, *C*-Pulmonary veins, *D*-Left auricle, *E*-Tricuspid valves, *F-Left* ventricle, *G*-Right ventricle, *H*-Inferior vena cava, *I*-Right auricle, *J*-Semilunar valves, *K*-Superior vena cava

(c) *A-Aorta, B*-Superior vena cava, *C*-Inferior vena cava, *D*-Right ventricle, *E*-Tricuspid valves, *F-Right* auricle, *G*-Left auricle, *H*-Pulmonary vein, *I-Left* ventricle, *J*-Semilunar valves, *K*-Pulmonary artery

(d) *A-Aorta, B*-Superior vena cava, *C*-Inferior vena cava, *D*-Left ventricle, *E*-Semilunar valves, *F-Left* auricle, *G*-Right auricle, *H*-Pulmonary artery, *I*-Right ventricle, *J*-Tricuspid valves, *K*-Pulmonary vein

8. Identify the correct match wrt clotting factors and their specific characters.

(a) Prothrombin — Lipoprotein synthesised in liver by vitamin K

(b) Fibrinogen — Glycoprotein deficiency causes haemophilia-A

(c) Hageman factor — Glycoprotein deficiency causes delayed blood clotting

(d) Fibrin stabilising factor — Lipoprotein deficiency causes haemophilia-B

9. In which one of the following pairs of terms both represent one and the same thing?

(a) Plasma — Serum

(b) Atrioventricular node — Pacemaker

(c) Leucocytes — Lymphocytes

(d) Mitral valve — Bicuspid valve

10. Match the following columns.

Column-I	Column-II
A. P-wave	1. Atrial depolarisation
B. First heart sound	2. Ventricular depolarisation
C. Second heart sound	3. Ventricular repolarisation
D. QRS complex	4. Closure of the AV valves at the onset of systole
E. T-wave	5. Closure of the semilunar valves at the onset of diastole

Codes:

	A	B	C	D	E
(a)	1	4	5	2	3
(b)	1	2	3	4	5
(c)	5	4	3	2	1
(d)	3	5	1	2	4

11. Match the following columns.

Column-I	Column-II
A. Tricuspid valve	1. On the opening of inferior vena cava
B. Pulmonary valve	2. On the entrance of aorta
C. Eustachian valve	3. Between right atrium and right ventricle
D. Coronary valve	4. Entrance of pulmonary artery
	5. Over the opening of coronary sinus

Codes:

	A	B	C	D
(a)	3	5	4	1
(b)	3	4	1	5
(c)	4	2	1	5
(d)	4	3	1	3

12. Match the following columns.

Column-I	Column-II
A. Lymphatic system	1. Carries oxygenated blood
B. Pulmonary vein	2. Immune response
C. Thrombocytes	3. To drain back the tissue fluid to the circulatory system
D. Lymphocytes	4. Coagulation of blood

Codes:

	A	B	C	D
(a)	2	1	3	4
(b)	3	1	4	2
(c)	3	1	2	4
(d)	2	1	3	4

13. Different factors play important roles in coagulation of blood, some of the factors are listed in list -I and their nomenclatures are given in list-II. Find out the accurate matching

List -I	List - II
a factor II	1. Thromboplastin
b factor III	2. Prothrombin
c factor VIII	3. Hageman factor
d factor XII	4. Antiheaemophilic globulin

(a) a : 2, b : 1, c : 4, d : 3
(b) a : 1, b : 2, c : 3, d : 4
(c) a : 3, b : 4, c : 2, d : 1
(d) a : 4, b : 4, c : 2, d : 1

14. Match the following columns and choose the correct answer from the options given below:

Column I	Column II
A. Erythrocytes	1. Most abundant white blood cells and the main phagocytic cell of the blood.
B. Eosinophils	2. Least abundant white blood cells
C. Neutrophils	3. Resist infections and are associated with allergic reaction
D. Lymphocytes	4. Blood cells that count haemoglobin and transport oxygen
E. Basophils	5. Specialized antibody producing white blood cells

	A	B	C	D	E
(a)	4	3	1	5	2
(b)	1	2	3	4	5
(c)	2	3	1	5	4
(d)	4	1	2	3	4

15. Match the items given in column I with those in column II and select the correct option given below:

Column I		**Column II**
A.	Fibrinogen	(i)	Osmotic balance
B.	Globulin	(ii)	Blood clotting
C.	Albumin	(iii)	Defence mechanism

(a) A-(iii), B-(ii), C-(i)
(b) A-(i), B-(ii), C-(iii)
(c) A-(i), B-(iii), C-(ii)
(d) A-(ii), B-(iii), C-(i)

16. Which of the following option is correctly matched with its category?

	Group	Type of Circulation	Blood is Oxygenated by
(a)	Fish	Single circulation	Skin
(b)	Amphibia	Double circulation	Gills
(c)	Reptilies	Incomplete double circulation	Lungs
(d)	Bird	Incomplete double circulation	Lungs

17. Match the blood vessels of human heart listed under column I with the functions given under column II and choose the answer.

Column I (Blood vessel)		**Column II** (Function)
A.	Superior vena cava	1. Carries deoxygenated blood to lungs
B.	Inferior vena cava	2. Carries oxygenated blood to lungs
C.	Pulmonary artery	3. Brings oxygenated blood from lower parts of the body to the right atrium
D.	Pulmonary vein	4. Brings oxygenated blood to the left atrium

5. Brings deoxygenated blood from upper parts of the body into the right atrium

(a) A-5, B-1, C-3, D-2
(b) A-5, B-3, C-1, D-4
(c) A-4, B-5, C-3, D-1
(d) A-5, B-1, C-2, D-3

18. Match the column I with column II and choose the correct combination from the options given.

Column I		**Column II**
A.	Eosinophils	(i)	Coagulation
B.	RBC	(ii)	Universal recipient
C.	AB group	(iii)	Resist infection
D.	Platelets	(iv)	Contraction of heart
E.	Systole	(v)	Gaseous exchange

(a) A-(iii), B-(v), C-(ii), D-(i), E-(iv)
(b) A-(v), B-(i), C-(iii), D-(iv), E-(ii)
(c) A-(iii), B-(i), C-(ii), D-(v), E-(iv)
(d) A-(iii), B-(v), C-(ii), D-(iv), E-(i)

19. Match the column I blood (components) with column II (their specific functions) and choose the correct option:

Column I	**Column II**
A. Globulin protein	- Involved in defense mechanism of body
B. Fibrinogen protein	- Needed for clotting of blood
C. Albumin protein	- Role is transport of gases
D. Basophils	- Involved in inflammatory reactions
E. Eosinophils	- Help in osmotic balance
F. Lymphocytes	- Responsible for immune responses of the body

How many are correctly matched

(a) Four
(b) Three
(c) Five
(d) Six

20. Match the terms given under column I with their functions given under column II and select the answer from the options given below:

Column I		Column II
A.	Lymphatic system	1. Carries oxygenated blood
B.	Pulmonary vein	2. Immune response
C.	Thrombocytes	3. To drain back the circulatory system
D.	Lymphocytes	4. Coagulation of blood

(a) A-2, B-1, C-3, D-4
(b) A-3, B-1, C-4, D-2
(c) A-3, B-1, C-2, D-4
(d) A-2, B-1, C-3, D-4

Solutions

1. **(d)** Red blood cell (blood) will first meet SAN in the right atrium. Then from the right atrium it passes into right ventricle through atrio ventricular valve. From the right ventricle it enters into pulmonary artery through semilunar valve.

2. (a)   3. (a)   4. (a)   5. (a)   6. (d)
7. (b)   8. (c)   9. (d)   10. (a)   11. (b)
12. (b)   13. (a)   14. (a)   15. (d)   16. (c)
17. (b)   18. (a)   19. (a)   20. (b)

Excretory Products and their Elimination

1. Select the correct combinations.

   I. Dysuria   – Painful urination

   II. Pyuria   – WBCs or pus in the urine

   III. Fructosuria   – Absence of glucose in urine

   IV. Albumin-uria – Absence of ketone bodies in urine

Choose the correct answer.

(a) Only I

(b) II and III

(c) I and II

(d) None of these

2. Match the following Columns.

Column I	Column II
A. Loop of Henle	1. Carries blood into the kidney
B. Renal artery	2. Area, where a considerable amount of reabsorption takes place
C. Proximal convoluted tubule	3. Main area of secretion
D. Glomerulus	4. Filtration of blood
E. Distal convoluted tubule	5. Plays a role in concentration of urine

Codes

	A	B	C	D	E
(a)	1	2	3	4	5
(b)	5	4	3	2	1
(c)	5	1	2	4	3
(d)	4	3	1	5	2

3. Match the following Columns.

Column I	Column II
A. Uremia	1. Excess of protein level in urine
B. Haematuria	2. The presence of high ketone bodies in urine
C. Ketonuria	3. The presence of blood cells in urine
D. Glycosuria	4. The presence of glucose in urine
E. Proteinuria	5. The presence of excess urea in urine

Codes

	A	B	C	D	E
(a)	5	3	2	4	1
(b)	4	5	3	2	1
(c)	5	3	4	2	1
(d)	3	5	2	1	4

4. Find the incorrectly matched pair of animal and its excretory structure.

(a) *Balanoglossus*   – Proboscis gland

(b) Earthworm   – Nephridia

(c) Grasshopper   – Malpighian tubules

(d) Prawn   – Flame cells

(e) *Amphioxus*   – Protonephridia

5. The correct match is

   I. DCT   – Secretion of H^+ and K^+ ions.

   II. Henle's loop – Reabsorption of glucose, water and Na^+ ions.

III. Podocytes   –   Attached to parietal layer of Bowman's capsule.

IV. JGA   –   Rise in glomerular blood pressure activates it to release renin.

(a) Only III   (b) Only II

(c) Only I   (d) Only IV

6. Select the option which shows correct matching of animals with its excretory organ and excretory product.

Animals	Excretory organ	Excretory product
(a) Labeo (Rohu)	Nephridial tubes	Ammonia
(b) Salamander	Kidneys	Urea
(c) Peacock	Kidneys	Urea
(d) Housefly	Renal tubules	Uric acid

7. Which one of the following options gives the correct categorisation of six animals according to the types of nitrogenous waste they give out?

	Ammonotelic	Ureotelic	Uricotelic
(a)	Pigeon, humans	Aquatic amphibia, lizards	Cockroach, frog
(b)	Frog, lizards	Aquatic amphibia, humans	Cockroach, Pigeon
(c)	Aquatic amphibia	Frog, human	Pigeon, lizards, cockroach
(d)	Aquatic amphibia	Cockroach, humans	Frog, pigeon, lizards

8. In which one of the following organisms its excetory organs are correctly stated?

(a) Humans   –   Kidneys, sebaceous glands and tear glnads

(b) Earthworm   –   Pharyngeal, integumentary and septal nephridia

(c) Cockroach   –   Malpighian tubules and enteric caeca

(d) Frog   –   Kidneys, skin and buccal epithelium

9. Match column I with column II regarding human excretory system. Choose the correct option.

Colum II	Column II
I. Epithelial cells of Bowman's capsule	A. Juxtamedullary nephron
II. Extension of cortex between the medullary pyramids as renal columns	B. Vasa recta
III. Nephrons with long loop of henle running deep into the medulla	C. Juxtaglomerular Apparatus
IV. A fine vessel of the periubular cappilaries running parallel to Henle's loop	D. Podocytes
V. A special sensitive regionin the DCT and afferent arteriole at the location of their contact	E. Columns of Bertin
	F. Cortical nephron

(a) I - C, II - B, III - A, IV - D, V - E

(b) I - E, II - A, III - B, IV - C, V - D

(c) I - D, II - C, III - F, IV - E, V - A

(d) I - D, II - E, III - A, IV - B, V - C

(e) I - B, II - D, III - F, IV - A, V - C

10.

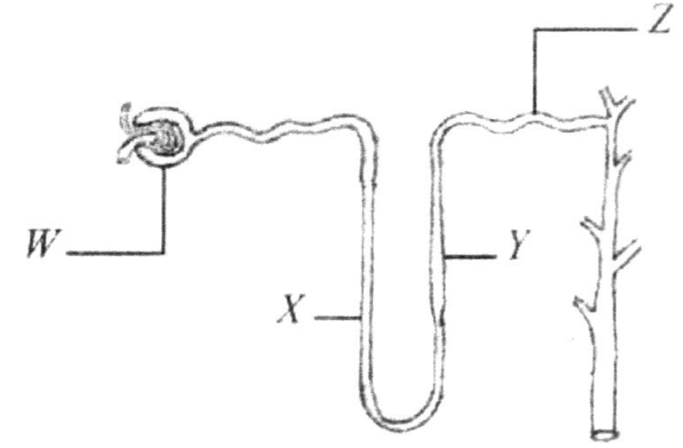

In the given diagram, water absorption does not occur in part labelled as ______.

(a) W (b) X

(c) Y (d) Z

11. Match the items given in column I with those in column II and select the correct options given below.

Column I (Function)	Column II (Part of excretory system)
A. Ultrafiltration	(i) Henle's loop
B. Concentration of urine	(ii) Ureter
C. Transport of urine	(iii) Urinary bladder
D. Storage of urine	(iv) Malpighian corpuscle
	(v) Proximal convoluted tubule

	A	B	C	D
(a)	(iv)	(v)	(ii)	(iii)
(b)	(iv)	(i)	(ii)	(iii)
(c)	(v)	(iv)	(i)	(ii)
(d)	(v)	(iv)	(i)	(iii)

12. Match the items given in column I with those in column II and select the correct options given below.

Column I	Column II
A. Glycosuria	(i) Accumulation of uric acid in joints
B. Gout	(ii) Mass of crystallised salts within the kidney
C. Renal calculi	(iii) Inflammation in glomeruli
D. Glomerular nephritis	(iv) Presence of glucose in urine

	A	B	C	D
(a)	(iii)	(ii)	(iv)	(i)
(b)	(i)	(ii)	(iii)	(iv)
(c)	(ii)	(iii)	(i)	(iv)
(d)	(iv)	(i)	(ii)	(iii)

13. Match the animals with their corresponding excretory structures

Animal	Excretory structure
1. Amphioxus	A. Pronephros kidney
2. Cockroach	B. Protonephridia
3. Prawn	C. Metanephridia
4. Earthworm	D. Green glands
	E. Malpighian tubules
	F. Antennal glands

(a) 1–B, 2–E, 3–D, 4–C

(b) 1–A, 2–C, 3–D, 4–B

(c) 1–B, 2–E, 3–F, 4–C

(d) None of these

14. Match the column I with the column II

Column I	Column II
A. Earthworm	I. Malpighian tubules
B. Cockroach	II. Green glands
C. Amphioxus	III. Solenocytes
D. Prawn	IV. Holonephridia
	V. Coxal glands

(a) A-IV, B-I, C-III, D-II

(b) A-I, B-V, C-IV, D-II

(c) A-IV, B-I, C-V, D-II

(d) A-III, B-I, C-II, D-V

15. Match the column-I with column-II and choose the correct option.

Column-I (Excretory organs)	Column-II (Animals)
A. Nephridia	I. Hydra
B. Malpighian tubules	II. Leech
C. Protonephridia	III. Shark
D. Kidneys	IV. Round worms
	V. Cockroach

(a) A-II, B-V, C-IV, D-III

(b) A-IV, B-II, C-I, D-V

(c) A-V, B-II, C-IV, D-III

(d) A-II, B-IV, C-V, D-I

16. A single load of insulin is injected into the bloodsteam. If the urine flow is constant, which graph best expresses the relationship between urine-insulin concentration and time?

(a) 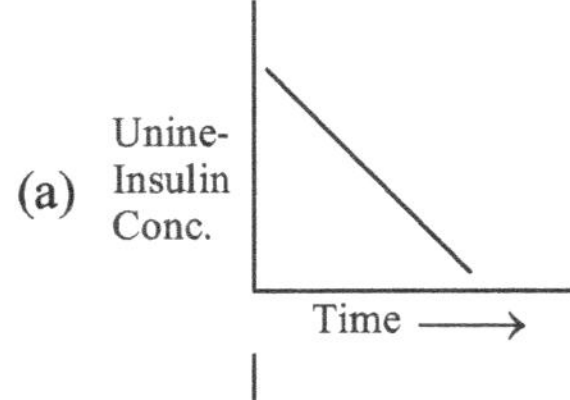

(b) 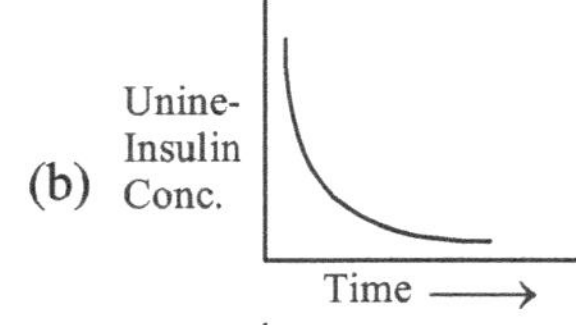

(c) 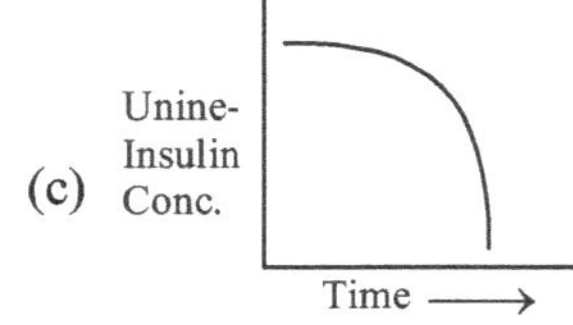

(d) 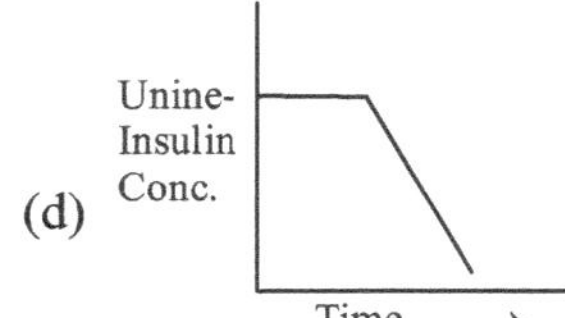

17. Select the correct match of the types of organs gives in column-I with their role in excretion given in column-II.

Column-I		Column-II
A. Lungs	I.	Secretes bile contaiing substances like bilirubin, biliverdin, cholesterol, degraded steroid hormones, vitamins and drugs.
B. Liver	II.	Eliminates water and salts in sweat and substances like sterols, hydrocarbons and waxes through sebum.
C. Skin	III.	Remove large amounts of CO_2 (18 litres/day) and also significant quantities of water everyday.
D. Kidney	IV.	Remove wastes (metabolic by products and regulate pH, ion concentration, volume and osmolarity of blood.

(a) A-I, B-II, C-III, D-IV
(b) A-III, B-I, C-II, D-IV
(c) A-III, B-I, C-IV, D-II
(d) A-IV, B-II, C-III, D-I

18. Which of the following hormone/enzyme is/are correctly paired with its function?

(i) Renin - Enzyme that catalyses the formation of angiotensin I.

(ii) Aldosterone ? Regulates water reabsorption at the distal convoluted tubule.

(iii) Anti-diuretic hormone (ADH) - It is a powerful vasoconstrictor that stimulates the secretion of aidosterone.

(iv) Angiotensin II ? Promotes reabsorption of sodium at distal convoluted tubule.

(a) Only (i)
(b) Only (iii)
(c) (i), (ii) and (iii)
(d) (ii), (iii) and (iv)

19. Match the column-I with column-II and choose the correct option.

Column-I		Column-II
A. Delivers blood	I.	Proximal convoluted tubules
B. Carries urine to pelvis	II.	Renal artery
C. Collects nitrate from Bowman's capsule	III.	Collecting duct
D. Loop of Henle	IV.	Ascending and descending limb

(a) A-IV, B-III, C-II, D-I
(b) A-I, B-II, C-III, D-IV
(c) A-II, B-III, C-IV, D-I
(d) A-II, B-III, C-I, D-IV

20. Match column-I with column-II regarding human excretory system and choose the correct option given below.

	Column-I		Column-II
A.	Epithelial cells of Bowman's capsule	I.	Juxtamedullary nephron
B.	Extension of cortex between the medullary pyramids as rental columns	II.	Vasa recta
C.	Nephrons with long loop of Henle running deep into the medulla	III.	Juxtaglomerular Apparatus
D.	A fine vessel of the peritubular capillaries running parallel to Henles loop	IV.	Podocytes
E.	A special sensitive region in the DCT and afferent arteriole at the location of their contact	V.	Columns of Bertini

(a) A-III, B-II, C-I, D-IV, E-V
(b) A-V, B-I, C-II, D-III, E-IV
(c) A-IV, B-III, C-I, D-II, E-V
(d) A-II, B-IV, C-VI, D-I, E-III

21. Match the following parts of a nephron with their function :

	Column-I		Column-II
(A)	Descending limb of Henle's loop	(i)	Reabsorption of salts only
(B)	Proximal convoluted tubule	(ii)	Reabsorption of water only
(C)	Ascending limb of Henle's loop	(iii)	Conditional reabsorption of sodium ions and water
(D)	Distal convoluted tubule	(iv)	Reabsorption of ions, water and organic nutrients

Select the correct option from the following :

(a) (A)-(iv), (B)-(i), (C)-(iii), (D)-(ii)
(b) (A)-(i), (B)-(iii), (C)-(ii), (D)-(iv)
(c) (A)-(ii), (B)-(iv), (C)-(i), (D)-(iii)
(d) (A)-(i), (B)-(iv), (C)-(ii), (D)-(iii)

22. Match the items given in Column I with those in Column II and select the correct option given below :

	Column I		Column II
A.	Glycosuria	I.	Accumulation of uric acid in joints
B.	Gout	II.	Mass of crystallised salts within the kidney
C.	Renal calculi	III.	Inflammation in glomeruli
D.	Glomerular	IV.	Presence of in nephritis glucose urine

	A	B	C	D
(a)	III	II	IV	I
(b)	I	II	III	IV
(c)	IV	I	II	III
(d)	II	III	I	IV

Solutions

1.   **(c)**   2.   **(c)**   3.   **(a)**   4.   **(d)**   5.   **(c)**

6.   **(b)**   In salamander, kidneys (mesonepheric) are the excretory organs and the excretory matter is urea. In *Labeo*, kidney is the excretory organ and is mesonephric. Excretion is ammonotelic. Peacock has metanephric kidneys with excretory matter being uric acid. In housefly, excretion takes place by Malpighian tubules. Excretory waste is uric acid chief.

7.   **(c)**

8.   **(b)**   Nephridia is the excretory organ of the earthworm. Earthworms have three types of nephridial structures called as septal, integumentary and pharyngeal nephridia. These three nephridial structures are present on different positions in the body and also vary in structures. Septal and pharyngeal nephridia are both enteronephric *i.e.*, nitrogen products are expelled in gut. Integumentary nephridia is exonephric *i.e.*, nitrogen waste products are directly discharged outside.

9.   **(d)**

10.   **(c)** W represents the glomerulus where ultrafiltration occurs. It is permeable to water and low molecular weight substancs. Water is reabsorbed by osmosis in PCT, DCT (Z) and descending limb of loop of Henle (X) except ascending limb of loop of Henle (Y).

11.   **(b)**   12.   **(d)**   13.   **(c)**   14.   **(a)**   15.   **(a)**

16.   **(c)**   17.   **(b)**   18.   **(a)**   19.   **(d)**   20.   **(d)**

21.   **(c)**   22.   **(c)**

Locomotion and Movement

1. Which one of the following pairs of chemical substances, is correctly categorised?

(a) Calcitonin and thymosin – Thyroid hormones

(b) Pepsin and prolactin – Two digestive enzymes secreted in stomach

(c) Troponin and myosin – Complex proteins in striated muscles

(d) Secretin and rhodopsin – Polypeptide hormones

2. Choose the wrongly matched pair.

(a) Portion of myofibril between two - Sarcomere 'Z' lines

(b) Isotropic band - Actin

(c) Anisotropic band - Myosin

(d) Central part of I-band - M-line

(e) Central part of A-band - H-zone

3. Select the correct matching of the type of the joint with the example in human skeletal system.

Type of joint	Example
(a) Cartilaginous joint	– Between frontal and parietal
(b) Pivot joint	– Between third and fourth cervical vertebrae
(c) Hinge joint	– Between humerus and pectoral girdle
(d) Gliding joint	– Between carpals

4. Match the following joints with the bones involved.

(1) Gliding joint   (i) Between carpal and metacarpal of thumb

(2) Hinge joint   (ii) Between atlas and axis

(3) Pivot joint   (iii) Between the carpals

(4) Saddle joint   (iv) Between humerus and ulana

select the correct option from the following.

(a) (1)-(iii), (2)-(iv), (3)-(ii), (4)-(i)

(b) (1)-(iv), (2)-(i), (3)-(ii), (4)-(iii)

(c) (1)-(iv), (2)-(ii), (3)-(iii), (4)-(i)

(d) (1)-(i), (2)-(iii), (3)-(ii), (4)-(iv)

5. Select the correct match pair.

(a) Abductor – Triceps extending forearm

(b) Adductor – Biceps bending forearm towards upper arm

(c) Elevator – Latissimus dorsi

(d) Rotator – Pyriformis that raises thigh

6. Select the correct match pair.

(a) Synarthrosis – Movable joints

(b) Amphiarthrosis – Slightly movable joints

(c) Shoulder joint – Between humerus and glenoid cavity

(d) Gliding joint – Monoaxial joint

7. Match the following Columns.

Column I	Column II
A. Ball and socket joint	1. Radius and ulna
B. Hinge joint	2. Metacarpals of thumb
C. Gliding joint	3. Glenoid cavity of pectoral girdle
D. Saddle joint	4. Between radius and carpals at wrist
E. Condyloid joint	5. Phalanges of digits

Codes

	A	B	C	D	E
(a)	3	5	1	2	4
(b)	1	2	3	4	5
(c)	4	3	1	2	5
(d)	5	2	3	1	4

8. Match the following Columns.

Column I		Column II
(skeleton)		(Number of bones)
A. Sternum	1.	14
B. Ribs	2.	1
C. Pelvis	3.	24
D. Face	4.	3

Codes

	A	B	C	D
(a)	2	3	4	1
(b)	2	4	1	3
(c)	1	3	4	2
(d)	4	1	2	3

9. Match the following Columns.

Column I		Column II
A. Fast muscle fibres	1.	Myoglobin
B. Slow muscle fibres	2.	Lactic acid
C. Actin filament	3.	Contractile unit
D. Sarcomere	4.	I-band

Codes

	A	B	C	D
(a)	1	2	4	3
(b)	2	1	3	4
(c)	2	1	4	3
(d)	3	2	4	1

10. Match the following Columns.

Column I		Column II
A. Sternum	1.	Synovial fluid
B. Glenoid cavity	2.	Vertebrae
C. Freely movable joint	3.	Pectoral girdle
D. Cartilaginous joint	4.	Flat bones

Codes

	A	B	C	D
(a)	2	1	3	4
(b)	4	3	1	2
(c)	2	1	4	3
(d)	4	1	2	4

11. Match the following Columns.

Column I		Column II
A. Zygomatic bone	1.	Keystone bone of cranium
B. Lacrimal bone	2.	Cheek bone of cranium
C. Parietal bone	3.	Smallest bone of face
D. Sphenoid	4.	Root of crranium
	5.	Floor of cranium

Codes

	A	B	C	D
(a)	1	3	5	2
(b)	2	4	5	1
(c)	2	4	1	3
(d)	2	3	4	5

12. Match the bones of column A with their corresponding number in column B

Column A		Column B
A. True ribs	a.	14
B. Cervical vertebrae	b.	12
C. Cranium bones	c.	8
D Vertebrochondral ribs	d.	6

(a) Ab, Be, Ca, Dd   (b) Aa, Be, Cc, Dd
(c) Ab, Bc, Cd, Dc   (d) Aa, Bc, Cb, Dd

13. Which one of the following pairs of structures is correctly matched with their correct description ?

	Structures		Description
(a)	Tibia and fibula	–	Both form parts of knee joint
(b)	Cartilage and cornea	–	No blood supply but do require oxygen for respiratory need
(c)	Shoulder joint and elbow joint	–	Ball and socket type of joint
(d)	Premolars and molars	–	20 in all and 3–rooted

14. Which of the following pairs, is correctly matched?

(a)	Hinge joint	-	between vertebrae
(b)	Gliding joint	-	between zygapophyses of the successive vertebrae
(c)	Cartilaginous joint	-	skull bones
(d)	Fibrous joint	-	between phalanges

15. Which one of the following is the correct matching of three items and their grouping category ?

Items		**Group**
(a)	cytosine, uracil, thiamine –	pyrimidines
(b)	malleus, incus, cochlea –	ear ossicles
(c)	ilium, ischium, –	coxal bones of pelvic girdle
(d)	actin, myosin, rhodopsin –	muscle proteins

16. Which one of the following pairs of structures is correctly matched with their correct description?

Structures		**Description**
(a)	Tibia and fibula –	Both form parts of knee joint
(b)	Cartilage and cornea –	No blood supply but do require oxygen for respiratory need
(c)	Shoulder joint and elbow joint –	Ball and socket type of joint
(d)	Premolars and molars –	20 in all and 3– rooted

17. Three of the following pairs of the human skeletal parts are correctly matched with their respective inclusive skeletal category and one pair is not matched. Identify the non-matching pair.

	Pairs of skeletal parts	**Category**
(a)	Humerus and ulna	Appendicular skeleton
(b)	Malleus and stapes	Ear ossicles
(c)	Sternum and Ribs	Axial skeleton
(d)	Clavicle and Glenoid cavity	Pelvic girdle

18. The characteristics and an example of a synovial joint in humans is

	Characteristics	**Examples**
(a)	Fibrous cartilage between two bones, limited movements	Knee joint
(b)	Fluid filled between two joints, provides cushion	Skull bones
(c)	Fluid filled synovial cavity between two bones	Joint between atlas and axis
(d)	Lymph filled between two bones, limited movement	Gliding joint between carpals

19. Match the locomotory structure of column I with the name of phylum in column II

	Column I		**Column II**
A.	Parapodia	I.	Mollusca
B.	Muscular foot	II.	Echinodermata
C.	Pseudopodia	III.	Protozoa
D.	Tube feet	IV.	Annelida
		V.	Arthropoda

(a) A-V, B-IV, C-III, D-II
(b) A-IV, B-I, C-III, D-II
(c) A-V, B-I, C-III, D-II
(d) A-IV, B-II, C-III, D-V

Solutions

1. **(c)**
2. **(d)** In a myofibril the dark bands (A bands) and light bands (I bands) are present alternately. At the centre of A band a comparatively lass dark H zone is present. In the centre of H zone is the M line. Each I band has at its centre a dark membrane called Z line. The part of myofibril between two successive Z lines is called a sarcomere.

3. **(d)** Cartilaginous joint – Between the adjacent vertebae in vertebral column

            Pivot joint – Between atlas and axis.

            Hinge joint – Knee joint

4. **(a)**   5. **(d)**   6. **(a)**   7. **(a)**   8. **(a)**
9. **(c)**   10. **(b)**   11. **(d)**   12. **(b)**   13. **(b)**
14. **(b)**   15. **(c)**   16. **(b)**   17. **(d)**   18. **(c)**
19. **(b)**

Neural Control and Coordination

1. Select the answer with correct matching of the structure, its location and function

Structure	Location	Function
(a) Eustachian tube	Anterior part of internal ear	Equalizes air pressure on either sides of tympanic membrane
(b) Cerebellum	Mid brain	Controls respiration and gastric secretions
(c) Hypothalamus	Fore brain	Controls body temperature, urge for eating and drinking
(d) Blind spot	Near the place where optic nerve leaves the eye	Rods and cones are present but inactive here

2. Column I lists the parts of the human brain and colum II lists the functions. Match the two columns and identify the correct choice from those given.

Column I	Column II
A. Cerebrum	p. controls the pituitary
B. Cerebellum	q. controls vision and hearing
C. Hypothalamus	r. controls the rate of heart beat
D. Midbrain	s. seat of intelligence
	t. maintains body posture

(a) A – t; B – s; C – q; D – p
(b) A – s; B – t; C – r; D – p
(c) A – t; B – s; C – r; D – q
(d) A – t; B – t; C – p; D – q

3. Match the following human spinal nerves in column I with the number of pairs in column II and choose the correct options

Column I	Column II
A. cervical nerves	1. 5 pairs
B. thoracic nerves	2. 1 pair
C. lumbar nerves	3. 12 pairs
D. coccygeal nerves	4. 8 pairs

(a) A - 2, B - 4, C - 1, D - 3
(b) A - 4, B - 3, C - 1, D - 2
(c) A - 3, B - 1, C - 2, D - 4
(d) A - 4, B - 1, C - 2, D - 3

4. Given below is a table comparing the effects of sympathetic and parasympathetic nervous system for four features (1–4). Which one feature is correctly described?

Feature	Sympathetic nervous system	Parasympathetic nervous system
1. Salivary glands	stimulates secretion	inhibits secretion
2. Pupil of eye	dilates	constricts
3. Heart rate	decreases	increases
4. Intestinal peristalsis	stimulates secretion	inhibits secretion

5. Match the entries in column I with those in column II and choose the correct combination from the options given.

Column I	Column II
(A) diencephalon	1. cerebellum
(B) telencephalon	2. medulla
(C) myelencephalon	3. amygdala
(D) metencephalon	4. thalamus

(a) A–4, B–3, C–1, D–2

(b) A–3, B–4, C–1, D–2

(c) A–4, B–3, C–2, D–1

(d) A–1, B–2, C–3, D–4

6. Which one of the following is the correct difference between rod cells and cone cells of our retina.

		Rod Cells	**Cone Cells**
(a)	Distribution	More concentrated in centre of retina	Evenly distributed all over retina
(b)	Visual acuity	High	Low
(c)	Visual pigment contained	Iodopsin	Rhodopsin
(d)	Over all function	Vision in poor light	Colour vision and detailed vision in bright light

7. Choose the incorrect pair w.r.t conduction of nerve impulse through a nerve fibre:

(a) Depolarisation- Opening of Na+ channels and rapid influx of Na+ ions

(b) Polarisation- Ionisation gradient is maintained by Na+ -K- pump which transport Na+ outwards for 2K+ into the cell

(c) Depolarisation - High permeability of the axon membrane for K+

(d) Repolarisation - High permeability of the membrane for K+ and rapid influx of K+ ions.

8. Match the column I with column II and choose the correct options:

	Column I		**Column II**
A.	Electrical synapse	1.	Membranes of pre-and post-synaptic neurons are separated by fluid filled space
B.	Chemical synapse	2.	Membranes of pre- and post-synaptic neurons are in very close proximity
C.	Receptors	3.	Chemicals filled in the vesicle of axon terminals
D.	Neurotransmitter	4.	Sites where neurotransmitters bind
		5.	Adrenergic or cholinergic

	A	B	C	D
(a)	2	1	4	3
(b)	2	3	5	4
(c)	2	5	4	3
(d)	2	1	4	3

9. Match the columns and find out the correct combination:

	A		
A.	Resting phase	1.	Activation gates of Na+ open
B.	Depolarising phase	2.	Inactivation gates of Na+ open only
C.	Repolarising phase	3.	Inactivation gate and activation gate of Na+ is closed
D.	Hyperpolarising phase	4.	Both gates of Na+ open

	A	B	C	D
(a)	2	1	4	3
(b)	2	3	4	1
(c)	2	1	3	4
(d)	2	4	1	3

10. Match the column I with column II and choose the correct option:

	Column I		**Column II**
A.	Cerebrum	1.	Controls the pituitary
B.	Cerebellum	2.	Controls vision and hearing
C.	Hypothalamus	3.	Controls the rate of heart beat
D.	Midbrain	4.	Seat of intelligence
		5.	Maintains body posture

    (a) A- 5, B-4, C-2, D-1

    (b) A-4, B-5, C-2, D-1

    (c) A-5, B-4, C-1, D-2

    (d) A-4, B-5, C-1, D-2

11. Match the column I and column II and choose the correct option.

A.	Fovea	1.	Provides opening for entry of light
B.	Iris	2.	Transduces RGB light
C.	Pupil	3.	Transmits information to CNS
D.	Lens	4.	Controls amount of light entering
E.	Optic nerve	5.	Focuses light on the retina

    (a) A-2, B-4, C-1, D-5, E-3

    (b) A-1, B-2, C-3, D-4, E-5

    (c) A-5, B-1, C-4, D-3, E-2

    (d) A-3, B-1, C-4, D-5, E-2

12. Find out the correct labelling for A, B, C and D in diagram:

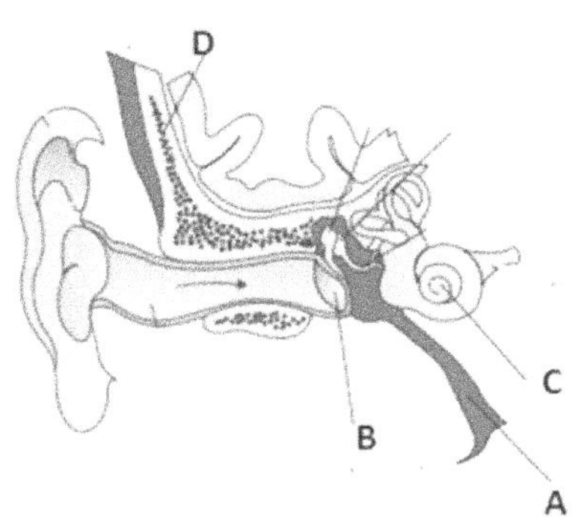

	A	B	C	D
(a)	External auditory Meatus	Tympanic membrane	Cochlea	Temporal bone
(b)	Temporal bone	Tympanic membrane	Cochlear nerve	Eustachian tube
(c)	Eustachian tube	Tympanic membrane	Cochlea	Temporal bone
(d)	Cochlea	Tympanic membrane	Auditory meatus	Temporal bone

13. Match the column I (various phase of an action potential) with column II (ionic activity associated) and choose the correct option.

	Column I		Column II
A.	Resting stage of a neuron	I.	Opening and then closing of the sodium channels
B.	Depolarization phase in the generation of an action potential.	II.	All voltage gated sodium and potassium channels are closed.
C.	Repolarization phase in the generation of action potential	III.	The sodium channels remain opened.
D.	Absolute refractory potassium phase.	IV.	Opening of gates and the rushing of potassium

    (a) A – II, B – I, C – IV, D – III

    (b) A – I, B – II, C – III, D – IV

    (c) A – III, B – IV, C – I, D – II

    (d) A – IV, B – II, C – III, D – I

14. Which of the following options correctly represents the name of 1, 2, 3 and 4 is the given diagram of neuron?

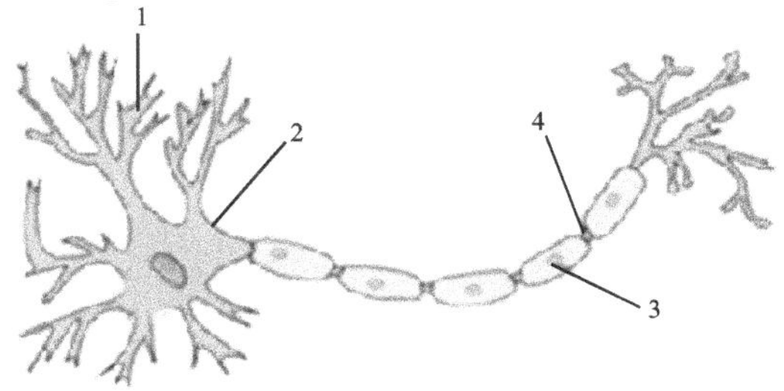

    (a) 1- Axon, 2- Dendrites, 3- Node of Ranvier, 4- Myelin sheath

    (b) 1- Dendrites, 2- Axon, 3- Node of Ranvier, 4- Myelin sheath

    (c) 1- Dendrites, 2- Cell body, 3- Myelin sheath, 4- Node of Ranvier

    (d) 1- Axon, 2- Cell body, 3- Dendrites, 4- Node of Ranvier

15. Unmyelinated nerve fibre is enclosed by an 'X' that does not form a myelin sheath around the 'Y', and is commonly found in 'Z' and the somatic neural systems. Identify 'X', 'Y' and 'Z'.

	X	Y	Z
(a)	Schwann cells	Axon	Autonomous
(b)	Nodes of Ranvier	Cell body	Synaptic knob
(c)	Synapse	Dendrites	Sympathetic
(d)	Meninges	Nerve impulse	Peripheral

16. Given below is a table comparing the effects of sympathetic and parasympathetic nervous system for four features (a – d). Which of the following feature is correctly described?

	Feature	Sympathetic nervous system	Parasympathetic nervous system
(a)	Salivary glands	Stimulates secretion	Inhibits secretion
(b)	Pupil of eye	Dilates	Constricts
(c)	Heart rate	Decreases	Increases
(d)	Intestinal peristalsis	Stimulates secretion	Inhibits secretion

17. 'X' is an important part of 'Y' which lies at the base of the structure which is a major coordinating centre for sensory and motor signalling. It contains a number of centre which control body temperature, urge for eating and drinking.

Identify X and Y from the options given below

(a) X -Cerebellum   ; Y - Hindbrain

(b) X -Hypothalamus   ; Y - Forebrain

(c) X -Corpora quadrigemina ; Y - Midbrain

(d) X -Pituitary gland   ; Y - Forebrain

18. Given below is a diagrammatic cross section of a single loop of human cochlea with few part labelled as A, B, C & D.

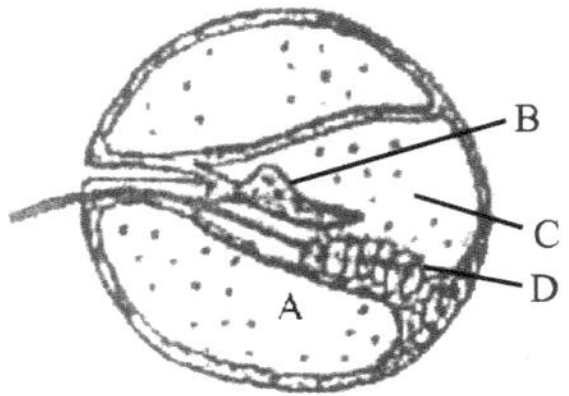

Which one of the following options correctly represents the name of three different parts?

(a) A: Perilymph, B: Tectorial membrane C: Endolymph

(b) B: Tectorial membrane, C:Perilymph, D: Secretory cells

(c) C: Endolymph, D: Sensory hair cells, A: Serum

(d) D: Sensory hair cells, A: Endolymph B: Tectorial membrane

19. Which of the following statements is/are functions of structure labelled as 'X' in the given diagram of eye?

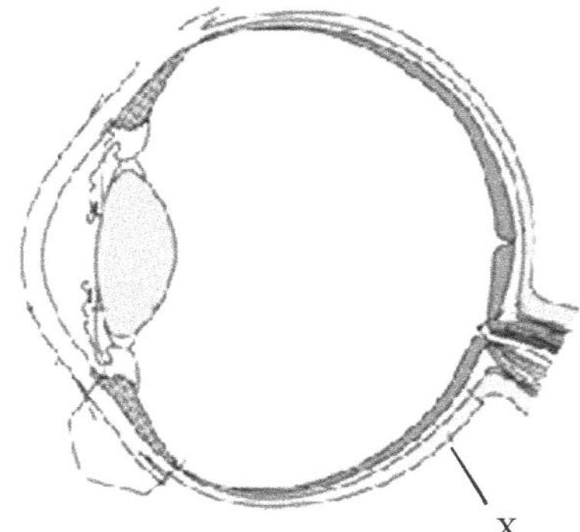

I.   It provides attachment points for muscles that move the eye.

II.   It maintains the shape of the eye ball.

III. It helps during accomodation.

IV. It is responsible for eye colour.

(a) I and II   (b) I, II and IV

(c) II, III and IV   (d) All of these

Solutions

1. (c) 2. (d) 3. (b) 4. (b) 5. (c)
6. (d) 7. (c) 8. (a) 9. (d) 10. (d)
11. (a) 12. (c) 13. (a)

14. **(c)** In the given diagram of neuron, the part marked as I, II, III and IV are respectively dendrites, cell body, myelin sheath and nodes of Ranvier. Neuron is a specialized, impulse-conducting cell that is the functional unit of the nervous system, consisting of the cell body and its processes, the axon and dendrites.

15. **(a)** Unmyelinated nerve fibre is enclosed by an Schwann cells that does not form a myelin sheath around the axon, and is commonly found in autonomous and the somatic neural systems.

16. **(b)**

	Features	Sympathetic nervous system	Parasympathetic nervous system
(a)	Salivary glands	Inhibits secretions	Stimulates secretions
(b)	Pupil of eye	Dilates	Constricts
(c)	Heart rate	Increases strength and rate of heart beat	Decreases strength and rate of heart beat
(d)	Intestinal peristalsis	Inhibits secretions	Stimulates secretions

17. **(b)** Hypothalamus is an important part of forebrain which lies at the base of the structure which is a major coordinating center for sensory and motor signaling. It contains a number of centers which control body temperature, urge for eating and drinking.

18. **(a)** In the given figure of cochlea, the correct labelling of A, B, C and D are respectively perilymph, tectorial membrane, endolymph and organ of corti.

The cochlea is the auditory portion of the inner ear. It is a spiral-shaped cavity in the bony labyrinth and receives sound in the form of vibrations, which cause the stereocilia to move. The stereocilia then convert these vibrations into nerve impulses which are taken up to the brain to be interpreted. Two of the three fluid sections are canals and the third is a sensitive 'organ of Corti' which detects pressure impulses which travel along the auditory nerve to the brain. The two canals are called the vestibular canal and the tympanic canal.

19. **(b)** The label X represents sclera. The white of the eye is called sclera. Choroid is responsible for eye colour. Ciliary muscles alters the shape of the lens during accomodation.

1. Identify A, B, C and D in the given flow chart and select the correct option.

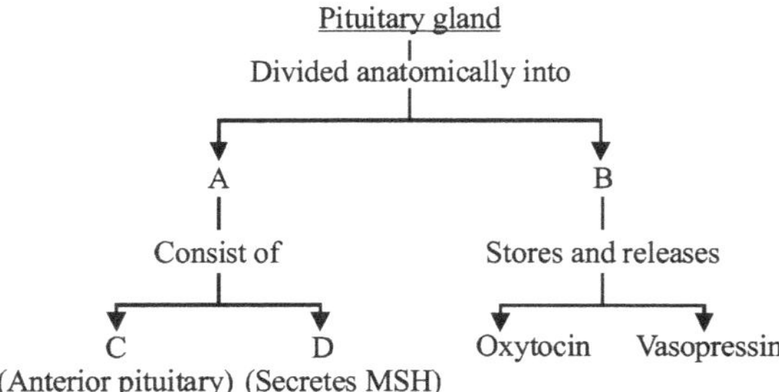

	A	B	C	D
(a)	Neuro-hypophysis	Adeno-hypophysis	Pars distalis	Pars intermedia
(b)	Adeno-hypophysis	Neuro-hypophysis	Pars intermedia	Pars distalis
(c)	Adeno-hypophysis	Neuro-hypophysis	Pars distalis	Pars intermedia
(d)	Neuro-hypophysis	Adeno-hypophysis	Pars intermedia	Pars distalis

2. Identify the parts labelled A, B and C in the given figure and select the correct option (second figure is the cross section of 'A').

	A	B	C
(a)	Adrenal gland	Cortex	Medulla
(b)	JGA	Cortex	Medulla
(c)	Adrenal gland	Medulla	Cortex
(d)	Adrenal gland	Pars distalis	Pars intermedia

3. Match column I with column II and select the correct option from the codes given below.

	Column I		Column II
A.	Thyroid	(i)	Acts on the renal tubules
B.	Adrenal	(ii)	Regulates blood calcium level
C.	Pituitary	(iii)	Maintains diurnal rhythm of our body
D.	Pineal	(iv)	Acts on the melanocytes

(a) A-(iv), B-(iii), C-(ii), D-(i)
(b) A-(iii), B-(iv), C-(i), D-(ii)
(c) A-(iv), B-(ii), C-(iii), D-(i)
(d) A-(ii), B-(i), C-(iv), D-(iii)

4. Match column I with column II and select the correct option from the given codes.

	Column I		Column II
A.	FSH	(i)	Transported axonally to neurohypophysis from hypothalamus
B.	MSH	(ii)	Acts on melanocytes and regulates pigmentation of skin
C.	Vasopressin (ADH)	(iii)	Stimulates the growth and development of ovarian follicles in female
D.	Pars intermedia	(iv)	In human, it is almost merged with pars distalis

(a) A-(iii), B-(ii), C-(i), D-(iv)
(b) A-(i), B-(ii), C-(iii), D-(iv)
(c) A-(iv), B-(iii), C-(ii), D-(i)
(d) A-(iii), B-(ii), C-(iv), D-(i)

5. Match the entries in Column - I with those of Column - II and choose the correct answer given below.

	Column-I		Column-II
(A)	FSH	(p)	Normal growth
(B)	GH	(q)	Ovulation
(C)	Prolactin	(r)	Parturition
(D)	Oxytocin	(s)	Water diuresis
		(t)	Milk secretion

(a) A - (q), B - (p), C - (t), D - (r)
(b) A - (q), B - (P), C - (t), D - (s)
(c) A - (P), B - (t), C - (r), D - (q)
(d) A - (q), B - (t), C - (s), D - (r)

6. Match the source gland with its respective hormone and function and select the correct option.

	Source gland	Hormone	Function
(a)	Anterior pituitary	Oxytocin	Contraction of uterus muscles during child birth
(b)	Posterior pituitary	Vasopressin	Stimulates resorption of water in the distal tubules in the nephron
(c)	Corpus luteum	Estrogen	Supports pregnancy
(d)	Thyroid	Thyroxine	Regulates blood calcium level

7. Match the hormones secreted by various endocrine structures and choose the correct option.

I.	Hypothalamus	A.	Melanocyte stimulating hormone
II.	Pars intermedia	B.	Aldosterone
III.	Pineal gland	C.	Gonadotrophin releasing hormone
IV.	Adrenal medulla	D.	Melatonin
V.	Adrenal cortex	E.	Catecholamines

(a) I - E, II - A, III - D, IV - B, V - C
(b) I - E, II - D, III - A, IV - B, V - C
(c) I - B, II - D, III - A, IV - C, V - E
(d) I - C, II - A, III - D, IV - B, V - E
(e) I - C, II - A, III - D, IV - E, V - B

8. Match Column I (hormone) with Column II (endocrine gland) and Column III (function).

	Column I	Column II	Column III
I.	Melatonin	A. Thyroid	i. Acts on the renal tubules
2.	MSH	B. Adrenal	ii. Regulates blood calcium levels
3.	Aldosterone	C. Pituitary	iii. Maintains diurnal rhythm of our body
4.	TCT	D. Pineal	iv. Acts on the melanocytes

(a) 4-A-iv; 3-D- iii; 1-B-ii; 2-C-i
(b) 1-D-iii; 2-C-iv; 3-B-i; 4-A-ii
(c) 1-B-i; 4-A-iii; 3-C-ii; 2-D-iv
(d) 2-D-ii; 1-B-i; 4-C-iv; 3-C-iii
(e) 2-C-iv; 3-A-ii; 1-D-iii; 4-B-i

9. Select the correct matching of a hormone, its source and function.

	Hormone	Source	Function
(a)	Vasopressin	Posterior pituitary	Increases loss of water through urine
(b)	Norepinephrine	Adrenal medulla	Increases heart beat, rate of respiration and alertness
(c)	Glucagon	Beta-cells of Islets of Langerhans	Stimulates glycogenolysis
(d)	Prolactin	Posterior pituitary	Regulates growth of mammary glands and milk fonnation in females

10. Select the option which correctly matches the endocrine gland with its hormone and its function.

	Endocrine gland	Hormone	Function
(a)	Placenta	Estrogen	Initiates secretion of the milk
(b)	Corpus luteum	Estrogen	Essential for maintenance of endometrium
(c)	Leydig's cells	Androgen	Initiates the production of sperms
(d)	Ovary	FSH	Stimulates follicular development and the secretion of estrogens

11. Match the Column I with Column II and select the correct option.

	Column I		Column II
A.	ANF	1.	Regulates blood calcium levels
B.	MSH	2.	Decreases blood pressure
C.	GIP	3.	Pigmentation
D.	TCT	4.	Inhibits gastric secretion

(a) A-4, B-1, C-*2,* D-3
(b) A-2, B-1, C-*4,* D-3
(c) A-4, B-1, C-*3,* D-2
(d) A-3, B-2, C-*4,* D-1
(e) A-2, B-3, C-*4,* D-1

11. In the given figure, what is indicated as 'X?

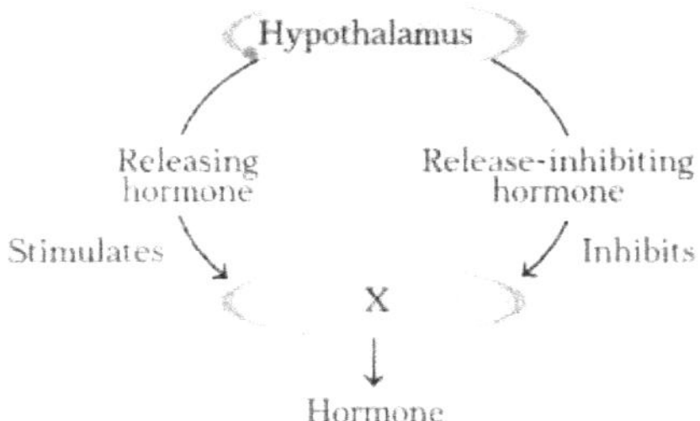

(a) Thyroid

(b) Parathyroid

(c) Anterior pituitary

(d) Gonads

12. Find out the correct labelling of the given figure.

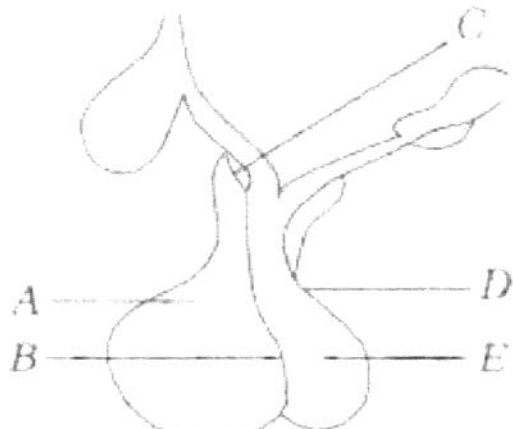

(a) A-Adenohypophysis, *B-Pars* intermedia, C-Hypothalamus, D-Infundibulum, E-Neurohypophysis

(b) A-Neurohypophysis, *B-Pars* intermedia, C-Hypothalamus, D-Infundibulum, *E*-Adenohypophysis

(c) A-Adenohypophysis, B-Infundibulum, C-Hypothalamus, D-Pars intermedia, E-Neurohypophysis

(d) A-Neurohypophysis, B-Infundibulum, C-Hypothalamus, D-Pars intermedia, *E*-Adenohypophysis

13. Which one of the following pairs is the correctly matched pair of the organ and the hormone it secretes?

(a) Thyroid   – Epinephrine

(b) Alpha cells of pancreas – Glucagon

(c) Anterior pituitary   – Adrenaline

(d) Stomach epithelium   – Secretin

14. Identify the hormones, labelled as *A*, Band C in the following figure.

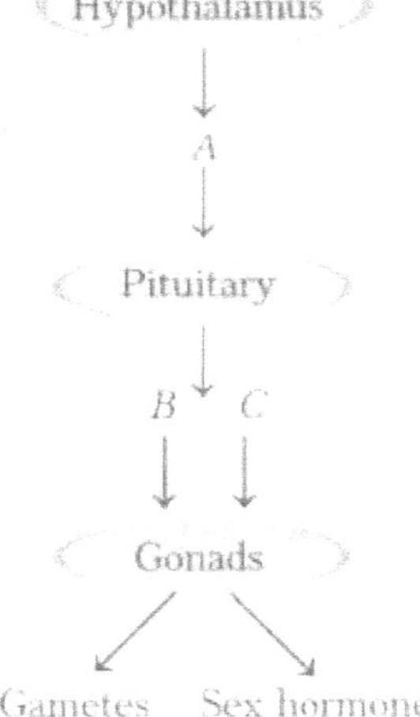

(a) *A*-GH,   B-*FSH*,   C-LH

(b) *A*-GnRH,   *B*-FSH,   C-LH

(c) *A*-GH,   *B*-GnRH,   C-PRT

(d) *A*-GnRH,   *B*-GH,   C-PRT

15. Match the source gland with its respective hormone and function.

	Source gland	Hormone	Function
(a)	Anterior piturity	Oxytocin	Contaction of uterus muscles during child birth
(b)	Posterior piturity	Vasopressin	Stimulates reabsoption of water in the distal tubules in nephron
(c)	Corpus luteum	Oestrogen	Supports pregnancy
(d)	Thyroid	Thyroxine	Reguulates blood calcium level

16. Match the following Columns.

	Column I		Column II
A.	Calcitonin	1.	Diabetes mellitus
B.	Gonadotrophin	2.	Rickets
C.	Erythropoietin	3.	Diabetes insipidus
D.	Insulin	4.	Formation of erythrocytes
E.	ADH	5.	Infertility

Codes

	A	B	C	D	E
(a)	3	1	4	2	5
(b)	3	2	1	5	4
(c)	4	3	2	1	5
(d)	2	5	4	1	3

17. Match the following Columns.

	Column I		Column II
A.	Pineal	1.	Epinephrine
B.	Thyroid	2.	Melatonin
C.	Ovary	3.	Oestrogen
D.	Adrenal medulla	4.	Tetraiodothyromine

Codes

	A	B	C	D
(a)	4	2	1	3
(b)	2	4	1	3
(c)	3	2	1	4
(d)	2	4	3	1

18. Match the following Columns.

	Column I		Column II
A.	Epinephrine	1.	Regulates blood calcium levels
B.	Testosterone	2.	Decreases blood pressure
C.	Glucagon	3.	Pigmentation
D.	Atrial natriuretric factor	4.	Increase heartbeat

Codes

	A	B	C	D
(a)	2	1	3	4
(b)	4	1	3	2
(c)	1	2	3	4
(d)	1	4	2	3

19. Given below is an incomplete table about certain hormones, their source glands and one major effect of each on the body in humans. Identify the correct option for the three blanks *A, B* and *C*.

Gland	Secretion	Effect on Body
A	Oestrogen	Maintance of secondary sexual characters
Alpha cells of islets Of Langerhans	B	Raises blood sugare level
Anterior pituitary	C	Over secretion leads to gigantism

	A	B	C
(a)	Placentra	Insulin	Vasopressin
(b)	Ovary	Insulin	Calcitonin
(c)	Placenta	Glucagon	Calcitonin
(d)	Ovary	Glucagon	Growth hormone

20. Identify the hormones A, B and C that are labelled in the given flowchart.

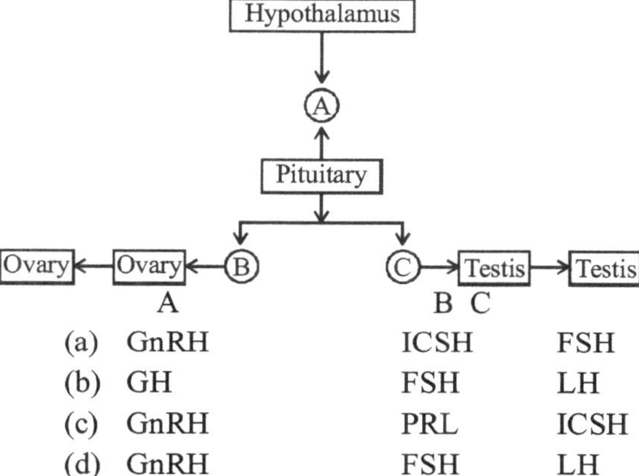

	A	B	C
(a)	GnRH	ICSH	FSH
(b)	GH	FSH	LH
(c)	GnRH	PRL	ICSH
(d)	GnRH	FSH	LH

21. Select the *correct* matching of a hormone, its source and function.

	Hormone	Source	Function
(a)	Vasopressin	Posterior pituitary	Increases loss of water through urine
(b)	Norepinephrine	Adrenal medulla	Increases heart beat, rate of respiration and alertness
(c)	Glucagon	Beta-cells of Islets of langerhans	Stimulates glycogenolysis
(d)	Prolactin	Posterior Pituitary	Regulates growth of mammary glands and milk formation in females

22. Match the list -I with list II

	List - I		List -II
(a)	adenohypophysis	(1)	epinephrine
(b)	adrenal medulla	(2)	somatotropin
(c)	parathyroid gland	(3)	thymosin
(d)	thymus gland	(4)	calcitonin

(a) a : 3, b : 1, c : 4, d : 2
(b) a : 1, b : 2, c : 3, d : 4
(c) a : 2, b : 1, c : 4, d : 3
(d) a : 4, b : 3, c : 2, d : 1

23. Match item in column A with those given in column B

	Column A		Column B
1.	ADH	A.	pituitary
2.	ACTH	B.	mineralocorticoid
3.	alsosterone	C.	diabetes mellitus
4.	insulin	D.	diabetes insipidus
5.	adrenaline	E.	vasodilator

(a) 1 - A, 2 - D, 3 - B, 4 - C, 5 - E
(b) 1 - D, 2 - B, 3 - A, 4 - C, 5 - E
(c) 1 - D, 2 - A, 3 - B, 4 - C, 5 - E
(d) 1 - D, 2 - A, 3 - C, 4 - B, 5 - E

24. Column I lists the endocrine structure and column II lists the corresponding hormones. Match the two columns. Identify the correct option from those given

	Column I		Column II
A.	hypothalamus	p.	relaxin
B.	anterior pituitary	q.	estrogen
C.	testis	r.	FSH and LH
D.	ovary	s.	testosterone
		t.	gonadotropin releasing hormone

(a) A = t, B = r, C = s, D = q
(b) A = t, B = r, C = q, D = s
(c) A = p, B = q, C = s, d = r
(d) A = r, B = t, C = s, D = q.

25. Given below is an incomplete table about certain hormones, their source glands and one major effect of each on the body in humans. Identify the correct option for the three blanks A, B and C

GLANDS	SECRETION	EFFECT ON BODY
A	Oestrogen	Maintenance of secondary sexual characters
Alpha cells of Islets of Langerhans Anterior pituitary	BC	Raises blood sugar levelOver secretion leads to Gigantism

Options:

	A	B	C
(a)	Placenta	Glucagon	Calcitonin
(b)	Ovary	Glucagon	Growth hormone
(c)	Placenta	Insulin	Vasopressin
(d)	Ovary	Insulin	Calcitonin

26. Mark the correct matching of the hormone and the endocrine cells

I.	C-Cell	A	Inhibin
II.	b-cell	B	Calcitonin
III.	Leydig cell	C	Insulin
IV.	Sertoli cells	D	Testosterone

(a) I-A, II-C, III-D, IV-B
(b) I-C, II-B, III-D, IV-A
(c) I-A, II-C, III-B, IV-D
(d) I-B, II-C, III-D, IV-A

Solutions

1. (c) 2. (a) 3. (d) 4. (a) 5. (a)
6. (b) 7. (e) 8. (b)
9. (b) Vasopressin reduces water loss through urine by stimulating resorption of water by the distal tubules of the kidney. Glucagon is released from a-cells. Prolactin is produced from anterior pituitary.

10. (c) Leydig's cells are present in between the seminiferous tubules which secrete androgens *(e.g.,* testosterone) that initiate the production of sperms. Theplacenta secretes into the mother's blood many hormones, such as estrogens and progesterone and these hormones supplement the hormones of same name produced by the ovary. Progesterone is secreted by corpus luteum. It brings about most of the pregnancy changes such as development of uterine lining and mammary glands, formation of placenta and also maintains pregnancy. Ovaries secrete two types of hormones - estrogens and progesterone.

11. (e) ANF pressure → Decreases blood
     MSH   → Pigmentation
     GIP   → Inhibits gastric secretion
     TCT   → Regulates blood calcium levels

11. (c) 12. (a) 13. (b) 14. (b) 15. (b)
16. (d) 17. (d) 18. (b) 19. (d) 20. (d)
21. (b) 22. (c) 23. (c) 24. (a) 25. (b)
26. (d)

Reproduction in Organisms

1. Match the column I with column II

Column I		Column II
A.	Animals which give birth to young one	I. *Hydra*
B.	Animal which produces bud	II. *Planaria*
C.	An animal which shows regeneration	III. Viviparous
D.	Provides nutrition to the developing embryo from the mother	IV. Placenta

(a) A-I, B-III, C-II, D-IV
(b) A-III, B-I,C-II, D-IV
(c) A-III, B-II, C-IV, D-I
(d) A-III,B-IV, C-I, D-II

2. Match the column I with column II and choose the correct option:

Column I		Column II
A.	Root tubers	1. *Curcuma* (Turmeric)
B.	Sucker	2. *Chrysanthemum*
C.	Rhizome	3. Sweet potato
D.	Corm	4. *Colocasia*

Codes

	A	B	C	D		A	B	C	D
(a)	2	3	4	1	(b)	3	1	2	4
(c)	3	2	1	4	(d)	1	3	4	2

3. Match the columns and find out the correct combination:

A.	Rose	1.	2 weeks
B.	Pinus	2.	5+ years
C.	*Wolffia*	3.	300+ years
D.	Banana	4.	1 year
		5.	About 2 year

(a) A-2, B-3, C-4, D-5
(b) A-3, B-2, C-1, D-5
(c) A-2, B-3,C-1, D-4
(d) A-2, B-3,C-1,D-5

4. Match the column I with column II and choose the correct option:

Column I		Column II
A.	Endothecium	1. Starting cell of male gametophyte
B.	Tapetum	2. Hypodermis in anther wall
C.	Microspore mother cell	3. Nutritive tissue of female gametophyte
D.	Pollen grain	4. Meiocytes
		5. More than one nucleus

(a) A-2, B-5, C-4, D-1
(b) A-2, B-3, C-4, D-1
(c) A-3, B-5, C-2, D-1
(d) A-3, B-2, C-1, D-5

5. Which form of reproduction is correctly matched?

(a) *Euglena* → transverse binary fission
(b) *Paramecium* → longitudinal binary fission
(c) *Amoeba* → multiple fission
(d) *Plasmodium* → binary fission

6. Match the items in column I with those in column II and choose the correct option.

Column I		Column II
A.	Binary fission	I. Algae
B.	Zoospore	II. *Amoeba*
C.	Conidium	III. *Hydra*
D.	Budding	IV. *Penicillium*
E.	Gemmules	V. Sponge

(a) A – I; B – IV; C – V; D – III; E – II
(b) A – II; B – I; C – IV; D – III; E – V
(c) A – II; B – IV; C – III; D – V; E – I
(d) A – I; B – IV; C – III; D – II; E – V

7. Match column I with column II and select the correct option.

Column I (Name of the organism)	Column II (Haploid chromosome number in gamete)
A. *Ophioglossum*	I. 23
B. Rice	II. 24
C. Potato	III. 12
D. Man	IV. 630

(a) A – I; B – II; C – III; D – IV
(b) A – II; B – III; C – IV; D – I
(c) A – III; B – IV; C – II; D – I
(d) A – IV; B – III; C – II; D – I

8. Match list I with list II and select the correct option.

List I	List II
A. Gemmules	I. *Agave*
B. Leaf-buds	II. *Penicillium*
C. Bulbil	III. Water hyacinth
D. Offset	IV. Sponges
E. Conidia	V. *Bryophyllum*

(a) A – IV; B – V; C – I; D – III; E – II
(b) A – IV; B – III; C – II; D – I; E – V
(c) A – III; B – V; C – IV; D – II; E – I
(d) A – IV; B – I; C – V; D – III; E – II

9. Match the following and choose the correct combination from the options given.

Column I (Organism)	Column II (Approximate life span)
A. Butterfly	I. 60 years
B. Crow	II. 140 years
C. Parrot	III. 15 years
D. Crocodile	IV. 1 – 2 years

(a) A – I; B – II; C – III; D – IV
(b) A – IV; B – III; C – I; D – II
(c) A – II; B – III; C – IV; D – I
(d) A – IV; B – III; C – II; D – I

10. Match the following and choose the correct combination from the options given.

Column I (Name of the organism)	Column II (Chromosome number in meiocyte (2*n*))
A. Housefly	I. 20
B. Fruit fly	II. 34
C. Apple	III. 8
D. Maize	IV. 12

(a) A – I; B – II; C – III; D – IV
(b) A – II; B – III; C – IV; D – I
(c) A – III; B – IV; C – II; D – I
(d) A – IV; B – III; C – II; D – I

11. Examine the figures given below and select the right options out of (1 - 4); in which all the 4 items A, B, C and D are identified correctly

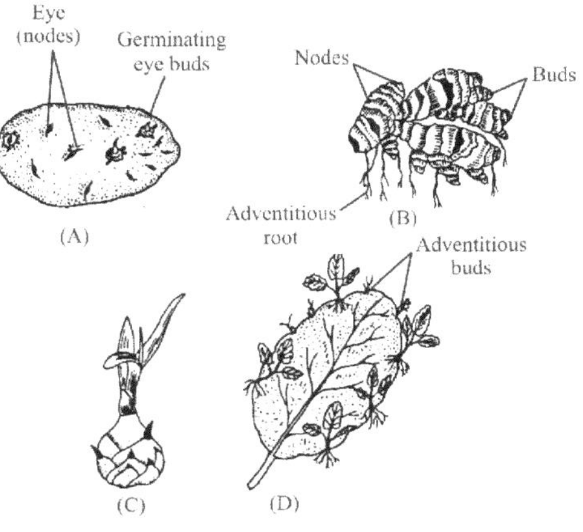

	(A)	(B)	(C)	(D)
(a)	Tuber	Rhizome	Bulb	Leaf buds
(b)	Offset	Sucker	Stolon	Leaf buds
(c)	Offset	Sucker	Stolon	Leaf buds
(d)	Tuber	Rhizome	Bulbil	Leaf buds

12. Pick the correct set

Column I	Column II
A. Bamboos	I. Bronchial allergy
B. Microspore	II. Die after flowering
C. Cleistozamous	III. Orchids
D. Micropropa-	IV. flowers which never gation open

(a) A–I; B–II; C–III; D–IV
(b) A–II; B–I; C–IV; D–III
(c) A–IV; B–II; C–III; D–I
(d) A–I; B–IV; C–II; D–III

13. Match the following and mark the correct set

Column I	Column II
A. Arum	I. Vegetative reproduction
B. Micropropagation	II. Fly-trap mechanism
C. Heterothallic	III. Entomophilly
D. Coloured petal and nectar	IV. Sexual reproduction

(a) A–I; B–II; C–III; D–IV
(b) A–II; B–I; C–IV; D–III
(c) A–III; B–II; C–IV; D–I
(d) A–I; B–III; C–IV; D–II

14. Match the columns

Column I	Column II
A. Phanerophytes	I. Buds are situated close to the ground
B. Chamaephytes	II. Buds completely hidden in the soil
C. Crytophytes	III. Buds naked or covered with scale
D. Therophytes	IV. Seasonal plants completing their life cycle in a single favourable season

(a) A – I; B–II; C–III; D–IV
(b) A–III; B–I; C–II; D–IV
(c) A–III; B–II; C–I; D–IV
(d) A–I; B–III; C–II; D–IV

Solutions

1. (b)   **2.** (c)   **3.** (d)   **4.** (a)

5. (3) Reproduction is the production of a new generation of individuals of the same species. It involves transfer of genetic material from one generation to the next. Asexual and sexual are the two types of reproduction. Fission and budding are two most common forms of asexual reproduction in animals. During adverse conditions, amoeba reproduces by multiple fission that gives rise to many amoeba. *Euglena* reproduces by longitudinal binary fission, *Paramecium* reproduces by transverse binary fission and *Plasmodium* reproduces by multiple fission.

6. (b)   **7.** (d)   **8.** (a)   **9.** (d)   **10.** (d)

11. (d)   **12.** (b)   **13.** (b)   **14.** (b)

Sexual Reproduction in Flowering Plants

24

1. Match the items in column I with those in column II and choose the correct answer.

	Column-I		Column-II
1.	Funicle	A.	Small opening of ovule
2.	Integuments	B.	Stalk of ovule
3.	Chalaza	C.	Protective envelopes of ovule
4.	Hilum	D.	Junction part of ovule and stalk
5.	Micropyle	E.	Basal part of the ovule

   (a) 1-B; 2-C; 3-E; 4-D; 5-A

   (b) 1-A; 2-C; 3-B; 4-D; 5-E

   (c) 1-B; 2-C; 3-A; 4-D; 5-E

   (d) 1-B; 2-D; 3-E; 4-A; 5-C

   (e) 1-C; 2-D; 3-E; 4-A; 5-B

2. Match the entries in Column I with those of Column II and choose the correct answer.

	Column I		Column II
A.	Cleistogamy	m.	Insect pollination
B.	Geitonogamy	n.	Bud pollination
C.	Entomophily	o.	Pollination between flowers in the same plant
D.	Xenogamy	p.	Wind pollination
		q.	Cross pollination

   (a) A-o, B-m, C-q, D-n

   (b) A-m, B-q, C-n, D-o

   (c) A-n, B-o, C-m, D-q

   (d) A-q, B-p, C-o, D-n

3. Match the column I with column II and select the correct answer from the given codes.

	Column I		Column II
A.	Parthenocarpy	(i)	Seed formation without fertilisation
B.	Polyembryony	(ii)	More than one embryo in same seed
C.	Apomixis	(iii)	Seedless fruits without fertilisation
D.	Somatic	(iv)	Embryo develops from embryogenesis a somatic cell

   (a) A - (iv), B - (ii), C - (iii), D - (i)

   (b) A - (iii), B - (ii), C - (i), D - (iv)

   (c) A - (i), B - (iv), C - (iii), D - (ii)

   (d) A - (ii), B - (iii), C - (i), D - (iv)

4. Identity the parts labbled A, B, C and D in the given figure and select the correct option.

	A	B	C	D
(a)	Chalaza	Female gametophyte	Embryo sac	Micropyle
(b)	Chalaza	Nucellus	Embryo sac	Micropyle
(c)	Micropyle	Egg	Embryo sac	Chalaza
(d)	Micropyle	Nucellus	Embryo sac	Chalaza

5. Select the mismatched pair.

(a)	Storage of pollen grains	–	196°C
(b)	Pollen allergy	–	Carrot grass
(c)	Chasmogamous flowers	–	Exposed anthers and stigmas
(d)	Xenogamy	–	Self pollination

6. Match column I with column II and select the correct option from the given codes.

	Column I		Column II
A.	Anemophily	(i)	Grasses, Date palm
B.	Hydrophily	(ii)	Rose, Jasmine
C.	Entomophily	(iii)	*Butea, Bignonia*
D.	Ornithophily	(iv)	*Vallisneria, Ceratophyllum*

(a) A-(i), B-(iv), C-(ii), D-(iii)
(b) A-(i), B-(iv), C-(iii), D-(ii)
(c) A-(ii), B-(iii), C-(i), D-(iv)
(d) A-(ii), B-(i), C-(iii), D-(iv)

7. Match column I with column II and select the correct option from the given codes.

	Column I		Column II
A.	Tallest flower	(i)	Maize
B.	*Pronuba* moth	(ii)	*Amorphophallus*
C.	Anemophily	(iii)	*Salvia*
D.	Entomophily	(iv)	*Yucca*

(a) A-(ii), B-(iv), C-(i), D-(iii)
(b) A-(ii), B-(iv), C-(iii), D-(i)
(c) A-(iii), B-(ii), C-(i), D-(iv)
(d) A-(iv), B-(iii), C-(ii), D-(i)

8. Match column I with column II and select the correct . option from the given codes.

	Column I		Column II
A.	Monoecious	(i)	*Primula*
B.	Dioecious	(ii)	Maize
C.	Cleistogamous	(iii)	Date palm
D.	Heterostyly	(iv)	*Commelina*

	A	B	C	D
(a)	(iii)	(ii)	(iv)	(i)
(b)	(ii)	(iii)	(iv)	(i)
(c)	(ii)	(iii)	(i)	(iv)
(d)	(i)	(ii)	(iii)	(iv)

9. Given below are the events that are observed in an artificial hybridisation programme. Arrange them in the correct sequential order and select the correct option.

1. Re-bagging
2. Selection of parents
3. Bagging
4. Dusting the pollen on stigma
5. Emasculation
6. Collection of pollen from male parent

(a) $2 \to 3 \to 5 \to 6 \to 4 \to 1$
(b) $2 \to 5 \to 3 \to 6 \to 4 \to 1$
(c) $5 \to 2 \to 3 \to 6 \to 1 \to 4$
(d) $2 \to 3 \to 6 \to 4 \to 5 \to 1$

10. Match column I with column II and select the correct option from the given codes.

	Column I		Column II
A.	Ovary	(i)	Groundnut, mustard
B.	Ovule	(ii)	Guava, orange, mango
C.	Wall of ovary	(iii)	Pericarp
D.	Fleshy fruits	(iv)	Seed
E.	Dry fruits	(v)	Fruit

	A	B	C	D	E
(a)	(v)	(iv)	(iii)	(ii)	(i)
(b)	(i)	(ii)	(iii)	(iv)	(v)
(c)	(i)	(iii)	(ii)	(iv)	(v)
(d)	(v)	(iv)	(i)	(ii)	(iii)

11. Choose the correct match.
(a) Microspore   –   Pollen
(b) Megasporangium   –   Ovule
(c) Microsporangium   –   Anther lobes
(d) None of the above

12. Match the following Columns.

	Column I		Column II
A.	*Arum maculatum*	1.	Mosaic endosperm
B.	*Zea mays*	2.	Longest endosperm
C.	*Echinocystis lobata*	3.	Highest ploidy level of endosperm
D.	*Annona squamosa*	4.	Ruminate endosperm

Codes

	A	B	C	D
(a)	4	2	1	3
(b)	2	3	1	4
(c)	4	2	3	1
(d)	3	1	2	4

13. Match the following Columns.

	Column I		Column II
A.	Place where pollen grains land	1.	Spores
B.	The site, where the seeds develop	2.	Stigma
C.	Reproductive cells that have exactly the same number of chromosomes as the parent *plant*	3.	Microspore mother cells
D.	Meiotically dividing cells in the male reproductive tissues that make four microspores	4.	Ovary

Codes

	A	B	C	D
(a)	1	2	3	4
(b)	2	4	1	3
(c)	3	4	1	2
(d)	4	3	2	1

14. Match the following Columns.

	Column I		Column II
A.	*Salvia*	1.	*Pronuba*
B.	*Yucca*	2.	Moth
C.	*Arisaema*	3.	Insect
D.	*Ophrys*	4.	Snail

Codes

	A	B	C	D
(a)	1	2	3	4
(b)	1	3	2	4
(c)	3	1	4	2
(d)	4	2	1	3

15. Macth column I with column II and selcet the correct option using the codes given below.

	Column I		Column II
A.	Pistils fused together	1.	Gametogenesis
B.	Formation of gametes	2.	Pistillate
C.	Hyphae of higher ascomycetes	3.	Syncarpous
D.	Unisexual female flower	4.	Dikaryotic

Codes

	A	B	C	D
(a)	4	3	2	1
(b)	2	1	4	3
(c)	1	2	4	3
(d)	3	1	4	2

16. Which one of the following is mismatched in angiosperm?

(a) Pollen grains   –   Haploid
(b) Megaspore   –   Diploid
(c) Synergid   –   Haploid
(d) Endosperm   –   Triploid

17. Choose the mismatched option.

(a) Wind – *Cannabis* – Anemophily
(b) Water – *Zoostera* – Hydrophily
(c) Insects – *Salvia* – Entomophily
(d) Birds – *Adansonia* – Ornithophily
(e) Bats – *Kigelia* – Cheiropterophily

18. Match the following ovular structure with postfertilisation structure and select the correct alternative.

	Column I		Column II
A.	Ovule	1.	Endosperm
B.	Funiculus	2.	Aril
C.	Nucellus	3.	Seed
D.	Polar nuclei	4.	Perisperm

Codes

	A	B	C	D
(a)	2	3	4	1
(b)	2	3	1	4
(c)	3	2	4	1
(d)	3	2	1	4

19. Match the following ovular structure with post-fertilisation structure and select the correct alternative.

Column I	Column II
A. Ovule	1. Endosperm
B. Funiculus	2. Aril
C. Nucellus	3. Seed
D. Polar nuclei	4. Perisperm

Codes

	A	B	C	D
(a)	2	3	4	1
(b)	2	3	1	4
(c)	3	2	4	1
(d)	3	2	1	4

(a) 4000   (b) 10000

(c) 24000   (d) 48000

20. Match the following and choose the correct option

Column I	Column II
A. Ovary	I. Groundnut, mustard
B. Ovule	II. Guava, orange, mango
C. Wall of ovary	III. Pericarp
D. Fleshy fruits	IV. Seed
E. Dry fruits	V. Fruit

(a) A-V ; B-IV ; C-III ; D-II ; E-I

(b) A-I ; B-II ; C-III ; D-IV ; E-V

(c) A-I ; B-III ; C-II ; D-IV ; E-V

(d) A-V ; B-IV ; C-I ; D-II ; E-III

21. Match the following and choose the correct option.

Column I	Column II
A. Funicle	I. Mass of cells with in ovule with more food
B. Hilum	II. Basal part of ovule
C. Integument	III. One or two protective layers of ovule
D. Chalazal end	IV. Region where body of ovules fuses with funicle
E. Nucellus	V. Stalk of ovule

(a) A-I ; B-II ; C-III ; D-IV ; E-V

(b) A-V ; B-IV ; C-III ; D-II ; E-I

(c) A-IV ; B-II ; C-I ; D-III ; E-V

(d) A-I ; B-III ; C-V ; D-II ; E-IV

22. Match the following and choose the correct option.

Column I	Column II
A. Megasporogenesis	I. Monosporic development
B. Megagametogenesis	II. Fatty substance
C. Sporopollenin	III. Embryo sac formation
D. Typical embryo & ac	IV. Megaspore formation

(a) A-I ; B-II ; C-III ; D-IV

(b) A-IV ; B-III ; C-II ; D-I

(c) A-IV ; B-I ; C-II ; D-III

(d) A-III ; B-II ; C-I ; D-IV

23. Match the following columns.

Column I	Column II
A. Calyx	I. Female gamete
B. Corolla	II. Protection
C. Stamen	III. Attraction
D. Carpel	IV. Male gamete

Codes

(a) A-I; B-II; C-III; D-IV

(b) A-II; B-III; C-IV; D-I

(c) A-IV; B-III; C-II; D-I

(d) A-I; B-II; C-IV; D-III

Solutions

1. (a) 2. (c) 3. (b)

4. (d) Given figure represents an anatropous ovule where A, B, C and D represent micropyle, nucellus, embryo sac and chalaza respectively.

5. (d) Xenogamy or cross pollination is the transfer of pollen grains from the anther of one flower to the stigma of a genetically different flower. Cross pollination is performed with the help of an ecternal agency.

6. (a)	7. (a)	8. (b)	9. (b)	10. (a)
11. (d)	12. (d)	13. (b)	14. (c)	15. (d)
16. (b)	17. (c)	18. (c)	19. (c)	20. (a)
21. (b)	22. (b)	23. (b)		

Human Reproduction  25

1. The given table shows differences between spermatogenesis and spermiogenesis. Select the incorrect option.

	Spermatogenesis	Spermiogenesis
(a)	Process of formation of spermatozoa.	Process of differentiatin of spermatozoon form a spermatid.
(b)	It changes a haploid stucture into another haploid structure.	It involves conversion of a diploid structure into haploid structure.
(c)	Growth and divisions occur.	Divisions and growth are absent.
(d)	A spermatogonium forms four spermatozoa.	A spermatid forms a single spermatozoon.

2. Match column I with column II and select the correct option from the codes given below.

	Column I		Column II
A.	Acrosome	(i)	Rudimentary erectile tissue
B.	Endometrium	(ii)	Uterus
C.	Polar body	(iii)	Oogenesis
D.	Clitoris	(iv)	Spermatozoon

   (a) A-(ii), B-(i), C-(iv), D-(iii)
   (b) A-(iv), B-(ii), C-(iii), D-(i)
   (c) A-(iv), B-(iii), C-(ii), D-(i)
   (d) A-(iv), B-(iii), C-(i), D-(ii)

3. Which of the following options is correct?

	Haploid	Diploid
(a)	Secondary oocyte	Primary spermatocyte
(b)	Secondary spermatocyte	Secondary oocyte
(c)	Primary oocyte	Secondary spermatocyte
(d)	Ovum	Spermatid

4. Match column I with column II and select the correct option from the codes given below.

	Column I		Column II
A.	Cleavage	(i)	Fertilisation
B.	Morula	(ii)	Mitotic divisions
C.	Polyspermy	(iii)	Endometrial
D.	Implantation	(iv)	Little mulberry

   (a) A-(ii), B-(iv), C-(i), D-(iii)
   (b) A-(i), B-(iv), C-(ii), D-(iii)
   (c) A-(iv), B-(ii), C-(i), D-(iii)
   (d) A-(ii), B-(iv), C-(iii), D-(i)

5. Match column I with column II and select the correct option from the codes given below.

	Column I		Column II
A.	Fertilisation	(i)	Isthmus of oviduct
B.	Cleavage	(ii)	Later part of oviduct
C.	Morula	(iii)	Cervix
D.	Blastocyst	(iv)	Ampulla of oviduct
E.	Parturition	(v)	Uterine wall

   (a) A-(iv), B-(i), C -(ii), D-(iii), E-(v)
   (b) A-(ii), B-(i), C -(iv), D-(iii), E-(v)
   (c) A-(ii), B-(i), C -(v), D-(iv), E-(iii)
   (d) A-(iv), B-(i), (-(ii), D-(v), E-(iii)

6. Match column I (terms) with column II (definitions) and select the correct option from the codes given below.

Column I	Column II
A. Parturition	(i) Attachment of embryo to endometrium
B. Gestation	(ii) Release of egg from Graafian follicle
C. Ovulation	(iii) Delivery of baby from uterus
D. Implantation	(iv) Duration between pregnancy and birth
E. Conception	(v) Formation of zygote by fusion of the egg and sperm
	(vi) Stoppage of ovulation and menstruation

(a) A-(ii), B-(iv), C-(i), D-(v), E-(vi)
(b) A-(iv), B-(iii), C-(i), D-(v), E-(ii)
(c) A-(v), B-(vi), C-(ii), D-(iii), E-(iv)
(d) A-(iii), B-(iv), C-(ii), D-(i), E-(v)

7. Match column I with column II and select the correct option from the codes given below.

Column I	Column II
A. Hypothalamus	(i) Sperm lysins
B. Acrosome	(ii) Estrogen
C. Graafian follicle	(iii) Relaxin
D. Leydig's cells	(iv) GnRH
E. Parturition	(v) Testosterone

(a) A-(iv), B-(i), C-(ii), D-(iii), E-(v)
(b) A-(ii), B-(i), C-(iv), D-(iii), E-(v)
(c) A-(ii), B-(i), C-(v), D-(iv), E-(iii)
(d) A-(iv), B-(i), C-(ii), D -(v), E-(iii)

8. Match column I with column II and select the correct option from the codes given below.

Column I	Column II
A. Hyaluronidase	(i) Acrosomal reaction
B. Corpus luteum	(ii) Morphogenetic movements
C. Gastrulation	(iii) Progesterone
D. Capacitation	(iv) Mammary gland
E. Colostrum	(v) Sperm activation

(a) A-(v), B-(ii), C-(iv), D-(i), E-(iii)
(b) A-(i), B-(iii), C-(ii), D-(v), E-(iv)
(c) A-(iii), B-(ii), C-(v), D-(iv), E-(i)
(d) A-(i), B-(ii), C-(iii), D-(iv), E-(v)

9. Select the correct match.

Column I	Column II
(A) Seminal fluid	(i) Corpus spongiosum
(B) Prostate gland	(ii) Membranous urethra
(C) Ejaculatory duct	(iii) Clitoris
(D) Erectile tissues	(iv) Fructose
	(v) Prostaglandins

(a) (A)-(iv) (b) (B)-(v)
(c) (C)-(i) (d) (D)-(ii)

10. Match the items given in column I with those in column II and select the correct option given below.

Column I	Column II
A. Proliferative phase	(i) Breakdown of endometrial lining
B. Secretory phase	(ii) Follicular phasse
C. Menstruation	(iii) Luteal phase

	A	B	C
(a)	(iii)	(ii)	(i)
(b)	(i)	(iii)	(ii)
(c)	(ii)	(iii)	(i)
(d)	(iii)	(i)	(ii)

11. Column I contains terms and column II contains definitions. Match them correctly and choose the right answer.

Column I	Column II
A. Parturition	1. Attachment of zygote to endometrium
B. Gestation	2. Release of egg from Graffian follicle
C. Ovulation	3. Delivery of baby from uterus
D. Implantation	4. Duration between pregnancy and birth
E. Conception	5. Formation of zygote by fusion of the egg and sperm
	6. Stoppage of ovulation

(a) A - 2, B - 4, C - 1, D - 5, E - 3
(b) A - 4, B - 3, C - 1, D - 5, E - 2
(c) A - 5, B - 1, C - 2, D - 3, E - 4
(d) A - 3, B - 4, C - 2, D - 1, E - 5

12. Which is the correctly matched pair among the following?

I.	Colostrum	–	Secretion found in seminal fluid
II.	Areola	–	Pigmented circular area around the nipple
III.	Sexual intercourse	–	Coitus
IV.	Bartholin's gland	–	Erectile body in female homologous to glans penis of male.

Codes
(a) II and III
(b) III and IV
(c) I and IV
(d) II and IV

13. Match the following Columns.

Column I	Column II
A. Male reproductive organ	1. Semen
B. Site of sperm maturation and strage	2. Seminiferous tubules
C. Unit of tests	3. Testis
D. Substance containig sperm and other secretions	4. Epididymis

Codes

	A	B	C	D
(a)	3	1	2	4
(b)	1	2	3	4
(c)	3	4	2	1
(d)	4	3	1	2

14. Match the following Columns.

Column I	Column II
A. A hollow ball of cells	1. Cleavage
B. Outer germ layer	2. Seminiferous
C. Cavity within a blastula	3. Blastocoel
D. Division of embryo	4. Ectoderm

Codes

	A	B	C	D
(a)	2	4	3	1
(b)	1	4	3	2
(c)	4	3	2	1
(d)	3	1	4	2

15. Match the following Columns.

Column I	Column II
A. The process of start of menstrual cycle in the life of a human female.	1. Capacitation

B. The process of   2. Luteal phase
    maturation of
    sperms

C. The process of   3. Sperminogenesis
    transformation of
    ruptured Graafian
    follicle into corpus
    luteum.

D. The process of   4. Menarche
    activation of
    sperms in female
    reproductive system
    after their ejaculation
    inot it

Codes

	A	B	C	D
(a)	4	3	2	1
(b)	1	2	3	4
(c)	2	1	3	4
(d)	3	1	2	4

16. Which one of the following is the correct matching of the events occurring during menstrual cycle?

(a) Ovulation   – FH and FSH attain peak level and sharp fall in the secretion of progesterone

(b) Proliferative   – Rapid regeneration of myometrium and maturation of Graafian follicle

(c) Development of corpus luteum   – Secretory phase and increased secretion of progesterone

(d) Menstruation   – Breakdown of myometrium and ovum not fertilised

17. Match the hormones listed under column I with their functions listed under column II choose the answer, which gives the correct combination of the alphabets of the two columns.

Column I		Column II
A. Oxytocin	1.	Stimulates ovulation
B. Prolactin	2.	Implantation and maintenance of pregnancy
C. Luteinising hormone	3.	Lactation after child birth
D. Progesterone	4.	Uterine conraction ding labour
	5.	Reabsorption of water by nephrons

Codes

	A	B	C	D			A	B	C	D
(a)	4	2	3	5		(b)	5	3	1	4
(c)	4	3	1	2		(d)	2	3	1	4

18. Match the following with correct combination.

A.	hyaluronidase	p.	acrosomal reaction
B.	corpus luteum	q.	morphogenetic movements
C.	gastrulation	r.	progesterone
D.	capacitiation	s.	mammary gland
E.	colostrum	t.	sperm activation

(a) A - t, B - q, C - s, D - p, E - r
(b) A - p, B - r, C - q, D - t, E - s
(c) A - r, B - q, C - t, D - s, E - p
(d) A - p, B - q, C - r, D - s, E - t

19. Match column I with column II and select the correct option using the code given below

Column I		Column II
A. Mons pubis	I.	Embryo formation
B. Antrum	II.	Sperm
C. Trophectoderm	III.	Female external genitalia
D. Nebenkern	IV.	Graafian follicle

(a) A–I; B–IV; C–III; D–II
(b) A–III; B–IV; C–II; D–I
(c) A–III; B–IV; C–I; D–II
(d) A–III; B–I; C–IV; D–II

20. In the given columns, column I contain structures of male reproductive system and column II contains its feature. Select the correct match from the options given below.

Column I (Structure of Male Reproductive System)		Column II (Features)
A.	Seminiferous tubule	I. Network of seminiferous tubule
B.	Rete testis	II. Secondary sexual characters
C.	Leydig cells	III. Meiosis and sperm formation occurs
D.	Prepuce	IV. Place of implantation
		V. Terminal skin of penis

(a) A – I; B – II; C – III; D – V
(b) A – III; B – I; C – II; D – V
(c) A – III; B – I; C – IV; D – II
(d) A – II; B – IV; C – III; D – V

21. In the given columns, column-I contain structures of female reproductive system and column-II contain its feature. Select the correct match from the option given below.

Column-I (Structures of female reproductive system)		Column-II (Features)
A.	Ampulla	I. It undergoes cyclical changes during menstrual cycle.
B.	Labia majora	II. It helps in collection of ovum after ovulation.
C.	Oviduct	III. Wider part of fallopian tube where fusion of male and female gametes takes place.
D.	Fimbriae	IV. Larger hairy folds which extend down from the mons pubis and surrounds the vaginal opening.
E.	Endometrium	V. Also called fallopian tubes, which extend from the periphery of each ovary to the womb.

(a) A – I; B – II; C – III; D – V; E – IV
(b) A – III; B – I; C – II; D – V; E – IV
(c) A – III; B – IV; C – V; D – II; E – I
(d) A – II; B – IV; C – III; D – V; E – I

22. The given figure shows the diagrammatic sectional view of female reproductive system with few structures marked as A, B, C, D, E and F.

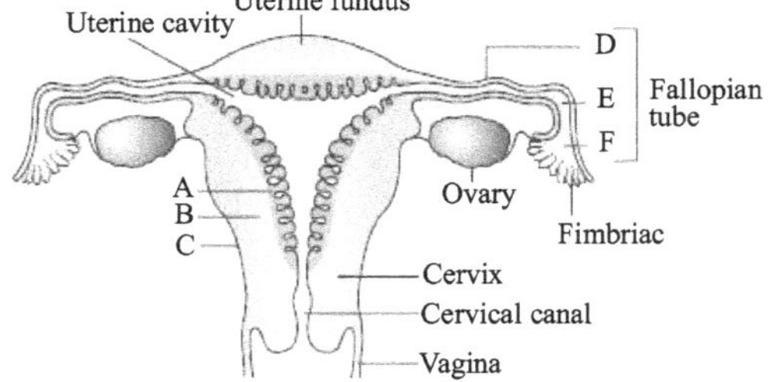

Which of the following options shows the correct labeling of A–F?

(a) A→Myometrium, B→Isthmus, C→Endometrium, D→ Perimetrium, E→Ampulla, F→ Infundibulum
(b) A→Infundibulum, B→Perimetrium, C→Endometrium, D→Myometrium, E→Ampulla, F→Isthmus
(c) A→Endometrium, B→Myometrium, C→Perimetrium, D→Isthmus, E→Ampulla, F→Infundibulum
(d) A→Perimetrium, B→Endometrium, C→Isthmus, D→Infundibulum, E→Ampulla, F→Myometrium

23. Refer the figure of mammary gland with few structures marked as A, B, C and D. Identify the marked structures.

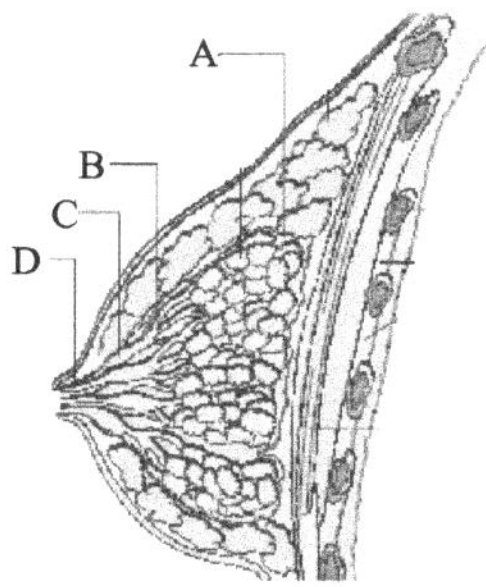

(a) Mammary lobe, mammary duct, ampulla and lactiferous duct.

(b) Ampulla, mammary duct, lactiferous duct and mammary lobe.

(c) Lactiferous duct, mammary lobe, mammary lobe and ampulla.

(d) Mammary duct, mammary lobe lactiferous duct and ampulla.

24. The figure given below shows the structure of sperm. Identify the correct feature corresponding to the marked structure A, B, C and D.

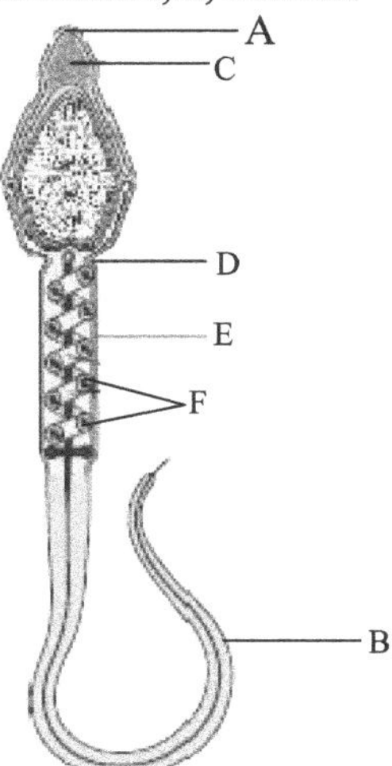

(a) A - plasma membrane, B - tail, C - Acrosome, D - Neck, E - middle piece and F - Mitochondria.

(b) A - middle piece, B - plasma membrane, C - Neck, D - Mitochondria, E - tail and F - Acrosome.

(c) A - Mitochondria, B - tail, C - Neck, D - plasma membrane, E - Acrosome and F - middle piece.

(d) A - Acrosome, B - middle piece, C - mitochondria, D - tail, E - plasma membrane and F - Neck.

25. The given figure shows the diagrammatic representation of oogenesis. Identify the option which shows the correct label marked as A, B, C and D.

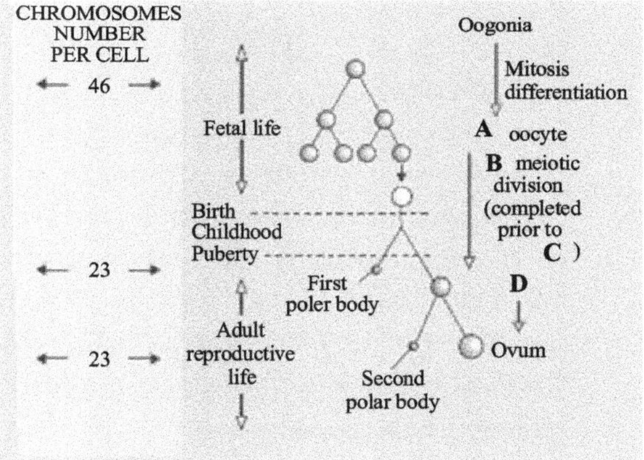

(a) A: Tertiary; B: I; C: Fertilization; D: Primary oocyte.

(b) A: Primary; B: II; C: Ovulation; D: Secondary oocyte.

(c) A: Secondary; B: II; C: Fertilization; D: Primary oocyte.

(d) A: Primary; B: I; C: Ovulation; D: Secondary oocyte.

Solutions

1. **(b)** Spermatogenesis involves conversion of a diploid structure (spermatogonia) into haploid structures (spermatozoa). Spermiogenesis changes a haploid structure (spermatid) into another haploid structure (spermatozoon).

2. **(b)**

3. **(a)** Secondary oocyte is formed by meiotic division of primary oocyte *(2n),* therefore, it is haploid. Primary spermatocyte is formed by mitotic division of spermatogonium *(2n),* therefore it is diploid.

4. **(a)** 5. **(d)** 6. **(d)** 7. **(d)** 8. **(b)**

9. **(a)** Seminal fluid is a viscous fluid which contributes about 60% of total volume of semen. It consists of fructose, fibrinogen and prostaglandins. Fructose provides energy to sperms for swimming. The prostaglandins stimulate contractions in the female reproductive tract to help the process of fertilisation. Fibrinogen helps in coagulation of semen after ejaculation.

10. **(c)** 11. **(d)** 12. **(a)** 13. **(c)** 14. **(a)**

15. **(a)** 16. **(c)** 17. **(c)** 18. **(b)** 19. **(c)**

20. **(b)** Seminiferous tubules are located in the testes, which are the specific location of meiosis, and the subsequent formation of sperms. Rete testis is a network of small tubules found in the part of the testicle that carries sperm. Leydig cells or interstitial cells of Leydig produce the hormone called testosterone which contributes to male secondary sexual characters. Prepuce is the foreskin, skin surrounding and protecting the head of the penis as well as clitoris.

21. **(d)** The menstrual cycle is the series of changes a woman's body goes through to prepare for a pregnancy. About once a month, the uterus grows a new lining (endometrium) to get ready for a fertilized egg. When there is no fertilized egg to start a pregnancy, the uterus sheds its lining. This is the monthly menstrual bleeding (also called menstrual period).

22. **(c)** In the given figure of female reproductive system, the marked structures (A to F) are the parts of uterus and fallopian tube. A to F are respectively endometrium, myometrium, perimetrium, isthmus, ampulla and infundibulum.

23. **(a)** The structures marked in the figure of mammary gland are A–mammary lobe, B–mammary duct, C–ampulla, and D–lactiferous duct. The mammary gland is a gland located in the breasts of females that is responsible for lactation. Mammary glands only produce milk after childbirth. Mammary lobe (A) contains clusters of cells called alveoli which secrete milk which is stored in the cavities of alveoli.

24. **(a)** In the given figure, A, B, C, D, E and F are marked as plasma membrane, tail, acrosome, neck, middle piece and mitochondria.

25. **(d)** A - Primary; B - I; C - Ovulation; D - Secondary oocyte

Reproductive Health 26

1. Given below are four methods (A-D) and their modes of action (i-iv) in achieving contraception. Select their correct matching from the four options that follow.

Method		Mode of Action
A. Oral pill	(i)	Prevents sperms reaching cerbix
B. Condom	(ii)	Suppresses sperm motelity
C. Vasectomy	(iii)	Prevents ovulation
D. Copper T	(iv)	Semen contains on sperms

(a) A-(ii), B-(iv), C-(i), D-(ii)
(b) A-(ii), B-(iii), C-(i), D-(iv)
(c) A-(iii), B-(i), C-(iv), D-(ii)
(d) A-(iv), B-(i), C-(ii), D-(iii)

2. Match the contraceptive methods given under column I with their examples given under column II and select the correct option form the given codes.

Column I		Column II
A. Chemical	(i)	Tubectomy and vasectomy
B. IUDs	(ii)	Copper T and loop
C. Barriers	(iii)	Condom and cervical cap
D. Sterilisation	(iv)	Spermicidal jelly and foam
	(v)	Coitus interruptus and calendar method

(a) A-(iv), B-(ii), C-(iii), D-(i)
(b) A-(iv), B-(v), C-(ii), D-(iii)
(c) A-(i), B-(iii), C-(ii), D-(v)
(d) A-(iv), B-(ii), C-(v), D-(i)

3. Which of the following contraceptive method correcty matches with its mode of action?

Contraceptive method	Mode of aciton
(a) Tubectomy	Makes the uterus unsuitable for implantation
(b) Oral pills	Inhibit ovulation and implantation
(c) Diaphragms	Spermicidal and increases phagocytosis of sperms within the uterus
(d) IUDs	Blocks gamete transport

4. Match column I with column II and select the correct option from the given codes.

Column I	Column II
A. Natural methods	(i) Coitus interruptus
B. IUDs	(ii) LNG - 20
C. Barrier methods	(iii) Diaphragms
D. Surgical methods	(iv) Multiload 375
E. Oral contraceptives	(v) Saheli
	(vi) Nirodh
	(vii) Sterilisation
	(viii) Vasectomy
	(ix) CuT

(a) A-(i), B-(ii); (iv); (ix) C-(iii);(vi), D-(vii); (viii), E- (v)

(b) A-(i), B-(ii); (iv), C-(iii);(vi); (ix), D-(vii);(viii), E-(v)

(c) A-(i), B-(ii); (iv), C-(iii);(ix), D-(vii); (viii), E-(v); (vi)

(d) A-(i), B-(iv); (ix), C-(ii);(iii); (vi), D-(vii); (viii), E-(v)

5. Match column I with column II and select the correct option from the given codes.

	Column I		**Column II**
A.	Syphilis	(i)	Huaman papilloma virus
B.	Chancroid	(ii)	*Haemophilus ducreyi*
C.	AIDS	(iii)	*Treponema pallidum*
D.	Genital warts	(iv)	HIV

      A   B   C   D

(a) (iii) (ii) (iv) (i)

(b) (ii) (i) (iii)(iv)

(c) (iv) (ii) (i) (iii)

(d) (i)   (iv) (iii) (ii)

6. Which of the following approaches does not give the defined action of contraceptive?

(a) Hormonal contraceptives — Prevent/retard entry of sperms, prevent ovulation and fertilisation

(b) Vasectomy — Prevents spermatogenesis

(c) Barrier methods — Prevent fertilisation

(d) Intra uterine — Increase phagocytosis of sperms, suppress sperm motility and fertilising capacity of sperms

7. Match the following.

	List I		**List II**
A.	Contraceptive pill	(i)	Prevents sperms reaching the female reproductive tract
B.	Condom	(ii)	Inhibits ovulation and implantation
C.	Vasectomy	(iii)	Increases phagocytosis of sperms
D.	Copper T	(iv)	Block gamete transport

(a) A-(iv), B-(i), C-(ii), D-(iii)

(b) A-(i), B-(ii), C-(iii), D-(iv)

(c) A-(ii), B-(i), C-(iii), D-(iv)

(d) A-(iv), B-(iii), C-(i), D-(ii)

(e) A-(ii), B-(i), C-(iv), D-(iii)

8. Given below are four methods (A-D) and their modes of action (i-iv) in achieving contraception. Select their correct matching from the four options that follow.

	Method		**Mode of action**
A.	The pilll	(i)	Pevents sperms reaching cervix
B.	Condom	(ii)	Prevents implantation
C.	Vasectomy	(iii)	Prevents ovulation
D.	Copper T	(iv)	Semen contains no sperms

(a) A-(ii), B-(iii), C-(i), D-(iv)

(b) A-(iii), B-(i), C-(iv), D-(ii)

(c) A-(iii), B-(iv), C-(i), D-(ii)

(d) A-(iv), B-(i), C-(ii), D-(iii)

9. Match the contraceptive methods given under column I with their examples given under column II. Select the correct choice from those given below.

Column I	Column II
A. Chemical	q. Tubectomy and Vasectomy
B. IUDs	q. Copper T and Loop
C. Barriers	r. Condom and Cervical cap
D. Sterilisation	s. Spermicidal jelly and foam
	t. Coitus interruptus and calendar method

(a) A-s, B-q, C-r, D-p   (b) A-s, B-t, C-q, D-r
(c) A-p, B-r, C-q, D-t   (d) A-s, B-q, C-t, D-p

10. Match the following sexully transmitted diseases (column I) with their causative agent (column II) and select the correct option.

Column I	Column II
(a) Gonorrhoea	(i) HIV
(b) Syphilis	(ii) *Neisseria*
(c) Genital warts	(iii) *Treponema*
(d) AIDS	(iv) Human papilloma virus

	A	B	C	D			A	B	C	D
(a)	(iii)	(iv)	(i)	(ii)		(b)	(iv)	(ii)	(iii)	(i)
(c)	(iv)	(iii)	(ii)	(i)		(d)	(ii)	(iii)	(iv)	(i)

11. Match the following Columns.

Column I	Column II
A. IUD	1. Intra Uterine Device
B. Spermicids	2. In vitro fertilisation
C. Temperature method	3. Kills the sperms
D. IVF	4. Natural birth control method

Codes

	A	B	C	D			A	B	C	D
(a)	1	3	4	2		(b)	2	1	3	4
(c)	4	3	1	2		(d)	3	2	1	4

12. Match the following Columns.

Column I	Column II
A. Gonorrhoea	1. HSV -1 and SHV-2 viruses
B. Syphilis	2. HIV virus
C. Chlamydia	3. *Treponema pallidum*
D. IVF	4. *Neisseria gonorrhoeae*
E. Herpes	5. *Chlamydia trachomatis*

Codes

	A	B	C	D	E
(a)	4	3	2	1	5
(b)	4	3	5	2	1
(c)	3	5	1	2	4
(d)	1	2	4	3	5

13. Which of the following approaches does not give the defined aciton of contraceptive?

(a) Intrauterine devices – Incrrease phagocytosis of sperms suppress sperm motility and fertilising capacity of sperms

(b) Hormonal – Prevent/retard entry of sperms, prevent ovulation and fertilisation

(c) Vasectomy – Prevents spermatogenesis

(d) Barrier methods – Prevents fertilisation

14. Match the following Columns.

	Column I		Column II
A.	Syphilis	1.	Human papilloma virus
B.	Genital warts	2.	HBV
C.	Hepatits-B	3.	*Treponema pallidum*
D.	Gonorrhoea	4.	HSV (Herpes Simplex Virus)
		5.	*Neisseria*

Codes

	A	B	C	D
(a)	2	1	4	5
(b)	3	1	4	2
(c)	3	1	2	5
(d)	2	3	4	5

15. Match the following Columns I, II with III.

	Column I		Column II		Column III
A.	Trichomoniasis	1.	*Herpes simplex*	(i)	Pain in lower abdomen
B.	Syphilis	2.	*Neissieria gonorrhoeae*	(ii)	Inflammation and itching in and around vagina
C.	Gonorrhoea	3.	*Treponema pallidum*	(iii)	Patchy hair loss
D.	Genital herpes	4.	*Trichomonas vaginalis*	(iv)	Feelling of uneasiness

Codes

	A	B	C	D
(a)	1-(iii)	2-(ii)	4-(iv)	3-(i)
(b)	4-(ii)	1-(iii)	2-(i)	3-(iv)
(c)	4-(i)	1-(iv)	2-(ii)	3-(iii)
(d)	4-(ii)	3-(iii)	2-(i)	1-(iv)

16. Given below are four methods (A-D) and their modes of action (I - IV) in achieving contraception.

Select their correct matching from the four options that follow :

	Method		Mode of Action
A.	The pill	I.	Prevents sperms reaching cervix
B.	Condom	II.	prevents implantation
C.	Vasectomy	III.	prevents ovulation
D.	Copper T	IV.	Semen contains no sperms

(a) A – II; B – III; C – I; D – IV
(b) A – III; B – I; C – IV; D – II
(c) A – IV; B – I; C – II; D – III
(d) A – III; B – IV; C – I; D – II

17. Match the following and choose the correct option

	Column I		Column II
A.	Non-medicated IUDs	I.	Lippes loop
B.	Hormone releasing IUDs	II.	Multiload 375
C.	Copper releasing IUDs	III.	CuT

IV. Cu7

V. LNG - 20

VI. Progestasert

(a) A – I; B– II,VI; C – III, IV, V

(b) A– I; B – V, VI; C – II, III, IV

(c) A – I; B – V, VI; C – I, III, IV

(d) A – II; B – I, VI; C – III, IV, V

18. Match the following and choose the correct option

Column-I		Column-II
A. Hepatitis B	I.	Vitamin E
B. Saheli	II.	7'April, 1948
C. Normal functioning	III.	CDRI, Lucknow of reproductive organs
D. World Health organisation	IV.	Detection of antibody/antigen
E. ELISA technique	V.	Hepatitis B virus

(a) A – V; B – III; C – I; D – II; E – IV

(b) A – V; B – II; C – I; D – III; E – IV

(c) A – V; B – III; C – IV; D – II; E – I

(d) A – V; B – II; C – IV; D – III; E – I

Solutions

1. **(c)** 2. **(a)**

3. **(d)**

Tubectomy	–	Blocks gamete transport
Oral pills	–	Inhibit ovulaiton and implantation
Diaphragms	–	Prevent sperms from reaching an ovum
IUDs	–	Increase phagocytosis of sperms within the uterus

4. **(a)** 5. **(a)** 6. **(b)** 7. **(e)** 8. **(b)**

9. **(a)** 10. **(d)** 11. **(a)** 12. **(b)** 13. **(c)**

14. **(c)** 15. **(d)** 16. **(b)** 17. **(b)** 18. **(a)**

CHAPTER 27

Principles of Inheritance and Variation

1. Match the following and choose the correct option–

Column-I		Column-II
A.	Linkage	I.	Recombination of genes
B.	Mutation	II.	More than two sets of chromosome
C.	Crossing over	III.	Morgan
D.	Polyploidy	IV.	Hugo de Vries

   (a) A – II; B – III; C –I; D – IV
   (b) A– III; B – IV; C–I; D – II
   (c) A – II; B – IV; C – III; D –I
   (d) A – II; B – IV; C –I; D – III

2. Match the following and choose the correct option –

Column – A		Column – B
A.	ABO blood	I.	Dihybrid cross groups
B.	Law of	II.	Monohybrid cross segregation
C.	Law of	III.	Base pairs substitution Independent assortment
D.	Gene mutation	IV.	Multiple allelism

   (a) A – II; B – I; C – IV; D – III
   (b) A – IV; B – I; C – II; D – III
   (c) A – IV; B – II; C – I; D – III
   (d) A – II; B – III; C – IV; D – I

3. Match the terms in Column- I with their description in Column- II and choose the correct option

Column- I		Column- II
A.	Dominance	I.	Many genes govern a single character
B.	Co-dominance	II.	In heterozygous only one allele expresses itself
C.	Pleiotropy	III.	In heterozygous organism both alleles express themselves
D.	Polygenic Inh.	IV.	Single gene influences many characters

   (a) A–IV; B–III; C–I; D–II
   (b) A–II; B–I; C–IV; D–III
   (c) A–II; B–III; C–IV; D–I
   (d) A–IV; B–I; C–II; D–III

4. Match the terms in column I with their description in column II and choose the correct option

Column I		Column II
A.	Dominance	(i)	Many genes govern a single character
B.	Co- dominance	(ii)	In a heterozygous organism only one allele expresses itself

C. Pleiotropy   (iii) In a heterozygous organism both alleles express themselves fully

D. Polygenic inheritance (iv) A single gene influences many characters

(a) A-(ii), B-(i), C-(iv), D-(iii)

(b) A-(iv), B-(iii), C-(iv), D-(iv)

(c) A-(iv), B-(i), C-(ii), D-(iii)

(d) A-(iv), B-(iii), C-(i), D-(ii)

5. Match the columns and find out the correct combination:

	Column I		Column II
A.	G.J Mendel	1.	Chromosomal theory of inheritance
B.	Sturtevant	2.	Discovered linkage in Drosophila
C.	T. H Morgan	3.	Prepared chromosome maps
D.	Sutton & Boveri	4.	Proposed laws of heredity

(a) A-4, B-3, C-2, D-1

(b) A-1, B-2, C-3, D-4

(c) A-2, B-3, C-4, D-1

(d) A-4, B-1, C-2, D-3

6. Match the columns and find out the correct combination:

	Column I		Column II
A.	Pod shape	1.	Wrinkled
B.	Pod colour	2.	Yellow
C.	Seed shape	3.	Constricted
D.	Seed colour	4.	Green
		5.	Grey

(a) A-4, B-5, C-2, D-1

(b) A-3, B-2, C-1, D-4

(c) A-2, B-3, C-1, D-4

(d) A-1, B-2, C-4, D-3

7. Match the following Column - I with Column -II.

	Column - I		Column - II
A.	Complementary ratio	I.	9 : 7
B.	Supplementary ratio	II.	9 : 3 : 4
C.	Epistatic ratio (Masking)	III.	12 : 3 :1
D.	Inhibitory ratio	IV.	13 : 3

(a) A – IV; B – I; C – III; D – II

(b) A – I; B – II; C – III; D – IV

(c) A – IV; B – I; C – II; D – III

(d) A – I; B – III; C – II; D – IV

8. Which one of the following pair is not correct?

(a) Mongolian idiocy - 21st chromosome

(b) Patau syndrome - 13th chromosome

(c) Cri-Du-Chat - 11th chromosome

(d) Edward syndrome - 18th chromosome

9. Select the correct match

(a) Phenylketonuria   –   Autosomal dominant trait

(b) Sickle cell anaemia – Autosomal recessive trait, chromosome-11

(c) Thalassemia   –   X linked

(d) Haemophilia   –   Y linked

10. Match the items of Column-I with Column-II :

	Column-I		Column-II
(A)	XX-XO method	(i)	Turner's syndrome of sex determination
(B)	XX-XY method	(ii)	Female heterogametic of sex determination
(C)	Karyotype-45	(iii)	Grasshopper
(D)	ZW-ZZ method of sex	(iv)	Female homogametic determination

Select the correct option from the following :

(a) (A)-(iv), (B)-(ii), (C)-(i), (D)-(iii)

(b) (A)-(ii), (B)-(iv), (C)-(i), (D)-(iii)

(c) (A)-(i), (B)-(iv), (C)-(ii), (D)-(iii)

(d) (A)-(iii), (B)-(iv), (C)-(i), (D)-(ii)

11. Which of the following is correct match?

(a) Down's syndrome — 21st chromosome

(b) Sickle cell anaemia — X-chromosome

(c) Haemophila — Y-chromosome

(d) Parkinson disease — X & Y chromosome

12. Match the column I with column II and select the correct option from the given codes.

Column I	Column II
A. Dihybrid test cross	(i) 9:3:3:1
B. Law of segregation	(ii) Dihybrid cross
C. Law of independent assortment	(iii) 1:1:1:1
D. ABO blood group	(iv) Purity of gametes in man
	(v) Multiple allelism

(a) A-(iii), B-(iv), C-(ii), D-(v)

(b) A-(i), B-(iv), C-(ii), D-(v)

(c) A-(iii), B-(ii), C-(iv), D-(v)

(d) A-(ii), B-(v), C-(iii), D-(i)

13. Match the column I with column II and select the correct option from the given codes.

Column I	Column II
A. Multiple allelism	(i) Tt x tt
B. Back cross	(ii) Tt x TT
C. Test cross	(iii) Human blood groups
D. Crossing over	(iv) Non-parental combination
E. Recombination	(v) Non-sister chromatids

(a) A-(iii), B-(i), C-(ii), D-(v), E-(iv)

(b) A-(iii), B-(ii), C-(i), D-(v), E-(iv)

(c) A-(iii), B-(ii), C-(i), D-(iv), E-(v)

(d) A-(iv), B-(ii), C-(i), D-(v), E-(iii)

14. Match the column I with column II and select the correct option from the given codes.

Column I	Column II
A. Gregor J. Mendel	(i) Chromosomal theory of inheritance
B. Sutton and Boveri	(ii) Laws of inheritance
C. Henking	(iii) Drosophila
D. Morgan	(iv) Discovered X-body

(a) A-(ii), B-(i), C-(iv), D-(iii)

(b) A-(iv), B-(i), C-(ii), D-(iii)

(c) A-(iv), B-(ii), C-(i), D-(iii)

(d) A-(ii), B-(iii), C-(iv), D-(i)

15. Match the column I with column II and select the correct option from the given codes.

Column I	Column II
A. Sickle cell anaemia	(i) 7th chromosome
B. Phenylketonuria	(ii) 4th chromosome
C. Cystic fibrosis	(iii) 11th Chromosome
D. Huntington's disease	(iv) X-chromosome
E. Colourblindness	(v) 12th chromosome

(a) A-(iii), B-(v), C-(ii), D-(i), E-(iv)

(b) A-(iii), B-(v), C-(i), D-(ii), E-(iv)

(c) A-(v), B-(iv), C-(ii), D-(iii), E-(i)

(d) A-(iv), B-(ii), C-(iii), D-(i), E-(v)

16. Match column I with column II and select the correct option from the given codes.

Column I	Column II
A. Autopolyploidy	(i) 2n+1
B. Trisomy	(ii) AAAA
C. Allopolyploidy	(iii) AABB
D. Nullisomy	(iv) 2n-2

(a) A-(ii), B-(i), C-(iii), D-(iv)

(b) A-(iv), B-(i), C-(ii), D-(iii)

(c) A-(ii), B-(iv), C-(iii), D-(i)

(d) A-(ii), B-(i), C-(iv), D-(iii)

17. Match the column I with column II and select the correct option from the given codes.

Column I		Column II
A.	Autosomal recessive trait	(i) Down's syndrome or mongolism
B.	Sex-linked recessive trait	(ii) Phenylketonuria
C.	Metabolic error linked to autosomal recessive trait	(iii) Haemophilia
D.	Additional 21st chromosome	(iv) Sickle cell anaemia

    (a) A-(ii), B-(i), C-(iv), D-(iii)
    (b) A-(iv), B-(i), C-(ii), D-(iii)
    (c) A-(iv), B-(iii), C-(ii), D-(i)
    (d) A-(iii), B-(iv), C-(i), D-(ii)

18. Which of the following is mismatched pair of disease and its related symptom?

Disease	Symptom
(a) Phenylketonuria	Urine turns black on exposure to air
(b) Down's syndrome	Physical and mental retardation

    (c) Klinefelter's syndrome — Sterile males
    (d) Turner's syndrome — Sterile female

19. Find out the mismatch pair:
    (a) Haemophilia — Sex linked recessive
    (b) Cystic fibrosis — Autosomal recessive
    (c) Down's syndrome — Trisomy 21
    (d) Turner's syndrome — Y-linked

20. Match the column I and column II and select the correct option from the given codes.

Column I		Column II
A.	Chromosomal aberration	(i) An additional sex chromosome
B.	Down's syndrome	(ii) Inversion
C.	Klinefelter's syndrome	(iii) Presence of an extra chromosome
D.	Turner's syndrome	(iv) Absence of sex chromosome

    (a) A-(ii), B-(iv), C-(i), D-(i)
    (b) A-(ii), B-(iv), C-(iii), D-(i)
    (c) A-(ii), B-(iii), C-(i), D-(iv)
    (d) A-(iii), B-(iv), C-(i), D-(ii)

Solutions

1. (b) 2. (c) 3. (c) 4. (b) 5. (c)
6. (b)
7. (b) Epistasis is an interaction between two or more genes to control a single phenotype. Dominant epistasis has a ratio 12 : 3 : 1 in the F_2 phenotype. Supplementary genes or recessive epistasis has a ratio of 9 : 3 : 4.

8. (c) Cri-Du-Chat (Cat Cry) syndrome was first described by Lejeune n 1963 in France. The affected newborn cries-like meowing of a cat. This condition appears due to a deletion in the short arm of the chromosome number 5.

9. (b) Phenylketonuria is an inborn error of metabolism is also inherited as the autosomal recessive trait. Sickle cell anemia is an autosomes linked recessive trait that can be transmitted from parents to the offspring when both the partners are carrier for the gene (or heterozygous). Thalassemia is an inherited blood disorder that causes your body to have less hemoglobin than normal. Hemoglobin enables red blood cells to carry oxygen. Thalassemia can cause anemia, leaving you fatigued. Haemophilia is a sex linked recessive disease, which shows its transmission from unaffected carrier female to some of the male progeny.

10. **(d)** XX- XO type of sex determination is seen in crickets, grasshoppers, and some other insects. In all these organisms the female is XX and is the homogametic sex. The male is the heterogametic sex but only has one sex chromosome. The male in XX-XO systems produce gametes with (X) or without (O) a sex chromosome.

In XX -XY method of sex determination, the sex of an individual is determined by a pair of sex chromosomes. Females typically have two of the same kind of sex chromosome (XX), and are called the homogametic sex. Males typically have two different kinds of sex chromosomes (XY), and are called the heterogametic sex.

Turner's syndrome is also known as 45, X or 45, X,. It is a condition that affects only females, and results when one of the X chromosme (sex chromosomes) is missing or partially missing. ZW-ZZ method of sex determination can be seen in some birds, butterflies, moths, and other organisms. Instead of X and Y chromosomes, they have Z and W chromosomes. The female is the heterogametic sex. In all these organisms female has a pair of dissimilar ZW chromosomes and male has two similar ZZ chromosomes.

11. **(c)** **12.** **(a)** **13.** **(b)** **14.** **(a)** **15.** **(b)**

16. **(a)** **17.** **(c)** **18.** **(a)** **19.** **(d)** **20.** **(c)**

Molecular Basis of Inheritance

1. Match the following and choose the correct option –

Column I	Column II
A. Helicase	(I) Joining of nucleotides
B. Gyrase	(II) Opening of DNA
C. Primase	(III) Unwinding of DNA
D. DNA polymerase III	(IV) RNA priming

   (a) A – II; B – I; C – III: D – IV
   (b) A – II; B – I; C – IV; D – III
   (c) A – IV; B – III; C – I; D – II
   (d) A – II; B – III; C – IV; D – I

2. Match the enzyme in column I with its function in column II and choose the correct option.

Column I	Column II
A. β-galactosidase	I. Joining of DNA fragments
B. Permease	II. Peptide bond formation
C. Ligase	III. Hydrolysis of lactose
D. Ribozyme	IV. Increases permeability to β-galactosidase

   (a) A – II; B – I; C – IV; D – III
   (b) A – III; B – II; C – I; D – IV
   (c) A – II; B – IV; C – I; D – III
   (d) A – I; B – II; C – IV; D – III

3. Match the following columns.

Column I	Column II
A. Topoisomerase	I. Relieves strain of unwinding by DNA helicase this is a specific type of topoisomerase
B. DNA gyrase	II. Relaxes the DNA from its super-coiled nature
C. DNA ligase	III. Provides a starting point of RNA or DNA for DNA polymerase to begin synthesis of the new DNA strand.
D. Primase	IV. Re-anneals the semi conservative strands and joins Okazaki fragments of the lagging strand.
E. Telomerase	V. Lengthens telomeric DNA by adding repetitive nucleotide sequences to the ends of eukaryotic chromosomes.

   (a) A–I; B–II; C–V; D–IV; E–III
   (b) A–I; B–II; C–III; D–V; E–IV
   (c) A–V; B–IV; C–III; D–II; E–I
   (d) A–II; B–I; C–IV; D–III; E–V

4. Match the following:

Column I		Column II
A.	Lactose permease	I. Z gene
B.	Galactoside-transacetylase	II. Y gene
C.	Peptidyl transferase	III. A gene
D.	β-Galactosidase	

(a) D-I, A-I, B-III   (b) A-II, B-III, C-I
(c) A-II, B-I, D-III   (d) A-III, B-II, C-I

5. Match the enzyme in column I with its function in column II and choose the correct option.

Column I		Column II
A.	β-galactosidase	I. Joining of DNA fragments
B.	Permease	II. Peptide bond formation
C.	Ligase	III. Hydrolysis of lactose
D.	Ribozyme	IV. Increases permeability to β-galactosidase

(a) A – II; B – I; C – IV; D – III
(b) A – III; B – II; C – I; D – IV
(c) A – II; B – IV; C – I; D – III
(d) A – I; B – II; C – IV; D – III

6. Select the correct option.

Direction of RNA synthesis	**Direction of reading of the template strand**
(a) $5'\rightarrow3'$	$3'\rightarrow5'$
(b) $3'\rightarrow5'$	$5'\rightarrow3'$
(c) $5'\rightarrow3'$	$5'\rightarrow3'$
(d) $3'\rightarrow5'$	$3'\rightarrow5'$

7. Match the codons given in column-I with their respective amino acids given in column-II and choose the correct answer.

Column-I (Codons)		**Column-II (Amino acids)**
A.	UUU	I. Serine
B.	GGG	II. Methionine
C.	UCU	III. Phenylalanine
D.	CCC	IV. Glycine
E.	AUG	V. Proline

(a) A – III; B – IV; C – I; D – V; E – II
(b) A – III; B – I; C – IV; D – V; E – II
(c) A – III; B – IV; C – V; D – I; E – II
(d) A – II; B – IV; C – I; D – V; E – III

8. Match column-I to the column-II and select the option having correct matching.

Column-I		**Column-II**
A.	Bacteriophage nucleotides	(I) 5386
B.	_E.coli_	(II) 3.3×10^9 bp
C.	Human genome	(III) 4.6×10^6 bp
D.	$\phi \times 174$	(IV) 48502 bp

(a) A – (IV), B – (III), C – (II), D – (I)
(b) A – (III), B – (II), C – (I), D – (IV)
(c) A – (IV), B – (III), C – (I), D – (II)
(d) A – (IV), B – (I), C – (II), D – (III)

9. Select the correct match
(a) Alec Jeffreys - _Streptococcus pneumoniae_
(b) Alfred Hershey and - TMV
      Martha Chase
(c) Francois Jacob and - _Lac_ operon
      Jacques Monod
(d) Matthew Meselson - _Pisum sativum_
      and F. Stahl

10. Match the following genes of the Lac operon with their respective products:

(A) i gene	(i) β-galactosidase
(B) z gene	(ii) Permease
(C) a gene	(iii) Repressor
(D) y gene	(iv) Transacetylase

Select the **correct** option.

	(A)	**(B)**	**(C)**	**(D)**
(a)	(i)	(iii)	(ii)	(iv)
(b)	(iii)	(i)	(ii)	(iv)
(c)	(iii)	(i)	(iv)	(ii)
(d)	(iii)	(iv)	(i)	(ii)

11. Select the correct option:

	Direction of RNA synthesis the template	Direction of reading of DNA strand
(a)	5′—3′	3′—5′
(b)	3′—5′	5′—3′
(c)	5′—3′	5′—3′
(d)	3′—5′	3′—5′

12. Study the following table to identify the correct combination.

	Type of nitrogen base	Group	Systemic chemical name
I.	Adenine	Pyrimidine	6 aminopurine
II.	Guanine	Purine	2-amino-6-oxypurine
III.	Cytosine	Purine	6 amino-2-oxypurine
IV	Thymine	Pyrimidine	5 methyle-2, 4-dioxypyrimidine

(a) II and IV   (b) I and IV
(c) III and IV   (d) I and IV

13. Match the following:

Column I	Column II
A. Fredrick Griffith	1. A sequence of three nucleotides codes for single amino acid
B. Gamow	2. Double helical structures
C. Watson and Crick	3. Induced mutation
D. Meselson and Stahl	4. Semiconservation replication of DNA
	5. Phenomenon of transformation.

(a) A-5, B-1, C-2, D-4
(b) A-1, B-5, C-4, D-2
(c) A-1, B-2, C-3, D-4
(d) A-5, B-1, C-4, D-2

14. Study the following table and choose the correct combination

	Scientist	Proved	By Using
I.	Hershey and Chase	Proved that DNA is the genetic material	Bacteriophage
II.	Watson and Crick	Double helix model for the structure of DNA	X-ray diffraction
III.	Avery, Macleod and McCarty	Genetic material through a protein	Virus
IV.	Griffith	Transformation in bacteria	*Streptococcus pneumonia*

(a) I and III only
(b) II, III and IV only
(c) I, II and IV only
(d) All of these

15. Match the column-I with column-II and select the correct answer:

Column-I	Column-II
(A) Replication	(i) RNA → DNA
(B) Transcription	(ii) mRNA → protein
(C) Translation	(iii) DNA → RNA
(D) Reverse transcription	(iv) DNA → DNA
(E) Ribosome	(v) mRNA + protein
	(vi) DNA + protein
	(vii) t-RNA
	(viii) r-RNA
	(ix) SnRNA + protein
	(x) rRNA + protein

(a) A-(i), B-(ii), C-(iii), D-(iv), E-(v)
(b) A-(ii), B-(i), C-(iii), D-(iv), E-(vi)
(c) A-(iii), B-(iv), C-(ii), D-(i), E-(vii)
(d) A-(iv), B-(iii), C-(ii), D-(i), E-(x)

16. Match the columns and find out the correct combination:

A.	Reverse transcription	1.	Protein
B.	At 5' end of polynucleotide chain	2.	Splicing
C.	Removal of introns and joining of exons	3.	Phosphate group is attached
D.	Exon helps in synthesis of	4.	Fatty acids
		5.	RNA dependent DNA polymerase

(a) A-5, B-1, C-2, D-3
(b) A-5, B-1, C-3, D-2
(c) A-1, B-2, C-3, D-4
(d) A-5, B-3, C-2, D-1

17. The given figure shows *lac* operon and its functioning. Select the option which correctly labels A, B, X, Y and Z.

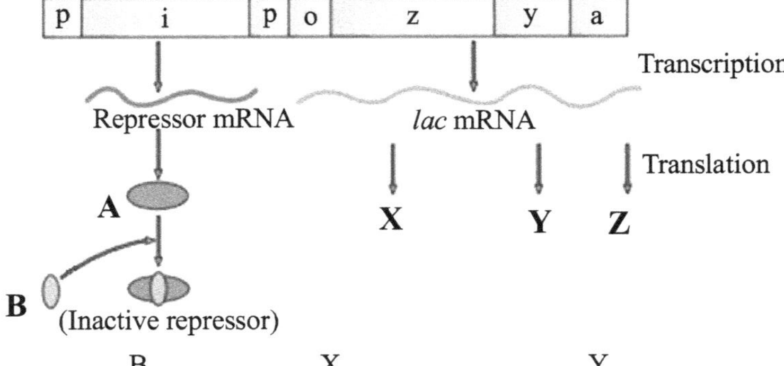

	A	B	X	Y	Z
(a)	Repressor	Inducer	Permease	Beta-galactosidase	Transacetylase
(b)	Inducer	Repressor	Beta-galactosidase	Permease	Transacetylase
(c)	Inducer	Repressor	Beta-galactosidase	Transacetylase	Permease
(d)	Repressor	Inducer	Beta-galactosidase	Permease	Transacetylase

18. Given diagram represent the components the components of a transcription unit. Select the correct answer regarding it.

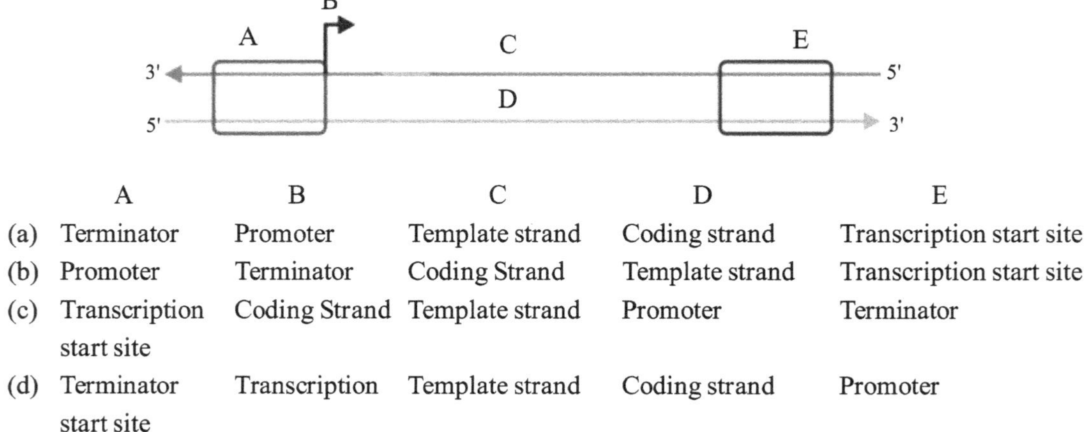

	A	B	C	D	E
(a)	Terminator	Promoter	Template strand	Coding strand	Transcription start site
(b)	Promoter	Terminator	Coding Strand	Template strand	Transcription start site
(c)	Transcription start site	Coding Strand	Template strand	Promoter	Terminator
(d)	Terminator	Transcription start site	Template strand	Coding strand	Promoter

19. Which of the following is/are correct matching(s)?

	Codon	**Amino acid**
(i)	5' AUG 3'	Serine
(ii)	5' AUC 3'	Tyrosine
(iii)	5' AUG 3'	Methionine
(iv)	5' GUG 3'	Valine

(a) (i) and (iii)
(b) All of these
(c) (ii), (iii) and (iv)
(d) (i), (ii) and (iii)

20. Match column-I with column-II and select the correct answer using the codes given below:

	Column-I		**Column-I**
A.	Operator site	I.	Binding site for RNA polymerase
B.	Promoter site	II.	Binding site for repressor molecule
C.	Structural gene	III.	Codes for enzyme protein
D.	Regulator gene	IV.	Codes for repressor molecules

(a) A-II, B-I, C-III, D-IV
(b) A-II, B-I, C-IV, D-III
(c) A-IV, B-III, C-I, D-II
(d) A-II, B-III, C-I, D-IV

21. Identify the labels A, B, C and D in the given structure of tRNA and select the correct option.

	A	**B**	**C**	**D**
(a)	Anticodon loop	TψC loop	AA binding site	DHU loop
(b)	AA binding site	TψC loop	Anticodon	DHU loop
(c)	AA binding site	DHU loop	Anticodon loop	TψC loop
(d)	AA binding site	DHU loop	TψC loop	Anti-codon loop

22. Match the enzymes given in column-I with its function given in column-II and select the correct option.

	Column-I		**Column-II**
A.	β-galactosidase	I.	Joining of DNA fragments
B.	Permease	II.	Peptide bond formation
C.	Ligase	III.	Hydrolysis of lactose
D.	Ribozyme	IV.	Increase permeability of galactosidase

(a) A-II, B-I, C-IV, D-III
(b) A-III, B-IV, C-I, D-II
(c) A-II, B-IV, C-I, D-III
(d) A-I, B-II, C-IV, D-III

23. Match column-I with column-II and select the correct answer using the codes given below:

	Column-I		**Column-II**
A.	Helicase	I.	Joining of nucleotides
B.	Gyrase	II.	Opening of DNA
C.	Primase	III.	Unwinding of DNA
D.	DNA polymerase	IV.	RNA priming

(a) A-II, B-I, C-III, D-IV
(b) A-II, B-I, C-IV, D-III
(c) A-IV, B-III, C-I, D-II
(d) A-II, B-III, C-IV, D-I

24. Match column-I with column-II and choose the correct option.

	Column-I		**Column-II**
A.	Exon	I.	Coding sequence
B.	Intron	II.	Cistron
C.	Genetic code	III.	Triplet bases on mRNA

D.	DNA packaging	IV.	Nucleosome
		V.	Non-codding sequence

(a) A-I, B-III, C-II, D-V
(b) A-I, B-IV, C-II, D-III
(c) A-I, B-V, C-III, D-IV
(d) A-IV, B-I, C-V, D-III

25. Choose the sequence in which the following enzymes take part in DNA replication.

(i) Helicase
(ii) Primase
(iii) SSB
(iv) DNA polymerase
(v) DNA ligase

(a) (i) → (v) → (iv) → (iii) → (ii)
(b) (i) → (ii) → (iii) → (iv) → (v)
(c) (i) → (iii) → (ii) → (iv) → (v)
(d) (i) → (iv) → (iii) → (ii) → (v)

26. Match column-I with column-II and select the correct combination from the given options.

	Column-I		**Column-II**
A.	Sigma factor	I.	5'-3'
B.	Capping	II.	Initiation
C.	Tailing	III.	Termination
D.	Codding strand	IV.	5' end
		V.	3' end

(a) A-III, B-V, C-IV, D-II
(b) A-II, B-IV, C-V, D-I
(c) A-II, B-IV, C-V, D-III
(c) A-III, B-V, C-IV, D-I

27. Match column-I with column-II and select the correct answer using the codes given below.

	Column-I		**Column-II**
A.	Termination	I.	Aminoacyl tRNA synthetase
B.	Translation	II.	Okazaki fragments
C.	Transcription	III.	GTP dependent release factor
D.	DNA replication	IV.	RNA polymerase

(a) A-II, B-I, C-III, D-IV
(b) A-III, B-I, C-IV, D-II
(c) A-IV, B-III, C-I, D-II
(d) A-II, B-III, C-I, D-IV

Solutions

1. **(d)**

2. **(b)** β-gal is primarily responsible for the hydrolysis of the disaccharide lactose into its monomeric units, galactose and glucose. It is coded by Z structural gene.

3. **(d)** 4. **(a)**

5. **(b)** β-gal is primarily responsible for the hydrolysis of the disaccharide lactose into its monomeric units, galactose and glucose. It is coded by Z structural gene.

6. **(a)** Synthesis of RNA exhibits several features that are synonymous with DNA replication. RNA synthesis requires accurate and efficient initiation, elongation proceeds in the $5'\rightarrow 3'$ direction (i.e., the polymerase moves along the template strand of DNA in the $3'\rightarrow 5'$ direction), and RNA synthesis requires distinct and accurate termination. Transcription exhibits several features that are distinct from replication.

7. **(a)**

UUU	–	Phenylalanine
GGG	–	Glycine
UCU	–	Serine
CCC	–	Proline
AUG	–	Methionine

8. **(a)**

9. **(c)** Francois Jacob and Jacque Monod proposed the model of gene regulation known as operon model/lac operon. Alec Jeffreys gave DNA fingerprinting technique. Matthew Meselson and F. Stahl gave semi-conservative DNA replication in E.coli. Alfred Hershey and Martha Chase proved DNA as genetic material not protein.

10. **(c)** Lac operon consist of one regulatory genes (*i* gene) and three structural genes (*z, y,* and *a*).
    - *i* gene codes for Repressor.
    - *z* gene codes for Beta-galactosidase.
    - *y* gene codes for Permease.
    - *a* gene codes for Transacetylase.

11. **(a)** Synthesis of RNA exhibits several features that are synonymous with DNA replication. RNA synthesis requires accurate and efficient initiation, elongation proceeds in the $5'\rightarrow 3'$ direction (i.e. the polymerase moves along the template strand of DNA in the $3'\rightarrow 5'$ direction), and RNA synthesis requires distinct and accurate termination.

12. **(a)** 13. **(a)** 14. **(d)** 15. **(d)** 16. **(d)**

17. **(d)** 18. **(d)** 19. **(c)** 20. **(a)**

21. **(b)** tRNA or transfer RNA is a single stranded molecule and takes the shape of a clover leaf. In the process of transcription tRNA brings amino acid and reads the genetic code and acts as an adapter molecule. In the given structure of tRNA, the labels A, B, C and D are respectively AA binding site (amino acid binding site), TψC loop, anticodon loop (codon recognition site) and DHU loop (amino acid recognition site).

22. **(b)** 23. **(d)** 24. **(c)** 25. **(c)** 26. **(b)**

27. **(c)**

CHAPTER 29

Evolution

1. Match the following column I with column II

Column I	Column II
A. Darwin	I. Use and disuse theory
B. Lamarck	II. Origin of species
C. Hugo De Vries	III. Origin of life
D. A. I. Oparin	IV. Mutation theory

   (a) A – I; B – II; C – III; D – IV
   (b) A – II; B -A; C – III; D – IV
   (c) A – IV; B – I; C – II; D – III
   (d) A – II; B – I; C – IV; D – III

2. Match the following

Column-I	Column-II
A. Mesozoic	I. First land vertebrates
B. Devonian	II. Proliferation of reptiles
C. Palaeocene	III. Raise of modern mammals
D. Permian	IV. Radiation of primitive mammals
	V. 160 million years

   (a) A–V; B–IV; C–III; D–II
   (b) A–V; B–I; C–IV; D–II
   (c) A–V; B–I; C–II; D–V
   (d) A–V; B–I; C–IV; D–III

3. Match the following

Column-I	Column-II
A. Pliocene	I. *Sinanthropus pekinensis*
B. Richard leaky	II. *Australopithecus*
C. Mid pleistocene	III. *Homo neanderthalensis*
D. Dussel Dorf	IV. *Homo habilis*
E. Raymond Dart	V. *Oreopithecus*

   (a) A–V; B – IV; C – I; D – III; E – II
   (b) A– V; B – I; C – IV; D – III; E – II
   (c) A– V; B – IV; C – I; D – II; E – III
   (d) A– V; B – IV; C – III; D – I; E – II

4. Which one of the following pairs of items correctly belongs to the category of organs mentioned against it?

   (a) Wings of honey bee and wings of crow - Homologous organs
   (b) Thorn of *Bougainvillea* and tendrils of Cucurbita - Analogous organs
   (c) Nictitating membrane and blind spot in human eye - Vestigial organs
   (d) Nephridia of earthworm and malpighian tubules of Cockroach - Excretory organs

5. Which one of the following scientist's name is correctly matched with the theory put forth by him?

   (a) Mendel – Theory of Pangenesis
   (b) Weismann – Theory of continuity of Germplasm
   (c) Pasteur – Inheritance of acquired characters
   (d) de Vries – Natural selection

6. Which one of the following scientists name is correctly matched with the theory put forth by him?

   (a) Weismann - Theory of continuity of germplasm

(b) Pasteur   -   Inheritance of acquired characters

(c) De Vries   -   Natural selection

(d) Mendel   -   Theory of Pangenesis

7. Match the columns

Column-I	Column-II
A. Hugo de Vries	1. Inheritcance of acquired characters
B. Julian Huxley	2. Multiplication of individual species in geographical proportion
C. Jean Baptiste	3. Mutation theory of evolution

	A	B	C
(a)	1	2	3
(b)	2	3	1
(c)	3	1	2
(d)	3	2	1

8. Which one of the following options gives one correct example each of convergent evolution and divergent evolution?

	Convergent evolution	Divergent evolution
(a)	Eyes of octopus and mammals	Bones of forelimbs and vertebrates
(b)	Thorns of Bougainvillea and tendrils of Cucurbita	Wings of butterflies and birds
(c)	Bones of forelimbs of vertebrates	Wings of butterfly and birds
(d)	Thorns of Bougainvillea and tendrils of Cucurbita	Eyes of octopus and mammals

9. Identify the incorrectly matched pair:

(a) Ramapithecus   More man like ape like

(b) Homo habilis   First human like being, the hominid

(c) Homo erectus   Probably did not eat meat

(d) Neanderthal   Buried their dead

10. Match column-I with column-II and select the correct option.

Column-I	Column-II
A. Saltation	I. Darwin
B. Formation of life was preceded	II. Louis Pasteur
C. Reproductive fitness	III. De Vries
D. Life comes from pre-existing life	IV. Oparin and haldance

(a) A-III, B-IV, C-I, D-II

(b) A-IV, B-III, C-II, D-I

(c) A-II, B-III, C-I, D-IV

(d) A-I, B-IV, C-III, D-II

11. Match the evolution concepts given in column-I with their description given in column-II and select the correct answer.

Column-I	Column-II
A. Mutation	I. Change in populations allele frequencies due to chance alone.
B. Gene flow	II. Differences is survival and reproduction among variant individuals.
C. Natural selection	III. Immigration, emigration change allele frequencies.
D. Genetic drift	IV. Source of new alleles.

(a) A-I, B-II, C-III, D-IV

(b) A-IV, B-II, C-III, D-I

(c) A-III, B-I, C-IV, D-II

(d) A-IV, B-III, C-II, D-I

12. Match the column-I with column-II and select the correct option.

Column-I (Name of the Scientist)	Column-II (Contributions)
A. Charles Darwin	I. Mutation theory
B. Lamarck	II. Germ plasm theory
C. Hugo De Vries	III. Philosophie Zoologique
D. Ernst Haeckel	IV. The Origin of species
E. August Weismann	V. Biogenetic law
	VI. Essay on population

(a) A-IV, B-III, C-I, D-V, E-II
(b) A-IV, B-III, C-V, D-I, E-VI
(c) A-IV, B-VI, C-V, D-III, E-I
(d) A-II, B-III, C-I, D-V, E-II

13. Which one of the following scientists name is correctly matched with the theory put forth by him?

(a) Weismann - Theory of continuity of germplasm
(b) Pasteur - Inheritance of acquired characters
(c) De Vries - Natural selection
(d) Mendel - Theory of Pangenesis

14. Match the hominids with their **correct** brain size:

(A) *Homo habilis*   (i) 900 cc
(B) *Homo neanderthalensis*   (ii) 1350 cc
(C) *Homo erectus*   (iii) 650 - 800 cc
(D) *Homo sapiens*   (iv) 1400 cc

Select the **correct** option.

	(A)	(B)	(C)	(D)
(a)	(iii)	(i)	(iv)	(ii)
(b)	(iii)	(ii)	(i)	(iv)
(c)	(iii)	(iv)	(i)	(ii)
(d)	(iv)	(iii)	(i)	(ii)

15. Which one of the following scientists name is correctly matched with the theory put forth by him?

(a) Weismann - Theory of continuity of Germplasm
(b) Pasteur - Inheritance of acquired characters
(c) De Vries - Natural selection
(d) Mendel - Theory of Pangenesis

16. Identify the correct match from column-I and column-II

Column-I	Column-II
A. Origin of universe	1. 3 bya
B. Origin of Earth	2. 20 bya
C. Origin of first cellular form of life	3. 20 bya
D. Origin of first noncellular form of life	4. 2 bya

(a) A-1, B-2, C-3, D-4
(b) A-2, B-3, C-4, D-1
(c) A-2, B-4, C-3, D-1
(d) A-1, B-3, C-2, D-4

17. Which two periods are correctly matched with the dominance of organisms in that particular period?

(a) (A) Jurassic – Amphibians
    (B) Carboniferous- Fishes
(b) (A) Jurassic – Amphibians
    (B) Devonian – Amphibians
(c) (A) Devonian – Amphibians
    (B) Jurassic –Dinosaurs
(d) (A) Devonian –fishes
    (B) Jurassic – Dinosaurs

18. Match column I with column II and select the correct option from the codes given below.

Column I	Column II
A. Edward Lewis	(i) Australopithecus
B. L.S.B Leakey	(ii) *Homo neanderthalensis*
C. C. Fuhlrott	(iii) *Homo habilis*
D. Raymond Dart	(iv) *Ramapithecus*

(a) A-(iv), B-(iii), C-(ii), D-(i)
(b) A-(ii), B-(i), C-(iv), D-(iii)
(c) A-(iii), B-(ii), C-(i), D-(iv)
(d) A-(i), B-(ii), C-(iii), D-(iv)

19. Match column I with column II and select the correct option from the given codes.

Column I	Column II
A. Wallace	(i) Essay of population
B. Malthus	(ii) Biston
C. Hardy-Weinberg law	(iii) $p^2 + q^2 + 2pq = 1$
D. Industrial melanism	(iv) Co-proposer of Natural selection

(a) A-(iii), B-(iv), C-(ii), D-(i)
(b) A-(ii), B-(i), C-(iv), D-(iii)
(c) A-(iv), B-(i), C-(ii), D-(iii)
(d) A-(iv), B-(i), C-(iii), D-(ii)

20. Match column I with column II and select the correct option from the codes given below.

Column I	Column II
A. Francesco Redi	(i) Theory of chemical evolution of life
B. L. Pasteur	(ii) Disproval of spontaneous generation
C. Richter	(iii) Swan necked flask experiment
D. Oparin	(iv) Mutation
	(v) Panspermia

(a) A-(v), B-(i), C-(iv), D-(ii)
(b) A-(ii), B-(iii), C-(v), D-(i)
(c) A-(v), B-(iv), C-(ii), D-(i)
(d) A-(i), B-(ii), C-(iii), D-(iv)

21. Match column I (containing list of scientists) with column II (their contributions) and choose the correct option.

Column-I (Name of the Scientist)	Column-II (Contributions)
A. Charles Darwin	I. Mutation theory
B. Lamarck	II. Germ plasm theory
C. Hugo de Vries	III. Philosophie Zoologique
D. Ernst Haeckel	IV. The Origin of species
E. August Weismann	V. Biogenetic law
	VI. Essay on population

(a) A – IV; B – III; C – I; D – V; E – II
(b) A – IV; B – III; C – V; D – I; E – VI
(c) A – IV; B – VI; C – V; D – III; E – I
(d) A – II; B – III; C – I; D – V; E – II

22. Following is the diagrammatic representation of the operation of natural selection of different traits. Which of the following options correctly identifies all the three graphs A, B and C?

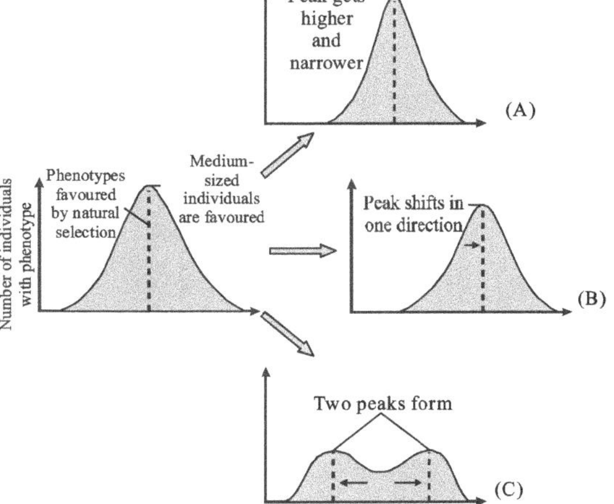

	A	B	C
(a)	Directional	Stabilizing	Disruptive
(b)	Stabilizing	Directional	Disruptive
(c)	Disruptive	Stabilizing	Directional
(d)	Directional	Disruptive	Stabilizing

23. Following is the diagrammatic representation of evolutionary history of vertebrates through geological periods. Identify the geological periods (A, B, C and D) and select the correct option.

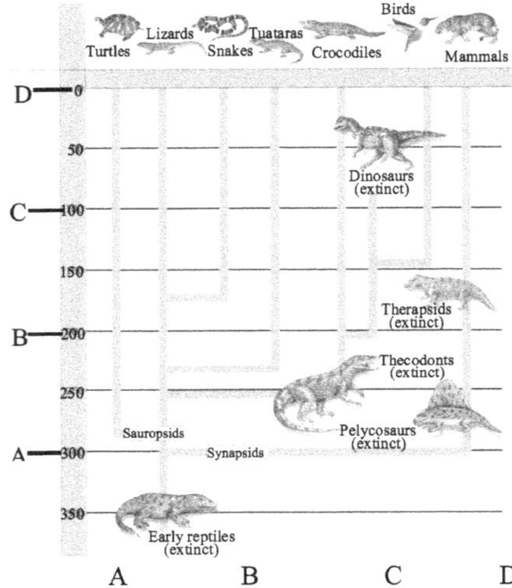

	A	B	C	D
(a)	Carboniferous	Triassic	Cretaceous	uaternary
(b)	Jurassic	Permian	Tertiary	retaceous
(c)	Permian	Jurassic	Quaternary	Tertiary
(d)	Cretaceous	Quaternary	Carboniferous	Jurassic

24. Identify the mammals from the diagrams of their respective skulls given below.

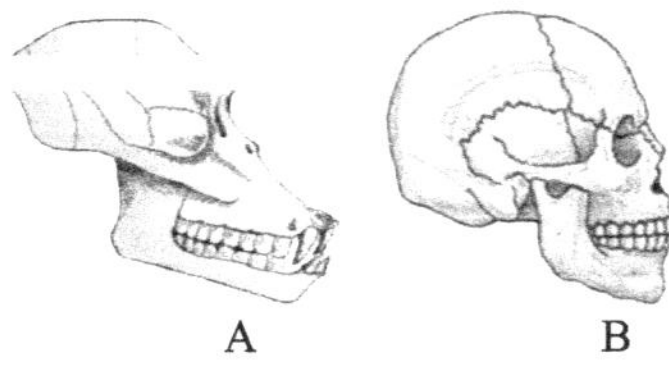

(a) Skull A : Human; Skull B : Old world monkey

(b) Skull A : Old world monkey; Skull B : Human

(c) Skull A : Ape; Skull B : Human

(d) Skull A : Human; Skull B : Ape

25. The diagram given below represents Miller's experiment. Choose the correct combination of labelling.

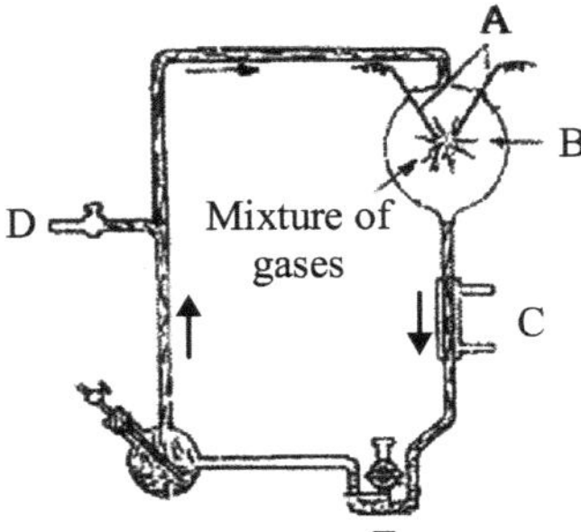

(a) A–electrodes, B– $NH_3 + H_2 + H_2O + CH_4$, C–cold water, D–vacuum, E–U trap

(b) A–electrodes, B–$NH_4 + H_2 + CO_2 + CH_3$, C–hot water, D–vacuum, E–U trap

(c) A–electrodes, B–$NH_3 + H_2O$, C–hot water, D–tap, E–U trap

(d) A–electrodes, B–$NH_3 + H_2 + H_2O + CH_4$, C–steam, D– vacuum, E–U trap

26. Match the name of scientists listed under column I with the ideas listed under column II.

Column I		Column II
A.	Darwin	I.	Abiogenesis
B.	Oparin	II.	Use and disuse of organs
C.	Lamarck	III.	Continental drift theory
D.	Wagner	IV.	Evolution by natural selection

(a) A – I, B – IV, C – II, D – III
(b) A – IV, B – I, C – II, D – III
(c) A – II, B – IV, C – III, D – I
(d) A – IV, B – III, C – II, D – I

Solutions

1. **(d)** 2. **(b)** 3. **(a)** 4. **(d)** 5. **(b)**
6. **(a)** The theory of the continuity of the germplasm was published by August Weismann (1834-1914) in 1886. It proposes that the contents of the reproductive cells (sperms and ova) are passed on unchanged from one generation to the next, unaffected by any changes undergone by the rest of the body. It thus rules out any possibility of the inheritance of acquired characteristics, and has become fundamental to Neo-Darwinian theory.
7. **(d)** 8. **(a)** 9. **(c)** 10. **(a)** 11. **(d)**
12. **(a)**
13. **(a)** The theory of the continuity of the germplasm was published by August Weismann (1834-1914) in 1886. It proposes that the contents of the reproductive cells (sperms and ova) are passed on unchanged from one generation to the next, unaffected by any changes undergone by the rest of the body. It thus rules out any possibility of the inheritance of acquired characteristics, and has become fundamental to Neo-Darwinian theory.
14. **(c)** The correct match of the hominids and their brain sizes are:
    Homo habilis – 650 - 800 c.c.
    Homo neanderthalensis –1400 c.c.
    Homo eractus –900 c.c.
    Homo sapiens –1350 c.c.
15. **(a)** The theory of the continuity of the germplasm published by August Weismann (1834-1914) in 1886. It proposes that the contents of the reproductive cells (sperms and ova) are passed on unchanged from one generation to the next, unaffected by any changes undergone by the rest of the body. It thus rules out any possibility of the inheritance of acquired characteristics, and has become fundamental to Neo-Darwinian theory.
16. **(b)** 17. **(d)** 18. **(a)** 19. **(d)** 20. **(b)**
21. **(a)**
22. **(b)** The graph A, B and C shows stabilizing, directional and disruptive traits of natural selection. In stabilizing selection, the median phenotype is selected during natural selection and which does not tilt the bell curve in any way. Instead, it makes the peak of the bell curve even higher than what would be considered normal. Directional selection of natural selection derives its name from the shape of the approximate bell curve that is produced when all individuals' traits are plotted. Instead of the bell curve falling directly in the middle of the axes on which they are plotted, it tilts either to the left or the right by varying degrees. Hence, it has moved in one direction or the other. In disruptive selection instead of the bell curve having one peak in the middle, it has two peaks with a valley in the middle of them.
23. **(a)** In the given diagrammatic representation of the evolutionary history of vertebrates through geological periods, the geological periods marked as A, B, C and D are respectively carboniferous, triassic, cretaceous and quaternary. A geologic period is a sub-division of geologic time enabling cross-referencing of rocks and geologic events from place to place.
24. **(c)** The diagrams of two skulls of two different mammals show that skull A is of an ape and skull B is of human.
25. **(a)**
26. **(b)** Darwin is related with evolution by natural selection. According to the theory in the struggle for existence, the individuals which have more favourable variations will survive and reproduce, while others, which have less favourable or unfavourable variations will not puripetuate.
    Oparin : Put forth abiogenesis theory.
    According to abiogenesis : Life is originated from the non-living things spontaneously.
    Lamarck : Use and disuse of organs is one of the important principle of Lamarckism.
    Wagner : Proposed continental drift theory.

CHAPTER 30

Human Health & Disease

1. Match the column I with column II and choose the correct option:

	Column I		Column II
A.	IgE	(i)	Can cross placenta to provide passive immunity to the foetus
B.	IgM	(ii)	Provides passive immunity to the infant
C.	IgD	(iii)	Produced early in the primary immune response and Antigen receptor cells are present on B-cells
D.	IgA	(iv)	Activates B-cells
E.	IgG	(v)	Mediate immediate hypersensitivity reaction and also provide host defense against helminths infection.

	A	B	C	D	E
(a)	(v)	(iii)	(iv)	(ii)	(i)
(b)	(iii)	(iv)	(ii)	(i)	(v)
(c)	(v)	(iv)	(i)	(ii)	(iii)
(d)	(iv)	(v)	(iii)	(i)	(ii)
(e)	(i)	(iii)	(iv)	(v)	(ii)

2. Match the disease in column I with column II and choose the correct option:

	Column I		Column II
A.	Amoebiasis	(i)	*Treponema pallidum*
B.	Diphtheria	(ii)	use only clean and sterilized food as well as water
C.	Cholera	(iii)	DPT vaccine
D.	Syphilis	(iv)	Use oral dehydration therapy

	A	B	C	D
(a)	A-(ii)	B-(i)	C-(iii)	D-(iv)
(b)	A-(ii)	B-(iii)	C-(iv)	D-(i)
(c)	A-(i)	B-(ii)	C-(iii)	D-(iv)
(d)	A-(ii)	B-(iv)	C-(i)	D-(iii)

3. Choose the correct option about given above:

	(A)	(B)
(a)	Hallucinogen	Depressant
(b)	Morphine	Datura
(c)	Heroine	Bhang
(d)	Datura	Morphine

4. Match the column I with column II and select the correct option:

	Column I		Column II
A.	Charas	(i)	*Claviceps purpuria*
B.	Cocaine	(ii)	Euphoria
C.	L.S.D	(iii)	Stimulant
D.	Amphetamine	(iv)	*Cannabis sativa*

	A	B	C	D
(a)	(iv)	(ii)	(iii)	(i)
(b)	(iv)	(ii)	(i)	(iii)
(c)	(iv)	(i)	(ii)	(iii)
(d)	(iii)	(iv)	(iv)	(ii)

5. Match the column I with column II and choose the correct option:

	Column I		Column II
A.	Histamine	(i)	Organ transplant
B.	Attract phagocytes to antigen	(ii)	Autoimmune disease
C.	Immunosuppression	(iii)	AIDS
D.	Reduction in helper T-lymphocytes	(iv)	Active immunity
E.	Myasthenia gravis	(v)	Killer T-cells
F.	Infection or Vaccination	(vi)	Inflammatory responses

(a) A-(vi), B-(v), C-(i), D-(iii), E-(iv), F-(ii)
(b) A-(vi), B-(v), C-(i), D-(iii), E-(ii), F-(iv)
(c) A-(vi), B-(v), C-(iv), D-(iii), E-(ii), F-(i)
(d) A-(i), B-(ii), C-(iv), D-(iii), E-(vi), F-(v)

6. Match the column I with column II and select the correct option.

	Column I		Column II
A.	Saliva in mouth and acid in the stomach	(i)	Cytokine barriers
B.	Mucus coating of the epithelium lining of the repiratory tract	(ii)	Cellular barriers
C.	Polymorphonuclear leucocytes and natural killer cells	(iii)	Physiological barriers
D.	Interferons	(iv)	Physical barriers

	A	B	C	D
(a)	(iii)	(iv)	(ii)	(i)
(b)	(ii)	(iii)	(i)	(iv)
(c)	(iv)	(iii)	(ii)	(i)
(d)	(iii)	(ii)	(i)	(iv)

7. Match the column I (Disease) with column II (vaccine) and choose the correct option:

	Column I		Column II
A.	Tuberculosis	(i)	Harmless virus
B.	Whooping cough	(ii)	Inactivated toxin
C.	Diphtheria	(iii)	Killed bacteria
D.	Polio	(iv)	Harmless Bacteria

(a) A-(iv), B-(iii), C-(ii), D-(i)
(b) A-(i), B-(ii), C-(iv), D-(iii)
(c) A-(ii), B-(i), C-(iii), D-(iv)
(d) A-(iii), B-(ii), C-(iv), D-(i)

8. Which one of the following options gives the correct matching of a disease with its causative organism and mode of infection?

	Disease	Causative organisms	Mode of Infection
(a)	Elephantiasis	Wuchereria bancrofti	With infected water and food
(b)	Malaria	Plasmodium vivax	Bite of male Anopheles mosquito
(c)	Typhoid	Salmonella typhi	With inspired air
(d)	Pneumonia	Streptococcus pneumoniae	Droplet infection

9. Match the column I with column II and chose the correct option:

	Column I		Column II
A.	Pneumonia	1.	Rhino viruses
B.	Common cold	2.	Haemophillus influenza
C.	Filariasis	3.	Microsporum
D.	Ringworms	4.	Wuchereria bancrofti

	A	B	C	D
(a)	1	2	3	4
(b)	3	1	4	2
(c)	2	1	4	3
(d)	1	2	4	3

10. Match each item in Column I with one item in Column II and choose your answer from the codes given below:

Column I (Type of secondary metabolite)		Column II (example)
I. Alkaloid	1.	Abrin
II. Toxin	2.	Morphine

III. Lectin   3. Vinblastin

IV. Drug   4. Concanavaline A

Codes

	I	II	III	IV
(a)	1	2	3	4
(b)	2	1	4	3
(c)	2	1	3	4
(d)	1	2	4	3

11. Match each item in Column I with one item in Column II and choose your answer from the codes given below:

	Column I		**Column II**
I.	Malaria	1.	Sporozoan
II.	Dysentary	2.	Amoeboid
III.	Sleeping sickness	3.	Cilliate
IV.	Balantidiasis	4.	Flagellate

Codes

	I	II	III	IV
(a)	1	2	3	4
(b)	2	1	4	3
(c)	2	1	3	4
(d)	1	2	4	3

12. Match the following columns

	Column I		**Column II**
A.	Psychotropic drug	1.	Cocaine
B.	Sedative	2.	LSD
C.	Opiates	3.	Barbiturates
D.	Stimulants	4.	Morphine
E.	Hallucinogens	5.	Pimozide

Codes

	A	B	C	D	E
(a)	5	3	4	1	2
(b)	5	2	1	4	3
(c)	2	5	4	1	2
(d)	4	3	4	2	1

13. Match the names of disease listed under column I with meanings given under column II, choose the answer which gives the correct combination of the alphabets of the columns.

	Column I		**Column II**
	(Name of disease)		**(Meanings)**
A.	Jaundice	p.	Allergic inflammation of nose
B.	Stenosis	q.	Loss of motor functions
C.	Rhinitis	r.	Heart vaive defect
D.	Paralysis	s.	Increase in bile pigments in the blood
		t.	Septal defect of heart

(a) A-q; B-t; C-r; D-p

(b) A- s; B-p; C-q; D-r

(c) A-s; B-r; C-p; D-q

(d) A-s; B-t; c-p; D-q

14. Match the disease in Column I with the appropriate items (pathogen/prevention/treatment) in Column II.

	Column I		**Column II**
1.	Amoebiasis	(i)	*Treponema pallidum*
2.	Diphtheria	(ii)	Use only sterilized food and water
3.	Cholera	(iii)	DPT Vaccine
4.	Syphilis	(iv)	Use oral rehydration therapy

(a) (1) - (i), (2) - (ii), (3) - (iii), (4) - (iv)

(b) (1) - (ii), (2) - (iv), (3) - (i), (4) - (iii)

(c) (1) - (ii), (2) - (i), (3) - (iii), (4) - (iv)

(d) (1) - (ii), (2) - (iii), (3) - (iv), (4) - (i)

15. Which one of the following sets of items in the options 1 - 4 are correctly categorized with one exception in it?

	Items	Category	Exception
(a)	UAA, UAG,UGA	Stop codons	UAG
(b)	Kangaroo, Koala, Wombat	Australian marsupials	Wombat
(c)	*Plasmodium,* Cuscuta, *Trypanosoma*	Protozoan parasites	Cuscuta
(d)	Typhoid, Pneumonia, Diphtheria	Bacterial diseases	Diphtheria

16. Identify the molecules (a) and (b) shown below and select the right option giving their source and use.

(a)

(b)

Options

	Molecule	Source	Use
(a)	Cocaine	*Erythroxylum coca*	Accelerates the transport of dopamine
(b)	Heroin	*Cannabis sativa*	"Depressant and slows down body functions"
(c)	Cannabinoid	*Atropabella dona*	Produces hallucinations
(d)	Morphine	*Papaver somniferum*	Sedative and pain killer

17. Match the following sexually transmitted diseases (Column –I) with their causative agents (Column- II) and select the correct option?

Column- I		Column -II
A.	Gonorrhoea	I. HIV
B.	Syphilis	II. Neisseria
C.	Genital warts	III. Treponema
D.	AIDS	IV. Human papilloma virus

(a) A–II; B–III; C–IV; D–I
(b) A–III; B–IV; C–I; D–II
(c) A–IV; B–II; C–III; D–I
(d) A–IV; B–III; C–II; D–I

18. Match the following bacteria with the diseases

Column-I		Column-II
A.	*Treponema pallidum*	I. Plague
B.	*Yersinia pestis*	II. Anthrax
C.	*Bacillus anthracis*	III. Syphilis
D.	*Vibrio*	IV. Cholera

(a) A – III; B – I; C – II; D – IV
(b) A – IV; B – I; C – II; D – III
(c) A – III; B – II; C – I; D – IV
(d) A – I; B – III; C – II; D – IV

19. Which one of the following is a correct match?
(1) Bhang   –   Analgesic
(2) Cocaine   –   Opiate narcotics
(3) Morphine   –   Hallucinogen
(4) Barbiturate   –   Tranquiliser

20. Match the following

Set I		Set II
A.	LSD	I. Euphorian effect
B.	Disulfiram	II. Parasympathetic
C.	Cocaine	III. *Cannabis*
D.	Scopolamine	IV. Ergot alkaloid
E.	Hashish	V. Antabuse

(a) A – IV; B – V; C – I; D – II; E – III
(b) A – IV; B – I; C – V; D – II; E – III
(c) A – IV; B – V; C – II; D – I; E – III
(d) A – V; B – IV; C – I; D – II; E – III

21. Column A represent diseases and column B represent their symptoms, which of the following pairs are correct match for them?

Column A	Column B
A. asthma	I. recurring of bronchitis
B. emphysema	II. accumulation of WBCs in alveolus
C. pneumonia	III. allergy

(a) A – III; B – I; C – II

(b) A – II; B – I; C – III

(c) A – III; B – II; C – I

(d) A – II; B – III; C – I

22. Column I lists the components of body defence and column II lists the corresponding descriptions. Match the two columns. Choose the correct option from those given.

Column I	Column II
A. active natural immunity	I. injection of gamma globulins
B. first line of defence	II. complement proteins and interferons
C. Passive natural immunity	III. direct contact with the pathogens that have entered inside
D. second line of defence	IV. surface barriers
	V. antibodies transferred through the placenta

(a) A – IV; B – III; C – V; D – II

(b) A – III; B – IV; C – II; D – V

(c) A – III; B – IV; C – V; D – II

(d) A – V; B – III; C – II; D – I

23. Column I lists some disorders associated with brain. Column II lists the causes for these disorders. Match the two columns and identify the correct option from those given.

Column I	Column II
A. Epilepsy	I. degeneration of neurons in the cerebral cortex
B. Alzheimer's disease	II. irregular electrical discharge in the neurons
C. Parkinson's disease	III. decreased production of acetylcholine
D. Huntington's chorea	IV. regeneration of dopamine releasing neurons
	V. formation of blood clots in brain

(a) A – V; B – IV; C – III; D – I

(b) A – II; B – III; C – I; D – IV

(c) A – II; B – III; C – IV; D – I

(d) A – II; B – IV; C – III; D – I

24. Match the disease given in column I with the appropriate items (pathogen/ prevention/ treatment) given in column II.

Column-I (Diseases)		Column-II (Pathogen/prevention/treatment)
A. Amoebiasis	I.	*Lassa virus*
B. Diphtheria	II.	Use only sterilized food and water
C. Cholera	III.	DPT vaccine
D. Rabies	IV.	Use oral rehydration therapy

(a) A – II; B – III; C – IV; D – I

(b) A – I; B – II; C – III; D – IV

(c) A – II; B – IV; C – I; D – III

(d) A – II; B – I; C – III; D – IV

25. Which one of the following options gives the correct matching of a disease with its causative organism and mode of infection?

	Disease	Causative organisms	Mode of Infection
(a)	Elephantiasis	*Wuchereria bancrofti*	With infected water and food
(b)	Malaria	*Plasmodium vivax*	Bite of male *Anopheles* mosquito
(c)	Typhoid	*Salmonella typhi*	With inspired air
(d)	Pneumonia	*Streptococcus pneumoniae*	Droplet infection

26. Select the correct match of the symptoms of diseases given in column I with their respective pathogen of the diseases given in column II.

	Column I		Column II
A.	Appearance of dry, scaly lesions on various parts of the body such as skin nails and scalp.	I.	*Entamoeba histolytica*
B.	Chronic inflammation of the lymphatic vessel of lower limbs.	II.	*Ascaris lumbricoides*
C.	Fever, chills, cough, headache and in severe cases the lips and finger nails may turn gray to bluish in colour.	III.	*Haemophilus influenzae*
D.	Constipation, abdominal pain and cramps, stool with excess mucous and blood clots.	IV.	*Wuchereria bancrofti*
E.	Internal bleeding, muscular pain, fever, anaemia and blockage of intestinal passage.	V.	*Microsporum*

   (a) A – I; B – II; C – III; D – IV; E – V
   (b) A – III; B – V; C – II; D – IV; E – I
   (c) A – III; B – I; C – V; D – II; E – IV
   (d) A – V; B – IV; C – III; D – I; E – II

27. Given figure shows the human lymphatic system with some part marked as A, B, C and D identify the correct part

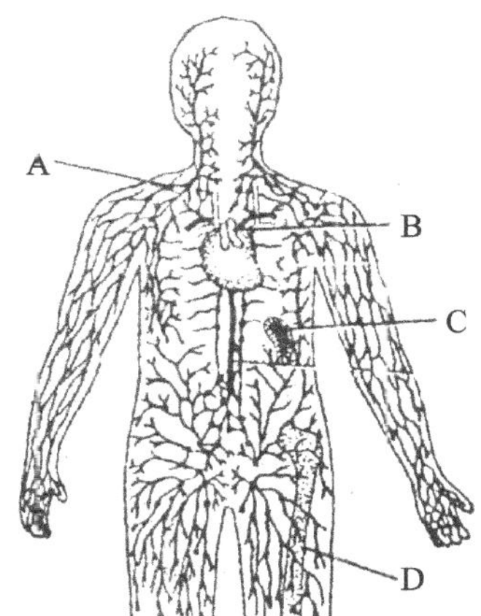

   (a) A - lymph nodes (primary lymphoid organ), B - thymus (primary lymphoid organ), C - spleen (secondary lymphoid organ), D - bone marrow (secondary lymphoid organ)

   (b) A - lymph nodes (primary lymphoid organ), B - thymus (secondary lymphoid organ), C - spleen (primary lymphoid organ), D - bone marrow (primary lymphoid organ)

   (c) A - lymph nodes (secondary lymphoid organ), B - thymus (primary lymphoid organ), C - spleen (secondary lymphoid organ), D - bone marrow (primary. lymphoid organ)

   (d) A - lymph nodes (primary lymphoid organ), B - thymus (secondary lymphoid organ), C - spleen (secondary lymphoid organ), D - bone marrow (secondary lymphoid organ)

28. The diagram given below shows an antibody molecule with their parts labelled as A, B, C, D, E & F. Identify the part marked as A, B, C, D, E and F.

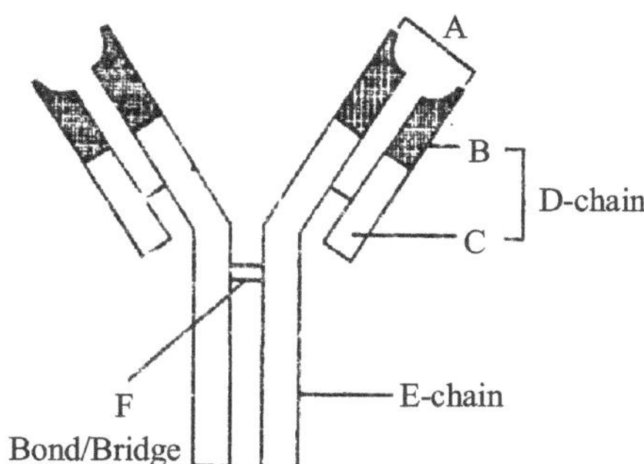

   (a) A-Antigen binding site; B-Variable region (of L-Chain); C - Constant region (of L-Chain); D - Light polypeptide chain (L-Chain); E-Heavy polypeptide chain (H-Chain); F - Disulfide bond.

   (b) A - Antigen binding site; B-Constant region (of L-Chain); C - Variable region (of L-Chain); D - Light polypeptide chain (L-Chain); E-Heavy polypeptide chain (H-Chain); F - Disulfide bond.

(c) A-Antigen binding site; B-Variable region (of L-Chain); C - Constant region (of L-Chain); D - Heavy polypeptide chain (L-Chain); E - Light polypeptide chain (H-Chain); F - Hydrogen bond

(d) A-Antigen binding site; B-Variable region (of L-Chain); C - Constant region (of L-Chain); D - Light polypeptide chain (L-Chain); E - Heavy polypeptide chain (H-Chain); F - Hydrogen bond

Solutions

1. (a) 2. (b) 3. (c) 4. (a) 5. (b)
6. (a) 7. (a) 8. (d) 9. (c) 10. (b)
11. (d) 12. (a) 13. (c)
14. (d)

Amoebiasis	:	Use only sterilized food and water
Diphtheria	:	DPT Vaccine
Cholera	:	Use oral rehydration therapy
Syphilis	:	*Treponema pallidum*

15. (c) UAG is also a stop codon. Wombats are also Australian marsupials. They are short-legged, muscular quadrupeds, approximately 1 metre (40 in) in length with a short, stubby tail. Diphtheria is an acute infectious disease caused by the bacteria *Corynebacterium diphtheriae*. Cuscuta, or Dodder plant, is not a protozoan. It is a parasitic vine that wraps around other plants for nourishment.

16. (d) Molecule (a) represents structure of morphine. Morphine is the most abundant alkaloid found in opium, the dried sap (latex) derived from shallowly slicing the unripe seedpods of the opium, or common and/or edible, poppy-*Papaver somniferum*. Morphine is a potent opiate analgesic drug that is used to relieve severe pain.

17. (a) 18. (a) 19. (d) 20. (a) 21. (a)
22. (c) 23. (c)
24. (a) A : Amoebiasis refers to infection caused by *Entamoeba histolytica*. It may cause dysentery and invasive extra-intestinal disease.

B : Diphtheria is a bacterial (*Corynebacterium diphtheria*) infection and spreads through respiratory droplets (such as from a cough or sneeze) of an infected person or someone who carries the bacteria but has no symptoms.

C : Cholera is an infectious disease that causes severe watery diarrhea, which can lead to dehydration and even death if untreated. It is caused by eating food or drinking water contaminated with a bacterium called *Vibrio cholerae*.

D : Rabies is a viral illness spread via the saliva of an infected animal. It is caused by the rabies (lassa) virus which infects the brain and ultimately leads to death.

25. (d) (a) Elephantiasis is caused by *Wuchereria bancrofti* which is transmitted from human to human via the female mosquito when it takes a blood meal. The parasite grows into an adult worm that lives in the lymphatic system of humans.

(b) Malaria is caused by protozoan species called *Plasomodium* that is passed from one human to another by the bite of infected female *Anopheles* mosquitoes.

(c) Typhoid fever (also known as enteric fever) is an infectious disease caused by the bacteria *Salmonella typhi*. It easily spreads through contaminated food and water supplies and close contact with others who are infected. It is characterized by very high fever, sweating, gastroenteritis, and diarrhoea.

26. **(d)** A : Appearance of dry, scaly lesions on various parts of the body such as skin nails and scalp is the symptoms of ringworm disease caused by *Microsporum*. Ringworm is a fungal disorder.

B : Chronic inflammation of the lymphatic vessel of lower limbs is the symptoms of elephantiasis disorder which is caused by *Wuchereria bancrofti*.

C : Fever, chills, cough, headache and in severe cases the lips and finger nails may turn gray to bluish in colour are the symptoms of pneumonia. Pneumonia is caused by *Haemophilus influenzae* and *Streptococcus pneumonia*.

D : Constipation, abdominal pain and cramps, stool with excess mucous and blood clots are the symptoms of amoebiasis. Amoebiasis is caused by *Entamoeba histolytica*.

E : Internal bleeding, muscular pain, fever, anaemia and blockage of intestinal passage are the symptoms of ascariasis which is caused by common roundworm, *Ascaris lumbricoides*.

27. **(c)** Lymphatic system is the network of vessels through which lymph drains from the tissues into the blood. In the given figure of human lymphatic system, the parts marked as A, B, C and D are respectively lymph nodes (secondary lymphoid organ), thymus (primary lymphoid organ), spleen (secondary lymphoid organ), and bone marrow (primary lymphoid organ).

28. **(a)** In the given diagram of an antibody molecule, the part marked as A, B, C, D, E and F are respectively antigen binding site, variable regions (of L chain), constant region (of L chain), light polypeptide chain (L chain), heavy polypeptide chain (H chain) and disulfide bond.

Strategies for Enhancement in Food Production

1. Match the column I with the column II and choose the correct option.

Column I		Column II
A.	Sericulture	I. Bee keeping
B.	Pisciculture	II. Rearing of silkworm
C.	Apiculture	III. Micropropagation
D.	Tissue culture	IV. Rearing of fishes
E.	Green Revolution	V. Fish production
F.	White Revolution	VI. Crop production
G	Blue Revolution	VII. Milk production

(a) A-IV, B-III, C-II, D-I, E-VI, F-VII, G-V

(b) A-IV, B-I, C-II, D-III, E-VII, F-VI, G-V

(c) A-I, B-II, C-III, D-IV, E-VI, F-VII, G-V

(d) A-II, B-IV, C-I, D-III, E-VI, F-VII, G-V

2. Match the column I with column II and choose the correction option.

Column I		Column II
A.	Many people have deficiencies as they cannot buy fruits & vegetables	I. Single cell proteins
B.	Crops with higher vitamins, proteins and fats	II. Micropropagation
C.	Growing microbes as the alternative source of proteins	III. Somaclones
D.	Capacity to generate plant from a single cell or explant	IV. Hidden hunger

| E. | Production of thousand plants through tissue culture | V. Biofortification |
| F. | Genetically identical plants | VI. Totipotency |

(a) A - IV; B - V; C - VI; D - I; E - II; F - III

(b) A - IV; B - V; C - VI; D - I; E - III; F - II

(c) A - IV; B - V; C - I; D - VI; E - II; F - III

(d) A - VI; B - V; C - I; D - IV; E - II; F - III

3. Which is correctly matched ?

(a) apiculture — honey bee

(b) pisciculture — silk moth

(c) sericulture — fish

(d) aquaculture — mosquito

4. Match the following columns and choose the correct option :

Column-I		Column-II
A.	Mutation breeding	I. Laborious and expensive process to obtain gene variation
B.	Selection	II. Hybrid vigour can be maintained for several generations
C.	Hybridisation	III. Simplest and easiest method of plant improvement
D.	Introduction	IV. Oldest breeding method
		V. Quick method to obtain gene variation

(a) A - V; B - IV; C - I; D - II

(b) A - V; B - IV; C - I; D - III

(c) A - IV; B - II; C - III; D - I

(d) A - I; B - II; C - IV; D - V

5. Consider the following two statements:

I. An effective germplasm collection is the prerequisite of any successful plant breeding program.

II. enetic variability is the root of any breeding program.

(a) Both I and II are true and II explains I

(b) Both I and II are true and II dose not explains I

(c) I is true but II is false

(d) I is false but II is true

6. Identify the option where all columns are not correctly matched:

Crop	Variety	Resistant to diseases
(a) Wheat	Himgiri	Leaf rust
(b) *Brassica*	Pusa swarnim	White rust
(c) Cowpea	Pusa komal	Black rot
(d) Chilli	Pusa sadabahar	Leaf curl

7. Match each item in column I with one item in column II and chose your answer from the codes given below:

Column I		Column II
A. Pusa Swarnim	I.	Cauliflower
B. Pusa Shubhra	II.	Brassica
C. Pusa Koma	III.	Okra
D. Pusa Sawami	IV.	Cow pea

	A	B	C	D
(a)	I	II	III	IV
(b)	II	I	IV	III
(c)	II	I	III	IV
(d)	I	II	IV	III

8. Which one is the wrong pairing for the disease and its causal organism?

(a) Late blight of potato-Alternaria solani

(b) Black rust of wheat-Puccinia graminis

(c) Loose smut of wheat-Ustilago nuda

(d) Root-knot of vegetables-Meloidogyne sp.

9. In the following table identify the correct matching of the crop, its disease and the corresponding pathogen.

Crop	Disease	Pathogen
(a) Citrus	Canker	*Pseudomonas rubrilineans*
(b) Potato	Late blight	*Fusarium udum*
(c) Brinjal	Root-knot	*Meloidogyne incognita*
(d) Pigeon pea	Seed gall	*Phytophthora infestans*

10. Which one of the following pairs is mismatched?

(a) Bombyx mori   –   silk

(b) Pila globosa   –   pearl

(c) Apis indica   –   honey

(d) Kenia lacca   –   lac

11. Which one of the following pairs is mismatched?

(a) Apis indica   –   honey

(b) Kenia lacca   –   lac

(c) Bombyx mori   –   silk

(d) Pila globosa   –   pearl

12. Match Column-I with Column-II.

Column-I		Column-II
(A) Saprophyte	(i)	Symbiotic association of fungi with plant roots
(B) Parasite	(ii)	Decomposition of dead organic materials
(C) Lichens	(iii)	Living on living plants or animals

(D) Mycorrhiza   (iv) Symbiotic association of algae and fungi

Choose the correct answer from the options given below:

     A   B   C   D

(a)   (i)   (ii)   (iii)   (iv)

(b)   (iii)   (ii)   (i)   (iv)

(c)   (ii)   (i)   (iii)   (iv)

(d)   (ii)   (iii)   (iv)   (i)

13. Which of the following is a correct match between crop, variety and resistance to diseases?

Crop	Variety	Resistant to diseases
(a) Wheat	Himgiri	White rust
(b) *Brassica*	*Pusa sadabahar*	Black rot
(c) Cowpea	*Pusa komal*	Bacterial blight
(d) Chilli	*Pusa swarnim*	Chilly mosaic virus

14. Match column I with column II and select the correct option from given codes.

Column I		Column II
A. Brassica	I.	Himgiri
B. Okra	II.	Pusa Komal
C. Wheat	III.	Pusa Gaurav
D. Cowpea	IV.	Pusa Sawani

(a) A-III, B-IV, C-I, D-II

(b) A-I, B-III, C-II, D-IV

(c) A-IV, B-III, C-I, D-II

(d) A-II, B-IV, C-I, D-III

15. The process of protoplast isolation was primarily carried out by __________

(a) Henshel

(b) Bergman

(c) Klercher

(d) None of the above

16. Which statement is correct?

A. Somaclonal variations are the variations observed in plants generated from somatic cultures.

B. A transgenic crop is one that contains and expresses a transgene.

C. Chloromycetin is obtained from *Penicillium*.

D. Bioprospecting is the process of discovery and commercialization of new products basesd on biological resources.

(a) A, B, D   (b) B, C

(c) C, D   (d) A, B, C, D

17. Given flow chart represents different steps of MOET. Study the flow chart carefully and select the correct answer for (1), (2) and (3).

Cow is administered with (1) hormone

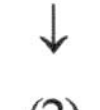

(2)

6-8 eggs per cycle are derived

Acritifically inseminated

Fertilised eggs at 8-32 cell stages are recovered

↓

(3)

(a) 1-FSH, 2-Super ovulation due to induced follicular maturation, 3-Transfer to surrogate mother.

(b) 1-LH, 2-Super ovulation due to induced follicular maturation, 3-Transfer to surrogate mother.

(c) 1-Progesterone, 2-Super ovulation due to induced follicular maturation, 3-Transfer to surrogate mother.

(d) 1-FSH, 2-Transfer to surrogate mother, 3-Super ovulation due to induced follicular maturation.

18. Study the flow chart and answer the following given questions respectively:

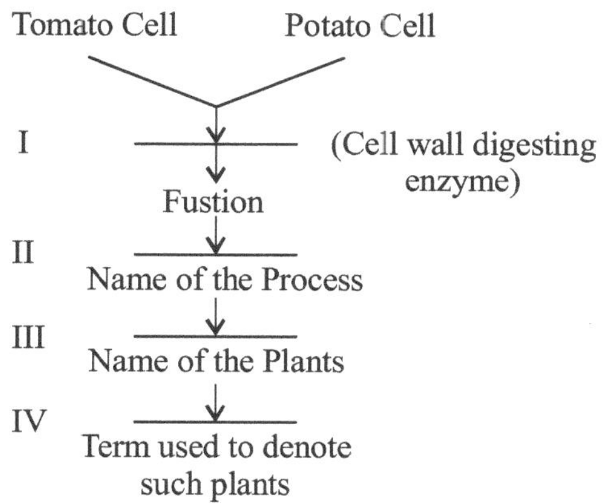

(a) I-Amylase, II-Protoplast fusion, III-Potato, IV-Somaclones

(b) I-Cellulase, II-Somatic hybridisation, III-Pomato, IV-Somatic hybrids.

(c) I-Amylase, II-Mristem culture, III-Pomato, IV-Somaclones.

(d) I-Polyethylene glycol, II-Somatic hybridisation, III-Pomato, IV-Somatic hybrids.

19. Find the wrong match.

(a) Wheat   – Pusa Shubra

(b) Cauliflower – Pusa Snowball K-1

(c) Chilli   – Pusa Sadabahar

(d) Brassica   – Pusa Swarnim

20. Find the mis-match:

(a) Explant – Plant part used for tissue culture

(b) Somaclones – Variations produced during micropropagation

(c) Callus – Undifferentiated mass of cells

(d) Totipotency – Capacity to generate a whole plant from any cell

21. ________ is an instrument that helps to achieve specific temperature and pressure for scientific/medical and industrial applications.

(a) Sterilizers   (b) Autoclave

(c) Electrosurgical unit (d) None of the above

22. ________ is the result of an artificial hybridization between radishand cabbage

(a) Brassicaceae   (b) Raphanobrassica

(c) Hirschfeldia incana (d) None of the above

Solutions

1. (a) 2. (c) 3. (a) 4. (b) 5. (a)
6. (c) 7. (b) 8. (a) 9. (c) 10. (b)
11. (d) 12. (d) 13. (c) 14. (a)
15. (c) 16. (a) 17. (a)
18. (b)

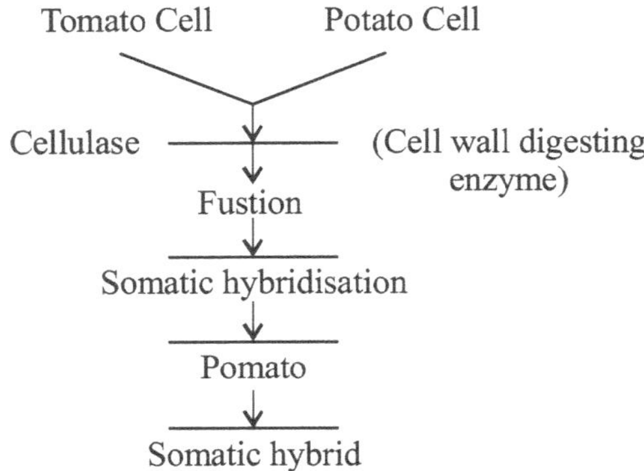

19. (a) 20. (b) 21. (b) 22. (b)

CHAPTER 32

Microbes in Human Welfare

1. Match different organisms in column I with their uses in coulmn II and select the correct answer from the given codes.

Column-I		Column-II
A.	*Lactobacillus acidophilus*	(i) Formation of dough
B.	*Saccharomyces cerevisiae*	(ii) Single cell proteins
C.	*Propionibacterium sharmanii*	(iii) Conversion of milk into curd
D.	*Spirulina*	(iv) Formtion of Swiss cheese

(a) A-(iii), B-(i), C-(ii), D-(iv)
(b) A-(iii), B-(i), C-(iv), D-(ii)
(c) A-(i), B-(iii), C-(iv), D-(ii)
(d) A-(i), B-(iii), C-(ii), D-(iv)

2. Which of the following antibiotics is not correctly matched with the source from which it is obtained?

	Antibiotic	Source
(a)	Penicillin	*Penicillium chrysogenum*
(b)	Bacitracin	*Bacillus licheniformis*
(c)	Griseofulvin	*Penicullium griseofulvum*
(d)	Streptomycin	*Bacillus griseus*

3. Identify the blank spaces A, B, C and D in the following table and select the correct answer.

Type of microbe	Scientific name	Commercial product
Bacteium	A	Streptokinase
B	*Aspergillus niger*	Citric acid
Fungus	*Trichoderma polysporum*	C
Bacterium	D	Butyric acid

(a) A-*Streptococcus* B-Fungus
    C-Cyclosporin A D-*Clostridium butylicum*
(b) A-*Clostridium butylicum* B-*Streptococcus*
    C-Fungus D-Cyclosporin A
(c) A-*Streptococcus* B-Yeast
    C-Cyclosporin A D-*Lactobacillus*
(d) A-*Streptococcus* B-Cyclosporin A
    C-Statins D-*Clostridium butylicum*

4. A drug used for patient A is obtained from the organism B. Identify A and B in the above statement and select the correct answer.

	A	B
(a)	Swine flu	*Monascus purpureus*
(b)	AIDS	*Pseudomonas denitrificans*
(c)	Heart	*Penicillium chrysogenum*
(d)	Organ transplant	*Trichoderma polysporum*

5. Identify the blak spaces A, B, C and D in the table given below and select the correct answer.

Type of micorbe	Scientific name	Product application	Medical
Fungus	A	Cyclosporin A	B
C	*Monascus purpureus*	Stain	D

(a) A-*Trichoderma polysporum*,
    B-As an immunosuppressive agent,
    C-Yeast (Fungus),
    D-Lowering of blood cholesterol
(b) A-*Trichoderma polysporum*,
    B-Lowering of blood cholesterol,
    C-Yeast (Fungus),
    D-As and immunosuppressive agent
(c) A-Yeast (Fungus),
    B-Lowering of blood cholesterol,
    C-*Trichoderma polysporum*,
    D-As an immunosuppressive agent
(d) A-*Streptococcus*,
    B-As an immunosuppressive agent,
    C-Barterium, D-Lowering of blood cholesterol

6. Identify the blank spaces A, B, C and D in the following table and select the correct answer.

Type of microbe	Scientific name	Commercial product
Bacterium	**A**	Lactic acid
Fungus	**B**	Cyclosporin A
C	*Monascus purpureus*	Statins
Fungs	*Penicillium notalum*	**D**

   (a) A-*Lactobacillus*   B-*Trichoderma polysporum*
       C-Yeast   D-Penicillin

   (b) A-*Acetobacter*   B-*Trichoderma polysporum*
       C-Yeast   D-Streptomycin

   (c) A-*Lactobacillus*   B-*Aspergillus niger*
       C-Alge   D-Penicillin

   (d) A-*Lactobacillus*   B-*Trichoderma polysporum*
       C-Agaricus   D-Penicillin

7. Match column I with column II and select the correct answer from the given codes

	Column-I		Column-II
A.	The stage in which of physical tretment of sewage is done	(i)	Anaerobic digestion activated sludge and production of biogas
B.	The stage in which biological treatment of sewage is done	(ii)	Activated sludge
C.	Name of the sediment in primary treatment	(iii)	Aeration tanks
D.	It is carried ot aeration tanks from primary settling	(iv)	Primary effluent
E.	Name of the sediment in secondary treatment	(v)	Primary sludge
F.	Site of flocs growth	(vi)	Secondary teatment
G	Function of sludge digester	(vii)	Primary treatment

(a) A-(vii), B-(vi), C-(v), D-(iv), E-(ii), F-(iii), G-(i)
(b) A-(i), B-(iii), C-(v), D-(vii), E-(ii), F-(iv), G-(vi)
(c) A-(i), B-(ii), C-(iii), D-(iv), E-(v), F-(vi), G-(vii)
(d) A-(vii), B-(vi), C-(i), D-(ii), E-(iii), F-(iv), G-(v)

8. Match column I with column II and select the correct answer from the given codes.

	Column-I		Column-II
A.	Methanogens	(i)	BOD
B.	Fermentors	(ii)	Methane rich fuel gas
C.	Organic waste in water	(iii)	Production of methane
D.	Biogas	(iv)	Large vessels for growing microbes

(a) A-(ii), B-(iv), C-(iii), D-(i)
(b) A-(iv), B-(iii), C-(iv), D-(i)
(c) A-(ii), B-(i), C-(iv), D-(iii)
(d) A-(iii), B-(iv), C-(i), D-(ii)

9. Match column I with column II and select the correct option from the codes given below.

	Column-I		Column-II
A.	Statins	(i)	Biogas
B.	Dung	(ii)	*Saccharomyces cerevisae*
C.	Ethanol production	(iii)	*Monascus purpureus*
D.	Cyclosporin A	(iv)	*Trichoderma polysporum*

(a) A-(iii), B-(i), C-(iv), D-(ii)
(b) A-(i), B-(iii), C-(iv), D-(ii)
(c) A-(iii), B-(ii), C-(iv), D-(i)
(d) A-(iii), B-(i), C-(ii), D-(iv)

10. Match clumn I with column II and select the correct answer from the given codes.

	Column-I		Column-II
A.	*Trichoderma*	(i)	Free living nitorgen fixing bacteria
B.	*Streptomyces*	(ii)	Biocontroal agent
C.	*Azospirillum*	(iii)	Lactic acid
D.	*Lactobacillus*	(iv)	Source of antibiotic

(a) A-(ii), B-(iii), C-(iv), D-(i)
(b) A-(ii), B-(iv), C-(i), D-(iii)
(c) A-(iii), B-(i), C-(ii), D-(iv)
(d) A-(iv), B-(ii), C-(i), D-(iii)

11. Match column I with column II and select the correct answer form the given codes.

Column-I	**Column-II**
A. Mycrrhizae	(i) Azadirachtin
B. *Bacillus thuringiensis*	(ii) Phosphorus nutrition
C. Root nodules	(iii) Leghaemoglobin
D. Biopesticide	(iv) Bioinsecticide

(a) A-(iii), B-(i), C-(ii), D-(iv)
(b) A-(ii), B-(iii), C-(iv), D-(i)
(c) A-(ii), B-(iv), C-(iii), D-(i)
(d) A-(iii), B-(iv), C-(ii), D-(i)

12. Match column I with column II and select the correct answer from the given codes.

Column-I	**Column-II**
A. Ganga action plan	(i) N_2fixing cyanobacterium
B. Bt cotton	(ii) Ministry of environment and forests
C. *Rhizobium*	(iii) Insect resistant plant
D. *Nostoc*	(iv) N_2 fixing bacterium

(a) A-(ii), B-(iii), C-(iv), D-(i)
(b) A-(iii), B-(ii), C-(iv), D-(i)
(c) A-(ii), B-(iv), C-(iii), D-(i)
(d) A-(i), B-(iii), C-(ii), D-(iv)

13. Match column I with coulmn II and select the correct answer from the given codes.

Column-I	**Column-II**
A. *Azolla*	(i) Symbiotic N_2-fixer
B. Rotenone	(ii) Symbiotic association with N_2-fixing cyanobacteria
C. *Crotolaria*	(iii) Natural *juncea* insecticide
D. *Frankia*	(iv) Green manure

(a) A-(ii), B-(iii), C-(iv), D-(i)
(b) A-(ii), B-(iv), C-(iii), D-(i)

(c) A-(ii), B-(i), C-(iv), D-(iii)
(d) A-(i), B-(iii), C-(iv), D-(ii)

14. Match column I with column II and setect the correct option from the given codes.

Column-I	**Column-II**
A. Streptokinase	(i) *Trichoderma Polysporum*
B. Statins	(ii) *Streptococcus*
C. Cyclosporin A	(iii) *Monasus purpureus*
D. Penicillin	(iv) *Penicillium*

(a) A-(ii), B-(iii), C-(i), D-(iv)
(b) A-(i), B-(ii), C-(iii), D-(iv)
(c) A-(iv), B-(i), C-(iii), D-(ii)
(d) A-(iii), B-(ii), C-(i), D-(iv)

15. Match column I with column II and select the correct option using the codes given below.

Column-I	**Cloumn-II**
A. Citric acid	(i) *Trichoderma*
B. Cyclosporin A	(ii) *Clostridium*
C. Statins	(iii) *Aspergillus*
D. Butyric acid	(iv) *Monascus*

(a) A-(iii), B-(i), C-(ii), D-(iv)
(b) A-(iii), B-(i), C-(iv), D-(ii)
(c) A-(i), B-(iv), C-(ii), D-(iii)
(d) A-(iii), B-(iv), C-(i), D-(ii)

16. Match the following:

List-I	**List-II**
(i) Statins	A. *Propionibacterium shermanii*
(ii) Swiss cheese	B. *Steptococcus*
(iii) Cyclosporin A	C. *Aspergillus niger*
(iv) Citric acid	D. *Trichoderma polysporum*
(v) Clot buster	E. *Monascus purpureus*

(a) (i)-E, (ii)-A, (iii)-D, (iv)-C, (v)-B
(b) (i)-B, (ii)-A, (iii)-D, (iv)-E, (v)-C
(c) (i)-E, (ii)-A, (iii)-B, (iv)-C, (v)-D
(d) (i)-C, (ii)-E, (iii)-A, (iv)-D, (v)-B
(e) (i)-E, (ii)-C, (iii)-A, (iv)-D, (v)-B

17. Match the microbes in column I with their commercial/industrial products in column II and choose the correct answer.

	Column-I		Column-II
A.	*Aspergillus niger*	1.	Ethanol
B.	*Clostridium butylicum*	2.	Statins
C.	*Saccharomyces cerevisiae*	3.	Citric acid
D.	*Trichoderma polysporum*	4.	Butyric acid
E.	*Monascus purpuerus*	5.	Cyclosporin A

18. Match the items in column I with those in column II and choose the correct answer.

	Column-I		Column-II
P.	Blue green algae as biofertilsers	i.	Ectomycorrhiza
Q.	Fungi as biofertilsers	ii.	*Thiobacillus* sp.
R.	Free living nitrogen fixing bacteria	iii.	*Anabaena* sp.
S.	Phosphate solubilising bacteria	iv.	*Clostridium* sp.
		v.	*Azospirillum* sp.

(a) P-iii, Q-i, R-v, S-ii

(b) P-v, Q-i, R-ii, S-iv

(c) P-v, Q-iv, R-i, S-ii

(d) P-iv, Q-ii, R-v, S-i

19. Match the following columns.

	Column-I		Column-II
A.	*Plasmodium ovale*	1.	Benign tertiary malaria
B.	*Plasmodium malariae*	2.	Wild teriary malaria
C.	*Plasmodium vivax*	3.	Malignant tertiary malaria
D.	*Plasmodium falciparum*	4.	Quartan malaria

Codes:

	A	B	C	D			A	B	C	D
(a)	1	2	3	4		(b)	3	1	2	4
(c)	2	1	3	4		(d)	2	4	1	3

20. Match the following columus.

	Column-I		Column-II
A.	African sleeping sickness	1.	*Sacculina*
B.	Dumdum fever	2.	*Haemophilus influenzae*
C.	Pneumonia	3.	*Leishmania donovani*
D.	Parasitic castration	4.	*Trypanosoma gambiense*
		5.	*Leishmania tropica*

Codes:

	A	B	C	D			A	B	C	D
(a)	4	3	2	1		(b)	3	4	1	2
(c)	3	1	2	4		(d)	4	3	1	5

21. Match the following columns.

	Column-I		Column-II
A.	Filariasis	1.	Amoebic dysentery
B.	Amoebiasis	2.	Whooping cough
C.	Trypanosomiasis	3.	Sleeping sickness
D.	Pertusis	4.	Elephantiasis

Codes:

	A	B	C	D			A	B	C	D
(a)	4	3	2	1		(b)	2	1	3	4
(c)	4	1	3	2		(d)	2	3	1	4

22. Match the following columns.

	Column-I		Column-II
A.	HIV infection	1.	Widal test
B.	Typhoid	2.	Biopsy
C.	Cancer	3.	Tuberculin analysis
D.	Tuberculosis	4.	ELISA

Codes:

	A	B	C	D			A	B	C	D
(a)	1	3	4	2		(b)	3	2	4	1
(c)	4	1	2	3		(d)	2	4	3	1

23. Match the following columns.

	Column-I		Column-II
A.	*Glossina sp.*	1.	Tse-tse fly
B.	*Panstrangylus sp.*	2.	Chagas disease
C.	*Coxiella*	3.	Q-fever
D.	*Closteidum sp.*	4.	Tetanospasmin

Codes:

	A	B	C	D			A	B	C	D
(a)	2	3	1	4		(b)	4	3	2	1
(c)	3	4	1	2		(d)	1	2	3	4

24. Watch each disease with its correct type of vaccine.

Column-I	Column-II
A. Tuberculosis	1. Harmless virus
B. Whooping cough	2. Inactivated toxin
C. Diphtheria	3. Killed bacteria
D. Pilio	4. Harmless bacteria

Codes:

	A	B	C	D			A	B	C	D
(a)	2	1	3	4		(b)	3	2	4	1
(c)	4	3	2	1		(d)	1	2	3	4

19. Match the microbes in column I with their commercial/industrial products in column II and choose the correct answer.

Column I	Column II
A. *Aspergillus niger*	I. Ethanol
B. *Clostridium butylicum*	II. Statins
C. *Saccharomyces cerevisiae*	III. Citric acid
D. *Trichoderma polysporum*	IV. Butyric acid
E. *Monascus purpureus*	V. Cyclosporin A

- (a) A – IV; B – V; C – II; D – I; E – III
- (b) A – V; B – IV; C – I; D – II; E – III
- (c) A – III; B – IV; C – I; D – V; E – II
- (d) A – III; B – IV; C – V; D – I; E – II

20. Match the following list of microbes and their importance:

A. *Sacharomyces*	I. Production of immunosuppressive agents *cerevisiae*
B. *Monascus Purpureus*	II. Ripening of Swiss cheese
C. *Trichoderma* ethanol	III. Commercial production of *polysporum*
D. *Propionibacterium sharmanii*	IV. Production of blood cholesterol lowering agents

- (a) A – IV; B – III; C – II; D – I
- (b) A – IV; B – II; C – I; D – III
- (c) A – III; B – I; C – IV; D – II
- (d) A – III; B – IV; C – I; D – II

21. Choose the right combination

Column-I	Column-II
A. *Escherichia coli*	I. Nif gene
B. *Rhizobium melilotae*	II. Digestive hydrocarbon of crude oil
C. *Bacillus thuringiensis*	III. Production of human insulin
D. *Pseudomonas putida*	IV. Biological control of fungal disease
	V. Bio-decomposed insectiside

- (a) A – III; B – I; C – V; D – IV
- (b) A – I; B – II; C – III; D – IV
- (c) A – II; B – I; C – III; D – IV
- (d) A – III; B – I; C – V; D – II

22. Match the items in Column 'I' and Column 'II' and choose correct answer.

Column-I	Column-II
A. Lady bird	I. *Methanobacterium*
B. Mycorrhiza	II. *Trichoderma*
C. Biological control	III. Aphids
D. Biogas	IV. *Glomus*

The correct answer is:

- (a) A-II, B-IV, C-III, D-I
- (b) A-III, B-IV, C-II, D-I
- (c) A-IV, B-I, C-II, D-III
- (d) A-III, B-II, C-I, D-IV

23. Match the column I and column II and choose the correct combination of alphabets of the two columns

Column-I Types of Bacteria	Column-II Activity
A. *Streptomyces*	I. Food poisoning
B. *Rhizobium*	II. Source antibiotics
C. *Nitrosomonas*	III. Nitrogen fixation
D. *Acetobacter*	IV. Nitrification
	V. Vinegar synthesis

- (a) A-IV, B-V, C-I, D-III
- (b) A-V, B-I, C-III, D-IV
- (c) A-II, B-III, C-I, D-V
- (d) A-II, B-III, C-IV, D-V

24. Match the following and choose the correct combination.

	Column-I		Column-II
A.	*Escherichia coli*	I.	'nif' gene
B.	*Rhizobium meliloti*	II.	Digests hydrocarbons of crude oil
C.	*Bacillus thuringiensis*	III.	Human insulin production
D.	*Pseudomonas putida*	IV.	Biocontrol of fungal disease
		V.	Biodegradable insecticide.

(a) A-III, B-I, C-V, D-II
(b) A-III, B-I, C-V, D-IV
(c) A-I, B-II, C-III, D-IV
(d) A-II, B-I, C-III, D-IV

25. Match the column I and column II and find the correct option.

	Column I		Column II
A.	Dextran	I.	Clarification of juices
B.	Invertase	II.	Used as clot buster
C.	Streptokinase	III.	Hydrolysis of sucrose
D.	Protease	IV.	Polymerization of simple sugar

(a) A – IV; B– III; C – II; D – I
(b) A– III; B– II; C– I; D– IV
(c) A– I; B– IV; C– III; D– II
(d) A– II; B– I; C – IV; D – III

Solutions

1. **(b)**

2. **(d)** Streptomycin is obtained from *Streptomyces griseus*. It is found useful in meningitis, pneumonia, tuberculosis and local infections.

3. **(a)**

4. **(d)** Cycolsporin A is a cyclic oligopeptide obtained through fermentative activity of fungs *Trichoderma polysporum*. It has anti-fungal, anti-inflammatory and immunosuppressive propeties. It inhibits activation of T-cells and therefore, prevents rejection reactions in organ transplantation.

5.	**(a)**	**6.**	**(a)**	**7.**	**(a)**	**8.**	**(b)**	**9.**	**(d)**
10.	**(b)**	**11.**	**(c)**	**12.**	**(a)**	**13.**	**(a)**	**14.**	**(a)**
15.	**(b)**	**16.**	**(a)**	**17.**	**(c)**	**18.**	**(a)**	**19.**	**(c)**
20.	**(d)**	**21.**	**(d)**	**22.**	**(b)**	**23.**	**(d)**	**24.**	**(c)**
19.	**(c)**	**20.**	**(d)**	**21.**	**(d)**	**22.**	**(b)**	**23.**	**(d)**
24.	**(a)**	**25.**	**(a)**						

Biotechnology: Principles and Processes

33

1. Select the correctly matched pair.
   (a) Cosmid – Cannot be used in human genome project
   (b) BAC – 300-350 kb of foreign DNA
   (c) YAC – Can clone fragments upto 45kb in length only
   (d) Phagemid – An RNA based cloning vector carrying an origin of relication derived from adenovirus.

2. Which of the following is correctly matched?
   (a) *Agrobacterium tumefaciens* – Tumour
   (b) *Thermus aquaticus* – Bt-gene
   (c) pBR322 – Enzyme
   (d) Ligase – Molecular scissors
   (e) *Hin*d II – Plasmid vector

3. Match the tissue/molecules mentioned in column I with those of their degrading enzymes mentioned in column II and select the correct option from the given codes.

Column I	Column II
A. Cell wall	(i) Proteases
B. RNA	(ii) Pectinases
C. Histone	(iii) Ribonucleases
D. Pectin	(iv) Cellulase

   (a) A-(iv), B-(iii), C-(i), D-(ii)
   (b) A-(ii), B-(i), C-(iv), D-(iii)
   (c) A-(i), B-(ii), C-(iii), D-(iv)
   (d) A-(iii), B-(iv), C-(ii), D-(i)

4. Match the items in column I with their uses in column II and choose the right option.

Column I	Column II
A. ELISA	(i) Antigen-antibody interaction
B. PCR	(ii) Gene amplification
C. Biolistics	(iii) Direct introduction of recombinant DNA
D. Micro-injection	(iv) Gold coated DNA

   (a) A-(iii), B-(iv), C-(i), D-(ii)
   (b) A-(ii), B-(i), C-(iv), D-(iii)
   (c) A-(iv), B-(i), C-(ii), D-(iii)
   (d) A-(i), B-(iv), C-(ii), D-(iii)
   (e) A-(i), B-(ii), C-(iv), D-(iii)

5. Match the items in column I with their uses in column II and choose the right option.

Column I	Column II
A. *Bacillus thuringiensis*	(i) Restriction endonuclease
B. *Agrobacterium tumefaciens*	(ii) Thermostable DNA polymerase
C. *Thermus aquaticus*	(iii) Insecticidal protein
D. *Escherichia coli*	(iv) Ti plasmid

   (a) A-(iii), B-(iv), C-(i), D-(ii)
   (b) A-(ii), B-(i), C-(iv), D-(iii)
   (c) A-(iv), B-(i), C-(ii), D-(iii)
   (d) A-(i), B-(iv), C-(ii), D-(iii)
   (e) A-(iii), B-(iv), C-(ii), D-(i)

6. Which of the following is not correctly matched for the organisms and its cell wall degrading enzyme?
   (a) Algae   –   Methylase
   (b) Fungi   –   Chitinase
   (c) Bacteria   –   Lysozyme
   (d) Plant cells –   Cellulase

7. Match the entries in column I with those of column II and choose the correct answer.

	Column I		Column II
A.	Restriction endo-nucleases	(p)	Kohler and Milstein
B.	Polymerase chain reaction	(q)	Alec Jeffreys
C.	DNA fingerprinting	(r)	Arber
D.	Monoclonal antibodies	(s)	Karry Mullis

(a) A - (r), B - (s), C - (q), D - (p)
(b) A - (r), B - (q), C - (s), D - (p)
(c) A - (q), B - (r), C - (s), D - (p)
(d) A - (q), B - (s), C - (r), D - (q)

8. Match column I with column II with respect to the nomeclature of restriction enzyme *Eco*RI and select the correct answer from the given codes.

	Column I		Column II
A.	E	(i)	Ist in order of identification
B.	co	(ii)	Name of genus
C.	R	(iii)	Name of species
D.	I	(iv)	Name of strain

(a) A – (iii), B – (i), C – (ii), D – (iv)
(b) A – (ii), B – (i), C – (iii), D – (iv)
(c) A – (i), B – (ii), C – (iii), D – (iv)
(d) A – (ii), B – (iii), C – (iv), D – (i)

9. Match column I with column II and select the correct answer form the given codes.

	Column I		Column II
A.	amp^R gene	(i)	Artificial plasmid
B.	Separation of DNA	(ii)	Selectable marker fragments
C.	*Hind*III	(iii)	Electrophoresis
D.	pBR322	(iv)	*Haemophilus influenzae*

(a) A – (iii), B – (ii), C – (i), D – (iv)
(b) A – (iv), B – (i), C – (iii), D – (ii)
(c) A – (ii), B – (iii), C – (iv), D – (i)
(d) A – (ii), B – (iv), C – (i), D – (iii)

10. Match the terms given in column I with their definitions in column II and select the correct answer from codes given below.

	Column II		Ciolmn II
A.	Transformation	(i)	Sequences cut by restriction enzymes
B.	Recognition site	(ii)	process by which DNA fragments are separated based on their size
C.	Gel electrophoresis	(iii)	Plasmid DNA that has incorporated human DNA
D.	Recombinant DNA	(iv)	Process by which bacteria take up pieces of DNA from the envirment

(a) A – (iii), B – (i), C – (ii), D – (iv)
(b) A – (iv), B – (i), C – (ii), D – (iii)
(c) A – (i), B – (ii), C – (iii), D – (iv)
(d) A – (ii), B – (iii), C – (iv), D – (i)

11. Match column I with column II and select the correct answer from the given codes.

	Column II		Ciolmn II
A.	Recombinant DNA techonology	(i)	Chilled ethanol
B.	Precipitation of DNA	(ii)	DNA staining
C.	Trajnsposons	(iii)	Jumping genes
D.	Ethidium bromide	(iv)	Genetic engineering

(a) A – (iv), B – (i), C – (iii), D – (ii)
(b) A – (i), B – (iii), C – (ii), D – (iv)
(c) A – (ii), B – (i), C – (iii), D – (iv)
(d) A – (iv), B – (ii), C – (i), D – (iii)

12. Match column I (enzyme) with column II (characteristic/activity) and select the correct answer from the given codes.

	Column II		**Ciolmn II**
A.	Taq DNA polymerase	(i)	Cleaves the ends of linear DNA
B.	Exonuclease	(ii)	Breakdown of fungal cell wall
C.	Protease	(iii)	Stable above 90°C
D.	Chitinase	(iv)	Made only by eukaryotic cells
		(v)	Degradation of proteins

(a) A – (iii), B – (iv), C – (i), D – (ii)
(b) A – (iv), B – (iii), C – (i), D – (ii)
(c) A – (ii), B – (i), C – (v), D – (iii)
(d) A – (iii), B – (i), C – (v), D – (ii)

13. Given table given an account of differences between PCR and gene cloning. Which of the following points shows the incorrect difference?

	Parameter	PCR	Gene cloning
1.	Efficient	More	Less
2.	Apparatus Requirement	DNA	Restriction enzyme, ligase, vector, bacterial cell
3.	Manipulation	*in vitro*	*in vitro* and *in vivo*
4.	Cost	More	Less
5.	Automation	Yes	No
6.	Error probability	Less	More
7.	Time for a typical experiment	2-4 days	4 hours
8.	Application	More	Less

(a) 1 and 3   (b) 4, 5 and 6
(c) 4 and 7   (d) 4, 7 and 8

14. Match the scientists in column I with their related discoverise in column II and select the correct option from the given codes.

	Column II		**Ciolmn II**
A.	Kary Mullis	(i)	Father of genetic engineering
B.	Paul Berg	(ii)	Nobel prize for the discovery of restriction endonucleases
C.	Stanley Cohen and Herbert Boyer	(iii)	Developed polymerase chain reaction
D.	Arber, Smitjh and Nathan	(iv)	Isolated an antibiotic resistant gene from a plasmid of the bacterium *Salmonella typhimurium*

(a) A – (iii), B – (i), C – (iv), D – (ii)
(b) A – (iii), B – (iv), C – (i), D – (ii)
(c) A – (iv), B – (ii), C – (iii), D – (i)
(d) A – (i), B – (iii), C – (iv), D – (ii)

15. Which of the following is correctly matched?

(a) *Agrobacterium tumefaciens*   – Tumour
(b) *Thermus aquaticus*   – *Bt* gene
(c) pBR322   – Enzyme
(d) Ligase   – Molecular scissors
(e) *Hind* II   – Plasmid vector

16. Match the following Columns.

	Column I		**Column II**
A.	Bacterial enzymes used to cut DNA at defined sequences	1.	Recognition sequences
B.	Sequences cut by restriction enzymes	2.	Plasmids
C.	Ends left on DNA segments cut by DNA restriction enzymes	3.	Sticky ends
D.	Circular pieces of DNA found in bacteria	4.	Restriction enzymes

Codes

	A	B	C	D
(a)	1	4	3	2
(b)	4	1	3	2
(c)	1	4	2	3
(d)	4	3	2	1

17. Match the following Columns.

Column I	Column II
A. Bacterial viruses	1. Transformation
B. Process by which bacteria take up pieces of DNA from the environment	2. Cloning vector
C. *Hind* II	3. *Haemophyllus influenzae*
D. vehicle that move DNA from one organism to another	4. Bacteriophges

Codes

	A	B	C	D
(a)	2	3	4	1
(b)	1	3	4	2
(c)	4	1	3	2
(d)	1	4	3	2

18. Match the following Columns.

Column I	Column II
A. A molecule used to carry foreign into bacteria	1. Restriction enzymes
B. A rapid way to amplify DNA in the laboratory	2. Recombinant DNA
C. A way to separate DNA fragments based on their size	3. PCR
D. Molecular scissors	4. Vector
E. A gene sequence from more than one origin	5. Gel electrophoresis

Codes

	A	B	C	D	E
(a)	4	3	5	1	2

(b)	2	4	3	1	5
(c)	5	4	3	2	1
(d)	1	5	4	2	3

19. Identify the correct match for the given apparatus.

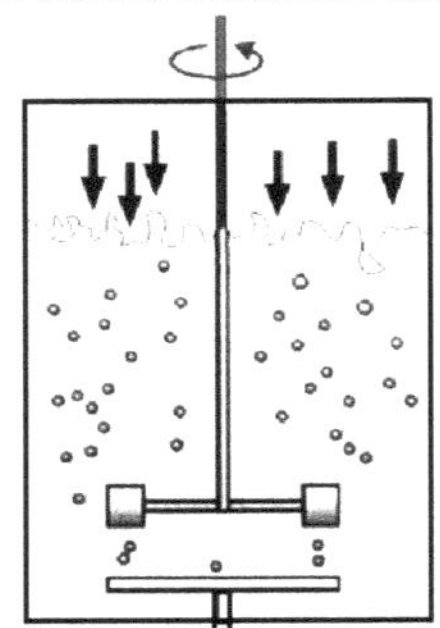

	Apparatus	Function
(a)	Gene gun	Vectorless direct gene transfer
(b)	Column chromatography	Separation of chlorophyll pigments
(c)	Sparged tank bioreactor	Carry out fermentation process
(d)	Respirometer	Finding out rate of respiration

20. Choose the correct option.

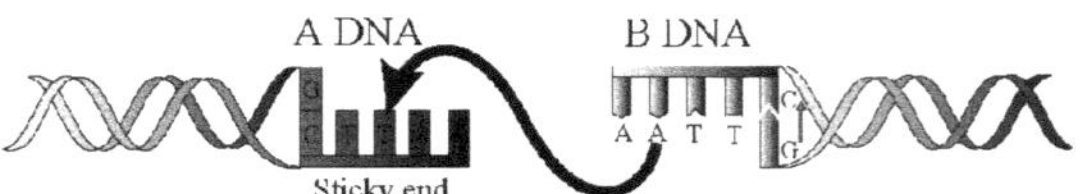

	A DNA	B DNA	Enzyme recognizing palindrome	Enzyme joining the sticky ends
(a)	Vector	Foreign	DNA ligase	EcoRI
(b)	Vector	Foreign	EcoRI	DNA ligase
(c)	Vector	Foreign	Exonuclease	DNA ligase
(d)	Vector	Foreign	DNA ligase	Exonuclease

21. Identify the correct match for the given figure.

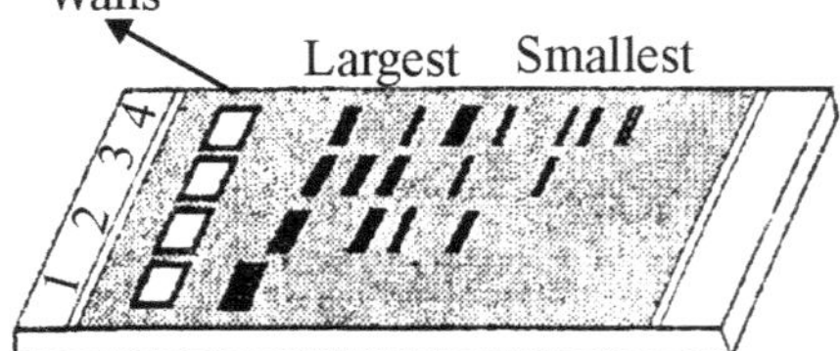

(a)	Electrophoresis	Differential migration of DNA fragments.
(b)	Column chromatography	Separation of chlorophyll pigments.
(c)	Gene cloning	Technique of obtaining identical copies of a particular DNA segment or a gene.
(d)	Microinjection	Technique of introducing foreign genes into a host cell.

22. Identify the correct option .

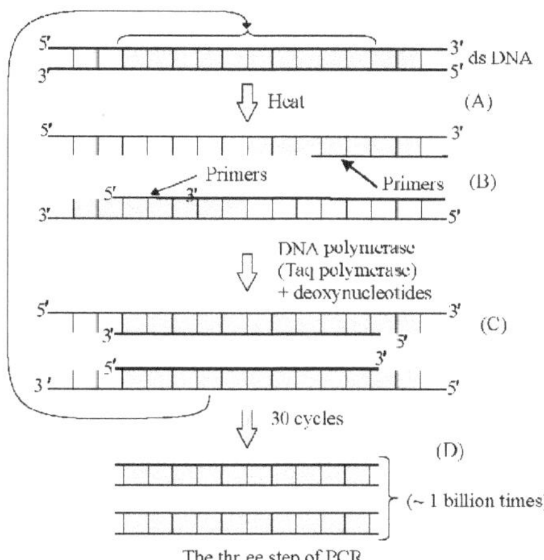

(a) A - Denaturation, B - Annealing, C - Extension, D - Amplified
(b) A - Annealing, B - Denaturation, C - Extension, D - Amplified
(c) A - Denaturation, B - Annealing, C - Amplified, D - Extension
(d) A - Annealing, B - Denaturation, C - Amplified, D - Extension

23. Match the following columns.

	Column I		**Column II**
A.	Plasmids	I.	Virus infecting bacteria
B.	Bacteriophages	II.	Natural polymer of D-galactose
C.	Cosmids	III.	Hybrid vector derived from plasmids
D.	Agarose	IV.	Circular extrachromosomal DNA

(a) A–II; B–I; C–III; D–IV
(b) A–IV; B–I; C–III; D–II
(c) A–III; B–II; C–I; D–IV
(d) A–I; B–IV; C–III; D–II

24. Match the following columns.

	Column I		**Column II**
A.	Arber, Nathan and Hamilton Smith	I.	Isolated first restriction endonuclease from bacteria
B.	Paul Berg	II.	Term biotechnology
C.	Herbert Boyer and Stanley Cohen	III.	Father of genetic engineering
D.	Karl Erkey	IV.	First recombinant DNA

(a) A–I; B–IV; C–III; D–II
(b) A–III; B–II; C–I; D–IV
(c) A–I; B–III; C–IV; D–II
(d) A–IV; B–III; C–I; D–II

25. Which of the following is correctly matched?
(a) *Agrobacterium tumefaciens* - tumour
(b) *Thermus aquaticus* - Bt-gene
(c) pBR322 - enzyme
(d) Ligase - molecular scissors

26. Which one of the following option is correct for A, B, C and D?

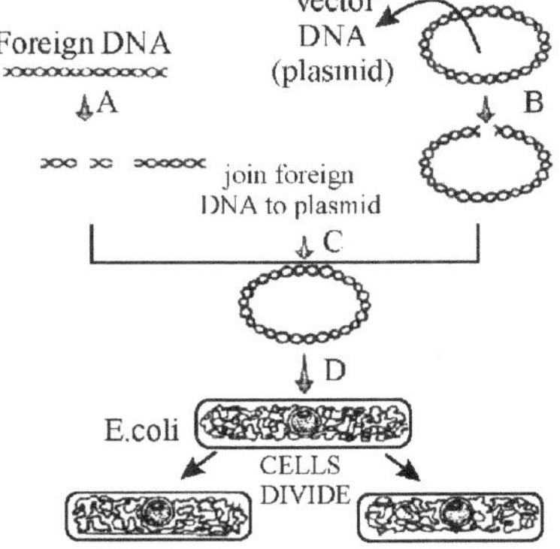

	A	**B**	**C**	**D**
(a)	Exonuclease	Endonuclease	DNA	Transformation ligase
(b)	Exonuclease	Exonuclease	DNA	Transformation ligase
(c)	Exonuclease	Endonuclease	Hydro-lase	Transduction
(d)	Restriction endonuclease	Restriction endonuclease	DNA	Transformation ligase

27. Which of the following pairs are correctly matched?

   (a) Central dogma   — Codon

   (b) Okazaki fragments — Splicing

   (c) RNA polymerase   — RNA primer

   (d) Restriction enzyme — Genetic engineering

28. Match List I with List II and select the correct option

	List I		**List II**
A.	*Bacillus thuringiensis*	I.	Production of chitinases
B.	*Rhizobium meliloti*	II.	Scavenging of oil spills
C.	*Escherichia coli*	III.	Incorporation of '*nif*' gene
D.	*Pseudomonas putida*	IV.	Production of *Bt* toxin
E.	*Trichoderma*	V.	Production of human insulin

   (a) A – II; B – IV; C – I; D – V; E – III

   (b) A – II; B – IV; C – V; D – I; E – III

   (c) A – IV; B – III; C – V; D – II; E – I

   (d) A – III; B – IV; C – V; D – I; E – II

29. Which one of the following pairs is not correctly matched?

   (a) Plasmid   Small piece of extrachromosomal DNA in bacteria

   (b) Interferon   An enzyme that interferes with DNA replication

   (c) Cosmid   A vector for carrying large DNA fragments into host cells

   (d) Myeloma   Antibody-producing tumour cells

30. Match the following columns.

	Column I		**Column II**
A.	*Eco RI*	I.	*E. Coli R 245*
B.	*Hind III*	II.	*Bacillus amylolique-faciens*
C.	*BamHi*	III.	*Haemophilus influenzae*
D.	*EcoRII*	IV.	*Escherichia coli RY13*

   (a) A–I; B–II; C–III; D–IV

   (b) A–III; B–II; C–I; D–IV

   (c) A–IV; B–III; C–II; D–I

   (d) A–IV; B–II; C–III; D–I

31. Match column I with column II with respect to the nomenclature of enzyme EcoRI and select the correct answer from codes given below.

	Column I		**Column II**
A.	*E*	I.	1st in order of identification
B.	*co*	II.	Name of genus
C.	R	III.	Name of species
D.	I	IV.	Name of strain

   (a) A–III; B–IV; C–I; D–II

   (b) A–II; B–III; C–IV; D–I

   (c) A–II; B–I; C–IV; D–III

   (d) A–II; B–III; C–I; D–IV

Solutions

1. **(b)** Bacterial artificial chromosome (BAC) vectors are based on natural, extra-chromosomal plasmid of *E.coli*. These vectors can accommodate upto 300-350 kb of foreign DNA and are also being used in genome sequencing project.

2. **(a)** Ti plasmid (tumour inducing) from the soil bacterium *Agrobacterium tumefaciens* is effectively used as vector for gene transfer to plant cells. The part of Ti plasmid transferred into plant cell DNA, is called the T-DNA. This T-DNA with desired DNA spliced into it, is inserted into the chromosome of the host plant where it produces copies of itself, by migrating from one chromosomal position to another at random.

3. **(a)** 4. **(e)** 5. **(e)**

6. **(a)** Cell wall of algae is made up of cellulaose, pectin and mucilage. These substances cannot be degraded by methylase. Methylase is a type of transferase enzyme that transfers a methyl group from a donor to a acceptor.

7. **(a)** 8. **(d)** 9. **(c)** 10. **(b)** 11. **(a)**

12. **(d)**

13. **(c)** The cost of gene cloning is far more than PCR because gene cloning requires many intricate steps. PCR takes less than 4 hours while gene cloning can take days.

14. **(a)**

15. **(a)** *Agrobacterium tumefaciens* (updated scientific name: *Rhizobium radiobacter*) is the causal agent of crown gall desease (the formation of tumour) in over 140 species of dicot. It is a rod-shaped, Gram negative soil bacterium (Smith, *et. al*, 1907). Symptoms are caused by the insertion of a small segment of DNA, knwon as T-DNA (transfer DNA) into the plant cell, which is incorporated at a semi-random location into the plant genome.

16. **(b)** 17. **(c)** 18. **(a)** 19. **(c)** 20. **(b)**

21. **(a)** 22. **(a)**

23. **(b)** Plasmid Circular - extrachromosomal DNA
Bacteriophages - Virus infecting bacteria
Cosmids - Hybrid vector derived from plasmids
Agarose - Natural polymer of D - galactose

24. **(c)** Arber, Nathan and Hamilton Smith - Isolated first restriction endonuclease from bacteria
Paul berg - Father of genetic engineering
Herbert Boyer and Stanley Cohen - First recombinant DNA
Karl Erkey - Term biotechnology

25. **(a)** 26. **(d)** 27. **(d)** 28. **(c)**

29. **(b)** Interferons are antiviral proteins which were produced by "Charles Weismann" (1980) by recombinant DNA technology in *E. coli*.

30. **(c)** *EcoRI* - *Escherichia coli RY13*
HindII - *Haemophilus infulenzae*
BamHI - *Bacillus amyloliquefaciens*
EcoRII - *E. coli R 245*

31. **(b)** E - Name of genus
co - Name of species
R - Name of strain
I - 1st in order of identification

Biotechnology and Its Applications

1. Select the correct set of the names for A, B, C and D.

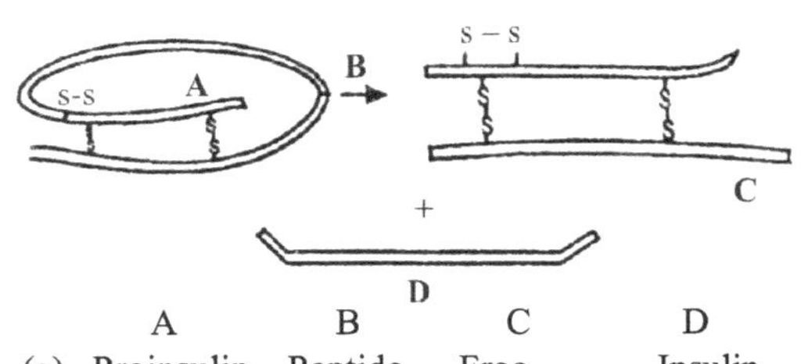

	A	B	C	D
(a)	Proinsulin	Peptide	Free C-Peptide	Insulin
(b)	Proinsulin	Peptidase	Insulin	Free C-Peptide
(c)	Proinsulin	Peptide	Insulin	Free C-Peptide
(d)	Insulin	Peptidase	Proinsulin	Free C-Peptide

2. Match the following and choose the correct option.

Column I		Column II
A. Golden Rice	I.	Cry protein
B. Bt toxin	II.	Rich in vitamin A
C. RNAi	III.	First trangenic cow
D. Rosie	IV.	Gene silencing

(a) A–II; B–I; C–IV; D–III
(b) A–II; B–I; C–III; D–IV
(c) A–II; B–III; C–I; D–IV
(d) A–IV; B–I; C–II; D–III

3. Match the following and choose the correct option.

Column I		Column II
A. Biopiracy	I.	Search for unknown compounds
B. Bioprospecting	II.	Hybridoma technology
C. Monoclonal antibodies.	III.	Mobile genetic element
D. Transposon	IV.	Bioresources

(a) A–II; B–I; C–IV; D–III
(b) A–II; B–I; C–III; D–IV
(c) A–II; B–III; C–I; D–IV
(d) A–IV; B–I; C–II; D–III

4. Match the following and choose the correct option.

Column I		Column II
A. Forensic science	I.	AIDS
B. ELISA	II.	First man made hormone
C. Humulin	III.	Emphysema
D. α-1-antitrypsin	IV.	DNA fingerprinting

(a) A–II; B–I; C–IV; D–III
(b) A–II; B–I; C–III; D–IV
(c) A–II; B–III; C–I; D–IV
(d) A–IV; B–I; C–II; D–III

5. Match the following columns.

Column I		Column II
A. Gene therapy	I.	Effort to fix functional gene
B. Humulin	II.	A single-stranded DNA of RNA tagged with a radioactive molecule
C. Probe	III.	Diabetes
D. ELISA	IV.	Diagnostic test

(a) A–I; B–III; C–II; D–IV
(b) A–IV; B–II; C–III; D–I
(c) A–II; B–III; C–I; D–IV
(d) A–III; B–I; C–IV; D–II

6. Which of the following is/are true ?

I. Biowar – Biowar is the use of biological weapons against humans and or their crops and animals.

II. Bioethics – Bioethics is the unauthorised use of bioresources and traditional knowledge related to bioresources for commercial benefits.

III. Biopatent – Exploitation of bioresources of other nations without proper authorization.

(a) II only   (b) I only

(c) I and II only   (d) I and III only

7. Which one of the following is the correctly matched pair of a product and the microorganism responsible for it ?

(a) Ethyl alcohol – Yeast

(b) Acetic acid – *Lactobacillus*

(c) Cheese – *Nitrobacter*

(d) Curd – *Azotobacter*

8. There are set of healthcare products. Match them with organisms which are genetically engineered for respective product

A.	Insulin	I.	*Escherichia coli / Saccharomyces*
B.	Somatotropin	II.	*Escherichia coli / yeast*
C.	Interferon	III.	GM *Escherichia coli*
D.	Interleukins	IV.	hGR in *Escheri chia coli*
		V.	Humulin through *Escherichia coli*

(a) A–V; B–IV; C–I; D–II

(b) A–V; B–I; C–II; D–IV

(c) A–V; B–III; C–IV; D–I

(d) A–V; B–IV; C–III; D–II

9. Match the column I with column II and choose the correct option:

Column I		Column II
A. *Cry IAc*	1.	*Escherichia coli*
B. *Cry I Ab*	2.	*Agrobacterium*
C. Hirudin	3.	Control cotton boll worms
D. Ti-plasmid	4.	Control corn borer
	5.	Introduced in *Brassica napus*

	A	B	C	D
(a)	2	3	1	5
(b)	3	2	4	1
(c)	1	2	3	4
(d)	3	4	5	2

10. Match the column I with column II and choose the correct option:

Column I		Column II
A. Bt- cotton	1.	Insecticide
B. Flavr-Savr tomato	2.	Delayed Ripening
C. Hirudin	3.	Prevents blood clotting
D. Golden rice	4.	Prevent Blindness
	5.	Vitamin B-rich

(a) A-2, B-3, C-1, D-5

(b) A-3, B-2, C-4, D-1

(c) A-1, B-2, C-3, D-4

(d) A-5, B-3, C-1, D-2

11. GM plants, whose genes have been altered by manipulation, are useful in many ways. Match the column I with column II and choose the correct option:

Column I		Column II
A. Reduce reliance on chemical pesticides	I.	Salt tolerant transgenic tomato
B. Enhanced nutritional value of food	II.	Flavr-savr tomato
C. Reduce post harvest losses	III.	Nematode resistant tobacco
D. Tolerant to abiotic stresses	IV.	Golden rice

(a) A-III, B-IV, C-I, D-II

(b) A-II, B-IV, C-III, D-I

(c) A-II, B-IV, C-I, D-III

(d) A-III, B-IV, C-II, D-I

Solutions

1. (b) 2. (a) 3. (d) 4. (d) 5. (a)
6. (b) 7. (a) 8. (a) 9. (d) 10. (d)
11. (d)

Organisms and Populations

35

1. Match the association in Column I with the type of interaction given in Column II and mark the correct option:

Column I		Column II
A.	Barnacles on whale	I. Predation
B.	Butterfly and birds	II. Parasitism
C.	Goats and tortoise	III. Competition
D.	Copepods on marine fish	IV. Commensalism

   (a) A- (I), B- (IV), C- (III), D- (II)
   (b) A- (IV), B- (I), C- (II), D- (III)
   (c) A- (III), B- (I), C- (IV), D- (II)
   (d) A- (IV), B- (I), C- (III), D- (II)

2. What is the sequence of phases in the growth curve?

	(a)	**(b)**	**(c)**
(a)	Lag	Log	Inflexion phase
(b)	Lag	Stationary	Log
(c)	Log	Lag	Stationary
(d)	Lag	Log	Stationary

   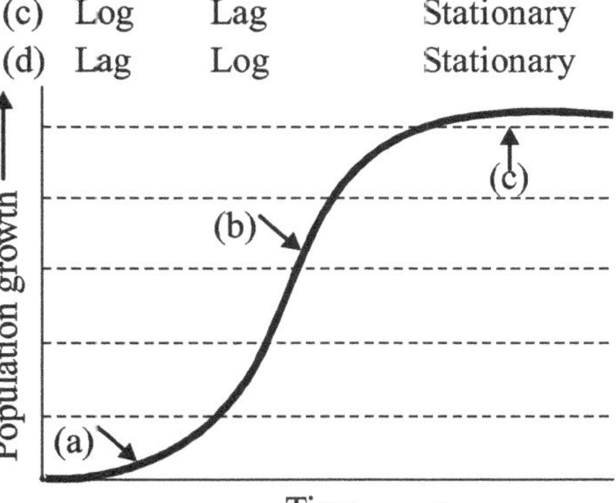

3. Match the columns and find out the correct combination:

A.	Bamboo	1.	Breeds many times in its lifetime
B.	Fish	2.	Produce a large number of small sized organization
C.	Mammal	3.	Breeds only once in its life time
D.	Bird	4.	Produce a small number of large sized organisms

   (a) A-3, B-2, C-4, D-1
   (b) A-1, B-2, C-3, D-4
   (c) A-2, B-4, C-1, D-3
   (d) A-4, B-1, C-3, D-2

4. Match the columns and find out the correct combination:

A.	Stable population	1.	Triangular
B.	Declining population	2.	Urn Shaped
C.	Growing population	3.	Bell shaped
D.	Migration	4.	Inward & outward movement

   (a) A-3, B-2, C-1, D-4
   (b) A-3, B-2, C-4, D-1
   (c) A-3, B-1, C-2, D-4
   (d) A-2, B-3, C-1, D-4

5. Match the column I with II and choose the correct option:

A.	Mutualism	1.	Ticks & lice
B.	Commensalism	2.	Liver fluke
C.	Ectoparasite	3.	Lichens
D.	Endoparasite	4.	Sea-anemone and clown fish

   (a) A-4, B-3, C-1, D-2
   (b) A-3, B-4, C-1, D-2
   (c) A-3, B-4, C-2, D-1
   (d) A-1, B-3, C-2, D-4

6. Identify the correct match from the column I, II and III regarding lake stratification:

Column I	**Column II**	**Column III**
1. Littoral zone	A. Maximum Phytoplankton	(i) Maximum Diversity
2. Limnetic zone	B. Aphotic zone	(ii) P/R = 1
3. Profundal zone	C. Ecotone	(iii) Euphotic zone
4. Compensation zone	D. Disphotic zone	(iv) Mainly occupied by heterotrophs

(a) 2-A-(ii), 1-C-(i), 3-B-(iv), 4-D-(iii)
(b) 1-C-(i), 2-A-(iv), 3-B-(iv), 4-D-(ii)
(c) 2-D-(iii), 2-B-(iv), 3-B-(i), 4-D-(ii)
(d) 2-B-(iii), 1-B-(iv), 3-A-(ii), 4-D-(iv)

7.

A **Mutualism**	**B** **Parasitism**	**C** **Commensalism**
(a) Barnacle & Whale	Loranthus & Mango	Yucca plant & pronuba moth
(b) Leech on cattle	Orchid & Bee	Pilot fish & shark
(c) Fig tree & wasp	Viscum & Oak	Orchid & mango
(d) Sucker fish & shark	Lichen	Ticks on dog

8. Which one is correct?

(a) Cold area animals	Small in size	Large surface area	Low volume
(b) Warm area animals	Small in size	Low surface area	Large volume
(c) Warm area animals	Small in size	Large surface area	Low volume
(d) Cold area animals	Large in size	Small surface area	Small volume

9. Match Column-I with Column-II.

Column-I	**Column-II**
(A) Saprophyte	(i) Symbiotic association of fungi with plant roots
(B) Parasite	(ii) Decomposition of dead organic materials
(C) Lichens	(iii) Living on living plants or animals
(D) Mycorrhiza	(iv) Symbiotic association of algae and fungi

Choose the correct answer from the options given below:

	(A)	**(B)**	**(C)**	**(D)**
(a)	(i)	(ii)	(iii)	(iv)
(b)	(iii)	(ii)	(i)	(iv)
(c)	(ii)	(i)	(iii)	(iv)
(d)	(ii)	(iii)	(iv)	(i)

10. The figure given below is a diagrammatic representation of response of organisms to abiotic factors. What do a, b and c represent respectively?

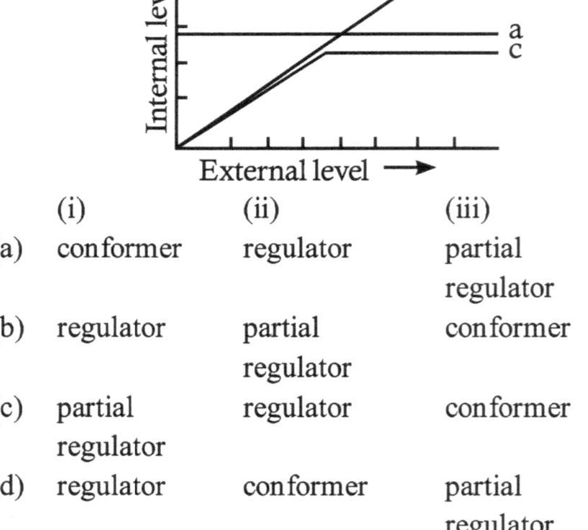

	(i)	(ii)	(iii)
(a)	conformer	regulator	partial regulator
(b)	regulator	partial regulator	conformer
(c)	partial regulator	regulator	conformer
(d)	regulator	conformer	partial regulator

11. Which one of the following pairs is mismatched?

    (a) Tundra   -   Permafrost

    (b) Savanna   -   Acacia trees

    (c) Prairie   -   Epiphytes

    (d) Coniferous forest -   Evergreen trees

12. Which of the following is a correct pair?

    (a) Cuscuta – parasite

    (b) Dischidia – insectivorous

    (c) Opuntia – predator

    (d) Capsella – hydrophyte

13. Match column-I with column-II and choose the correct answer.

Column-I	Column-II
A. Pacific Salmon fish	I. Produces a small number of large sized offspring
B. Mammals	II. Produces a large number of small sized offspring
C. Oysters	III. Breed only once in their lifetime
D. Birds	IV. Breed many times during their lifetime

    (a) A – III, B – IV, C – II, D – I

    (b) A – I, B – IV, C – II, D – III

    (c) A – IV, B – II, C – I, D – III

    (d) A – II, B – IV, C – III, D – I

14. Match Column - I with Column - II and choose the correct option.

Column I	Column II
A. Pacific salmon fish	I. Verhulst - pearl logistic growth
B. $N_t = N_0 e^{rt}$	II. Breed only once in life time
C. Oyster	III. Exponential growth

D. $dN/dt = rN \dfrac{[K-N]}{K}$ IV. A large number of small sized offsprings

    (a) A – IV; B – III; C – I; D – II

    (b) A – III; B – IV; C – I; D – II

    (c) A – III; B – I; C – IV; D – II

    (d) A – II; B – III; C – IV; D – I

15. The density of a population in a given habitat during a given period, fluctuates due to changes in four basic processes. On this basis choose the correct option to fill up A and B boxes in the given diagram.

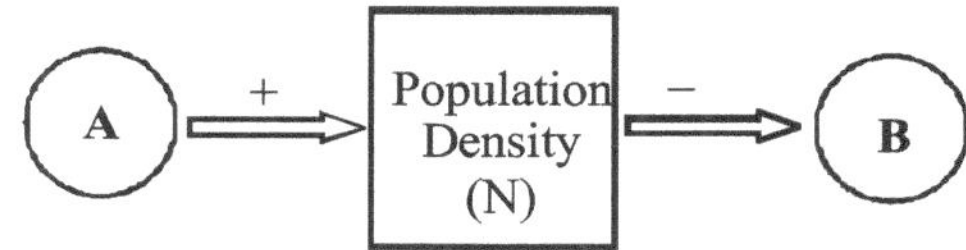

    (a) A = Natality + Immigration, B = Mortality + Emigration

    (b) A = Natality + Mortality, B = Immigration + Emigration

    (c) A = Birth rate + Death rate, B = Mortality + Emigration

    (d) A = Natality + Emigration, B = Mortality + Immigration

16. Identify I to IV which affect the population density.

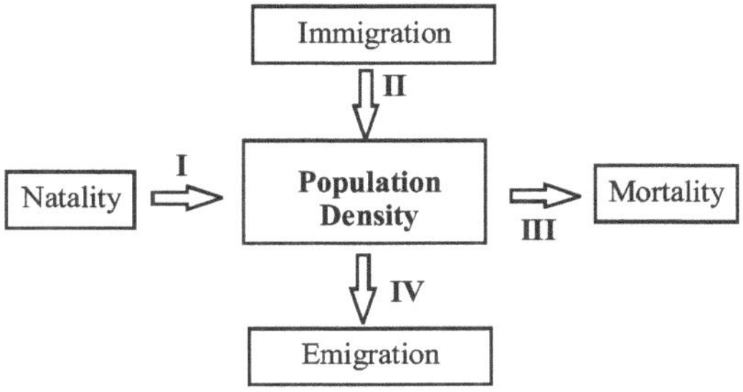

	I	II	III	IV
(a)	Increase	Decrease	Increase	Decrease
(b)	Decrease	Increase	Decrease	Increase
(c)	Increase	Increase	Decrease	Decrease
(d)	Decrease	Decrease	Increase	Increase

Solutions

1. (d) **2.** (d) **3.** (a) **4.** (a) **5.** (b)
6. (b) **7.** (c) **8.** (c)

9. **(d)** Saprophytes are organisms which live on dead organic matter and help in their decomposition.

Parasites is an organisms that live in or on other living plants and animals and dependent on them for their food.

Lichens represent a type of symbiotic association of algae and fungi, in which, both of them dependent on each other for their food and shelter.

Mycorrhiza is also a type of symbiotic association of fungi and plant roots, e.g., *Cycas* coralloid root.

10. **(d)** In the graph, the line 'a' represents regulator, line 'b' represents conformer and line 'c' represents partial regulator. Organism that are able to maintain homeostasis by physiological means that ensures constant body temperature are called regulators. Organism that are not able to maintain a constant internal temperature are called conformers.

Partial regulators are organisms that have the ability to regulate, but only over a limited range of environmental conditions, beyond which they simply conform.

11. **(c)** Prairie is a grass land, and epiphytes and ephemerals are found in desert. In Tundra, much of the ground stays frozen round the year, this condition is called permafrost. The *Acacia* trees are common in African savannas. In coniferous forest, all plants do not shed their leaves at the same time hence forest remain evergreen.

12. **(a)** *Opuntia* is a xerophyte. *Cuscuta* is a parasite. *Capsella* is not a hydrophyte.

13. **(a)** **14.** **(d)**

15. **(a)** Population density due to changes in the following basic process - A: Natality + Immigration; B: Mortality + Emigration

Natality is the proportion of births to the total population in a place in a given time. Immigration is the number of individuals of the same species that have come into the habitat from elsewhere during the time period under consideration. Mortality is the number of deaths in the population during a given period of time. Emigration is the number of individuals of the population who left the habitat and have gone elsewhere during a given period of time.

16. **(c)** According to the given figure, I, II, III and IV (which affects the basic process of population density) are respectively increase, increase, decrease and decrease.

Ecosystem

1. Identified A, B, C and D.

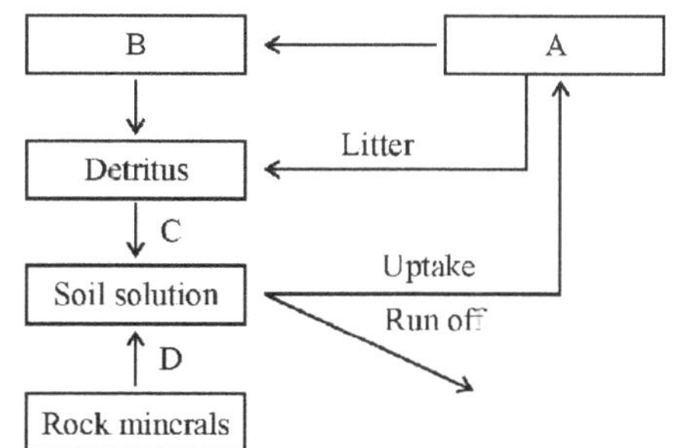

(a) A – Primary producer; B – Second consumer; C – Man / Lion; D – Plants

(b) A – Secondary consumer; B – Primary producer; C – Man / lion; D – Plants

(c) A – Primary producer; B – Secondary consumer; C – Plants; D – Man / lion

(d) A – Secondary consumer; B – Primary producer; C – Plants; D – Man / lion

2. Identified A, B, C and D of a nutrient cycle.

(a) A – Consumers; B – Decomposition; C – Producers; D – Weathering

(b) A – Consumers; B – Weathering;

C – Producers; D – Decomposition

(c) A – Producers; B – Consumers;

C – Decomposition; D – Weathering

(d) A – Consumers; B – Producers;

C – Decomposition; D – Weathering

3. Match the following and choose the correct option

A. Primary succession   I. Autotrophs

B. Climax community   II. Community that has com pleted succession

C. Consumer   III. Colonization of a new environment

D. Producer   IV. Animals

(a) A – III; B – II; C – IV; D – I

(b) A – III; B – I; C – IV; D – II

(c) A – I; B – III; C – II; D – IV

(d) A – II; B – III; C – IV; D – I

4. Match the following columns.

Column I	Column II
A. Scavengers	I. Autotrophs
B. Parasites	II. Heterotrophs
C. Producers	III. Consumers of dead bodies
D. Phagotrophs	IV. Consumers that feed on a small part of a living being

(a) A–III; B–V; C–I; D–II

(b) A–III; B–I; C–II; D–IV

(c) A–I; B–II; C–IV; D–III

(d) A–IV; B–III; C–II; D–I

5. Identify A, B and C from the given flow chart.

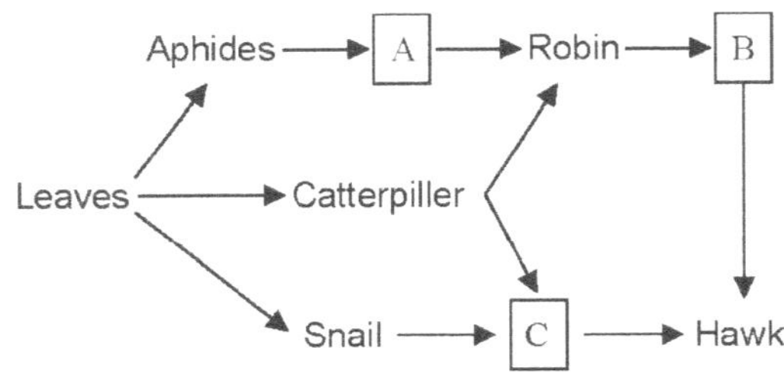

(a) A-Bulbul, B-Snake, C-Monkey

(b) A-Beetle, B-Lizard, C-Praying mantis

(c) A-Ladybird, B-Snake, C-Pigeon

(d) A-Lizard, B-Bird, C-Snake

6. Match the two sets

Column I		Column II
A.	Pioneers	I. Vegetation which modifies its own environment and thus causing its own replacement
B.	Autogenic	II. Replacement of existing community by external conditions.
C.	Allogenic	III. Establishment succession
D.	Ecesis	IV. Primary colonisers

(a) A – IV; B – I, C – II; D – III

(b) A – I; B – II, C – III; D – IV

(c) A – II; B – I, C – IV; D – III

(d) A – I; B – IV, C – III; D – II

7. Match the following columns.

Column I	Column II
A. Inorganic substances	I. Light, temperature and humidity
B. Organic compounds	II. Soil, pH and minerals.
C. Climatic factors	III. Proteins, carbohydrates and lipids, nucleic acid
D. Edaphic factors	IV. Carbon, nitrogen, oxygen and water.

(a) A–III; B–I; C–II; D–IV

(b) A–IV; B–III; C–I; D–II

(c) A–I; B–II; C–III; D–IV

(d) A–IV; B–II; C–I; D–III

8. Match the names of organisms given under column I with the ecological names given under column II. Choose the answer which gives the correct combinations of the two columns.

Column I (Organisms)	Column II (Ecological names)
A. Grass	I. Decomposer
B. Grasshopper	II. Secondary carnivore
C. Frog	III. Producer
D. Hawk	IV. Primary consumer
	V. Primary carnivore

(a) A–III; B–V; C–IV; D–II

(b) A–III; B–IV; C–V; D–II

(c) A–I; B–III; C–IV; D–V

(d) A–III; B–I; C–IV; D–V

9. Identify the likely organisms (I), (II), (III) and (IV) in the food web shown below.

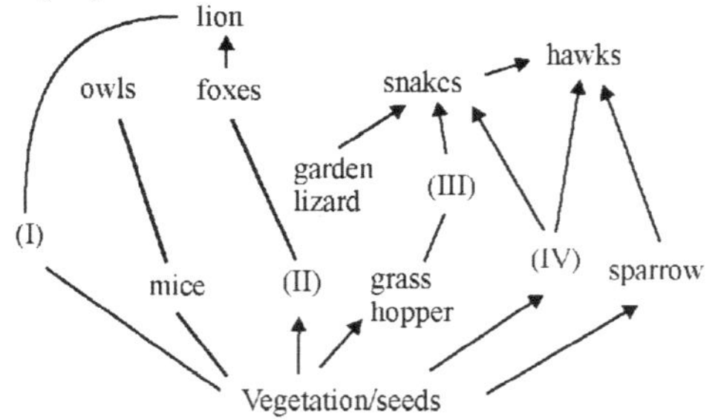

	(I)	(II)	(III)	(IV)
(a)	Deer	Rabbit	Frog	Rat
(b)	Dog	Squirrel	Bat	Deer
(c)	Rat	Dog	Tortoise	Crow
(d)	Squirrel	Cat	Rat	Pigeon

10. Match the following and select the correct option

(A) Earthworm	(I) Pioneer species
(B) Succession	(II) Detritivore
(C) Ecosystem service	(III) Natality
(D) Population growth	(IV) Pollination

	(A)	(B)	(C)	(D)
(a)	(I)	(II)	(III)	(IV)
(b)	(IV)	(I)	(III)	(II)
(c)	(III)	(II)	(IV)	(I)
(d)	(II)	(I)	(IV)	(III)

11. Given below is a simplified model of phosphorus cycling in a terrestrial ecosystem with four blanks (A-D). Identify the blanks:-

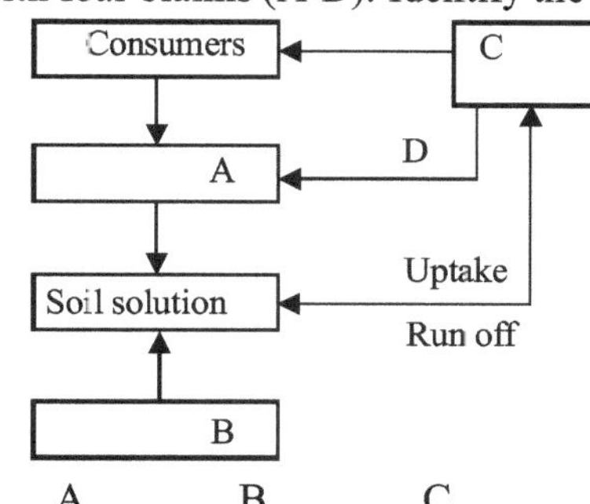

	A	B	C	D
(a)	Rock	Detritus minerals	Litter fall	Producers
(b)	Litter fall	Producers	Rock	Detritus minerals
(c)	Detritus minerals	Rock	Producer	Litter fall
(d)	Producers	Litter fall	Rock	Detritus minerals

12. In which of the following both pairs have correct combination ?

(a) Gaseous nutrient cycle — Carbon and sulphur

Sedimentary nutrient — Nitrogen and cycle — Phosphorus

(b) Gaseous nutrient cycle — Nitrogen and sulphur

Sedimentary nutrient cycle — Carbon and Phosphorus

(c) Gaseous nutrient cycle — Sulphur and Phosphorus

Sedimentary nutrient cycle — Carbon and Nitrogen

(d) Gaseous nutrient cycle — Carbon and Nitrogen

Sedimentary nutrient cycle — Sulphur and Phosphorus

13. Match the following and choose the correct option –

Column I	Column II
A. Standing state	I. Perfect
B. Gaseous cycles	II. Amount of nutrients
C. Standing crop	III. Imperfect
D. Sedimentary cycles	IV. Living matter at different trophic levels

(a) A – II, B – I, C – IV, D – III

(b) A – I, B – II, C – III, D – IV

(c) A – III, B – II, C – IV, D – I

(d) A – I, B – IV, C – III, D – II

14. Answer the correct set

Column I	Column II
A. Gross primary	I. Total assimilation productivity
B. Secondary productivity	II. Remains mobile and does not remain in-situ
C. Transducers	III. Green plants
D. Food web	IV. Interlocking pattern

(a) A–I; B–II; C–III; D–IV

(b) A–II; B–III; C–IV; D–I

(c) A–III; B–IV; C–I; D–II

(d) A–I; B–III; C–II; D–IV

15. Study the following columns and choose the correct option.

Column I		Column II
A.	Population	I. Parts of the earth consisting of all the ecosystems of the world.
B.	Community	II. Assemblage of all the individuals belonging to different species occurring in an area
C.	Ecosystem	III. Group of similar individuals belonging to the same species found in an area.
D.	Ecosphere	IV. Interaction between the living organisms and their physical environment components.
		V. Classification of organisms based on the type of environment.

(a) A–III; B–II; C–I; D–IV

(b) A–V; B–II; C–III; D–IV

(c) A–II; B–III; C–V; D–I

(d) A–III; B–II; C–IV; D–I

16. Choose the correct combination of labelling of the zones in water in a lake

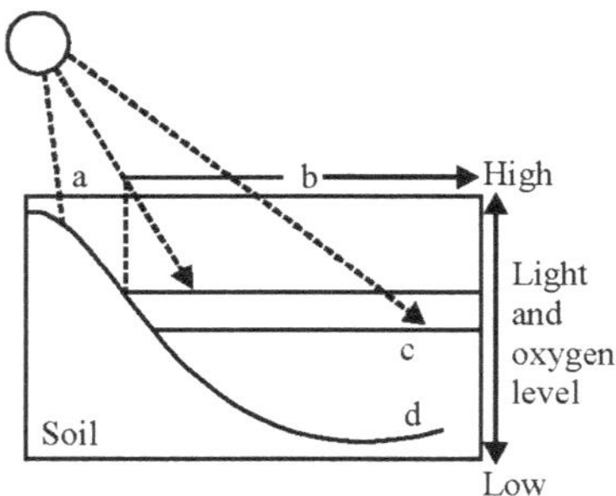

(a) a-Limnetic zone, b-Profundal zone, c-Littoral zone, d-Benthic zone

(b) a-Littoral zone, b-Benthic zone, c-Profundal zone, d-Limnetic zone

(c) a-Littoral zone, b-Limnetic zone, c-Profundal zone, d-Benthic zone

(d) a-Limnetic zone, b-Littoral zone, c-Benthic zone, d-Profundal zone

17. Match the following columns.

Column I		Column II
A.	Primary consumers	I. A meat eater that eats primary consumers.
B.	Secondary consumers	II. A meat eater that eats tertiary consumers.
C.	Tertiary consumers	III. A organism eater that eats producers.
D.	Quaternary consumers	IV. A meat eater that eats secondary consumers.

(a) A–I; B–IV; C–II; D–III

(b) A–III; B–I; C–IV; D–II

(c) A–IV; B–II; C–III; D–I

(d) A–II; B–III; C–I; D–IV

18. Select the options that correctly identifies A, B and C in the given table.

Organisms	Trophic Level	Type of Food Chain
Eagle	*A*	Grazing
Earthworm	Primary consumer	*B*
C	Secondary consumer	Grazing

(a) A-Secondary consumer, B-Grazing, C-Algae

(b) A-Top carnivore, B-Detritus, C-Frog

(c) A-Scavenger, B-Grazing, C-Hawk

(d) A-Decomposer, B-Detritus, C-Perch

19. Match the following columns.

	Column I		Column II
A.	Primary succession	I.	Colonisation of a new environment
B.	Climax community	II.	Ecosystem development
C.	Pioneer community on	III.	Crustose lichens lithosphere
D.	Ecological succession	IV.	Community that has completed succession

(a) A–III; B–II; C–I; D–IV
(b) A–IV; B–III; C–II; D–I
(c) A–I; B–II; C–III; D–IV
(d) A–IV; B–III; C–I; D–II

20. Match the following columns.

	Column I		Column II
A.	First trophic level	I.	Producer
B.	Decomposer	II.	Consumer
C.	Primary productivity	III.	Phytoplankton
D.	Secondary productivity	IV.	Stratification
		V.	Bacteria

(a) A–I; B–V; C–III; D–IV
(b) A–II; B–III; C–IV; D–V
(c) A–III; B–V; C–I; D–II
(d) A–III; B–V; C–II; D–I

21. Match the sets

	Column I		Column II
A.	*Artemisia tridentata*	I.	Grow better in over grazed area
B.	*Capparis spinosa*	II.	Dominate in areas destructed by fires
C.	*Pteridium aquilina* and *Pyronema*	III.	Indicates intense soil erosion
D.	*Amaranthus* and *Chenopodium*	IV.	Saline soils

(a) A–I; B–II; C–III; D–IV
(b) A–II; B–III; C–IV; D–I
(c) A–III; B–I; C–II; D–IV
(d) A–IV; B–III; C–II; D–I

22. Match column A with column B and select the correct option.

	Column I		Column II
A.	Pyramid of energy	I.	Xerosere
B.	First group of	II.	Always plant in bare area inverted
C.	Pyramid of biomass	III.	Hydrosere in aquatic habitat
D.	Succession in	IV.	Pioneers desert area
		V.	Always upright

(a) A – II; B – I; C – V; D – III
(b) A – V; B – IV; C – II; D – I
(c) A– V; B – III; C – II; D – IV
(d) A – II; B – III; C – V; D – I

23. Given food web contains some missing organisms A, B, C and D. Identify these organisms and select the correct answer.

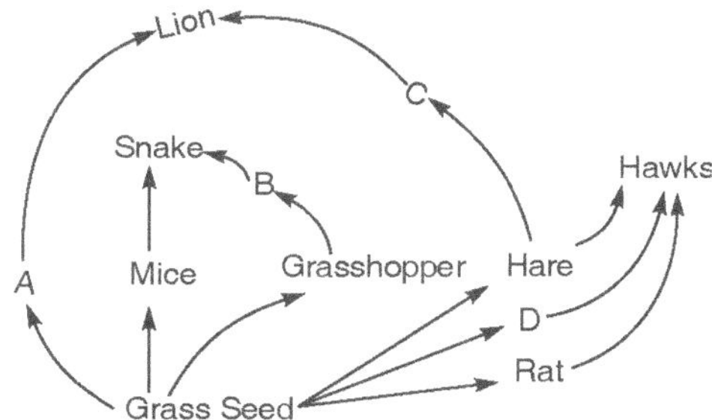

(a) A-Deer, B-Frog, C-Foxes, D-Sparrow
(b) A-Dog, B-Squirrel, C-Deer, D-Hawks
(c) A-Cat, B-Eagle, C-Cow, D-Rat
(d) A-Eagle, B-Sparrow, C-Dog, D-Cat

24. Match the following columns.

	Column I		Column II
A.	Xeroseres	I.	Ecological succession starts on terrestrial habitat.

B. Hydroseres	II. Succession begins from open water	(a) A – III; B – I, C – II; D – IV
		(b) A – IV; B – III, C – I; D – II
C. Lithoseres	III. Successions begin on sand	(c) A – I; B – II, C – IV; D – III
D. Psammoseres	IV. Succession start on a bare rock	(d) A – II; B – IV, C – III; D – I

Solutions

1. (d) **2.** (c) **3.** (a)

4. (a) Scavengers - Consumers of dead bodes
Parasites - Consumers that feed on a small part of a living being
Producers - Autotrophs
Phagotrophs - Heterotrophs

5. (c) *Leaves → Aphids → Ladybird → Robin → Snake → Hawk Leaves → Snail → Pigeon → Hawk*

6. (a)

7. (b) Inorganic substances - Carbon, nitrogen, oxygen and water.
Organic compounds - Proteins, carbohydrates, lipids and nucleic acid.
Climatic factors - Light, temperature and humidity.
Edaphic factors - Soil, pH, minerals.

8. (b)

9. (a) Food web is a network of food chains or feeding relationships by which energy and nutrients are passed on from one species of living organisms to another.

10. (d)

11. (c) Phosphorus is an important element for living beings. Consumers obtain phosphorus directly or indirectly from plants. Phosphorus is also present in phosphatic rocks. It is released during the decomposition of plant and animal remains. The released phosphorus may reach the deeper layers of soil and gets deposited as phosphate rocks. All plants and animals eventually die and in due time, their organic remains or debris decay through the action of micro-organism and the phosphates are released into the water for recycling.

12. (d) Carbon and Nitrogen are gaseous nutrient cycle. Sulphur and phosphorus are sedimentary nutrient cycle.

13. (a) **14.** (a)

15. (d) Population consists of organisms of same species, community have organisms of different species and ecosystem include biotic and abiotic components. Ecosphere is part of the earth consisting of all the ecosystems of the world.

16. (c)

17. (b) Primary consumer : That eats autotrophs.
Secondary consumer : A meat eater that eats primary consumers.
Tertiary consumer : A meat eater that eats secondary consumers.
Quaternary consumer : A meat eater that eats tertiary consumers.

18. (b) A-Top carnivore, B-Detritus, C-Frog.

19. (c) Primary – Colonisation of a new succession environment
Climas community – Community that has completed succession
Pioneer community – Crustose lichen on lithosphere
Ecological – Ecosystem development succession

20. (c) First trophic level - Phytoplankton
Decomposer – Bacteria
Primary productivity – Producer
Secondary productivity – Consumer

21. (c) **22.** (b)

23. (a) A-Deer, B-Frog, C-Foxes, D-Sparrow

24. (c) Xeroseres: Ecological succession start on terrestrial habitat
Hydroseres: Succession begins from open water
Lithoseres: Succession starts on a bare rock.
Psammoseres: Succession begins on sand.

Biodiversity and Conservation

1. Match items given in column I with those given in column II.

	Column I		Column II
A.	Rhinoceros	I.	Bharatpur
B.	Tiger project in Karnataka	II.	Tropical evergreen forest
C.	Assemblage protection	III.	Kaziranga
D.	Silent valley	IV.	National park
		V.	Bandipur

   (a) A–V; B–III; C–I; D–IV
   (b) A–II; B–IV; C–III; D–II
   (c) A–IV; B–III; C–II; D–V
   (d) A–III; B–V; C–I; D–II

2. Which one of the following is the correct matched pair of an endangered animal and National Park?

   (a) Rhinoceros - Kaziranga National Park
   (b) Wild ass - Dudhwa National Park
   (c) Great Indian - Keoladeo National Park bustard
   (d) Lion - Corbett National Park

3. Given below is the representation of the extent of global diversity of invertebrates. What groups the four portions (A-D) represent respectively?

   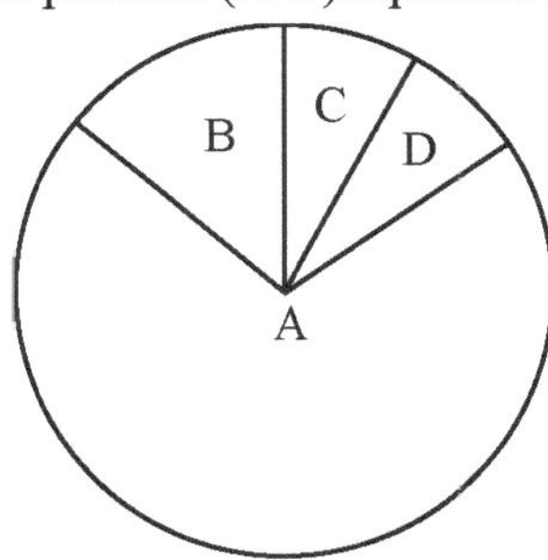

	A	B	C	D
(a)	Insects	Crustaceans	Other animal groups	Molluscs
(b)	Crustaceans	Insects	Molluscs	Other animal groups
(c)	Molluscs	Other animal groups	Crustaceans	Insects
(d)	Insects	Molluscs	Crustaceans	Other animal groups

4. Find the wrongly matched pair:

   (a) Endemism- Species confined to a region and not found anywhere else
   (b) Hot spots- Western Ghats
   (c) Sacred groves- Jaintia Hills of Rajasthan
   (d) *Ex-situ* conservation- Zoological park

5. Match the column -I with column -II

	Column I		Column II
A.	Bihar	I.	Indian elephant
B.	Rajasthan	II.	Gazello
C.	Madhya Pradesh	III.	Leopard
D.	Uttar Pradesh	IV.	Barasingha
E.	Gujarat	V.	Sloth Bear
		VI.	Asiatic Lion

   (a) A–I; B–III; C–V; D–II; E–IV
   (b) A–V; B–II; C–IV; D–III; E–VI
   (c) A–III; B–V; C–II; D–IV; E–I
   (d) A–VI; B–V; C–IV D–III; E–II

6. Which one of the following pairs is not correctly matched :
   (a) Manas Sanctuary   – Assam
   (b) Kanha National Park   – Madhya Pradesh
   (c) Dachigam Sanctuary – West Bengal
   (d) Bandipur Sanctuary   – Karnataka

7. Identify the correctly matched pair :
   (a) Rann of Kutch   – Wild ass
   (b) Corbett Park   – Bustard
   (c) Kaziranga   – Elephant
   (d) Gir Forest   – Rhino

8. Given below is the representation of the extent of global diversity of *invertebrates*. What groups the four portions (A-D) represent respectively?

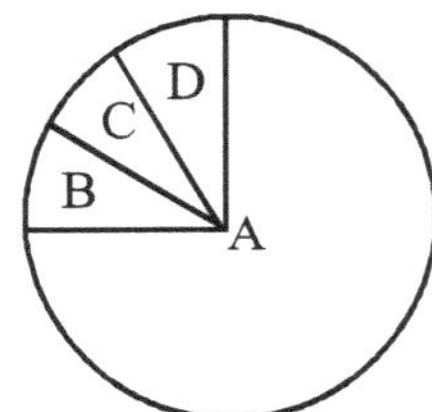

	A	**B**	**C**	**D**
(a)	Insects	Crustaceans	Other animal groups	Molluscs
(b)	Crustaceans	Insects	Molluscs	Other animal groups
(c)	Molluscs	Other animal groups	Crustaceans	Insects
(d)	Insects	Molluscs	Crustaceans	Other animal groups

9.

	Column-I		**Column-II**
1.	Silent valley	(A)	Kaziranga
2.	Rhinoceros	(B)	Bandipur
3.	Tiger project in Karnataka	(C)	In situ
4.	National Park	(D)	Tropical evergreen forest

   (a) I-B, II-A, III-D, IV-C
   (b) I-D, II-A, III-B, IV-C
   (c) I-A, II-C, III-B, IV-D
   (d) I-B, II-A, III-C, IV-D

10. Match the following columns and select the correct option:

A.	Alpha diversity	1.	Richness of different species in a habitat
B.	Beta diversity	2.	Richness of different species along with a gradient from one habitat to another habitat within the community.
C.	Gamma diversity	3.	Richness of different species in different habitat.

   (a) A-1,B-2, C-3
   (b) A-1,B-3, C-2
   (c) A-2, B-1, C-3
   (d) A-3,B-2,C-1

11. Match the following columns:

	Column I		**Column II**
A.	Lungs of planet	1.	*Lantana camara*
B.	Reserpine	2.	Amazon rain forest
C.	Anti-cancer drug	3.	Yew Tree
D.	Exotic species	4.	*Rauwolfia*

   (a) A-2, B-4,C-3,D-1
   (b) A-2,B-3,C-4,D-1
   (c) A-4,B-3,C-1,D-2
   (d) A-2,B-4,C-1,D-3

12. Given below are pie diagrams A, B and C related to proportionate number of species of major taxa of invertebrates, vertebrates and plants respectively. Critically study and fill in the blanks I, II, III and IV.

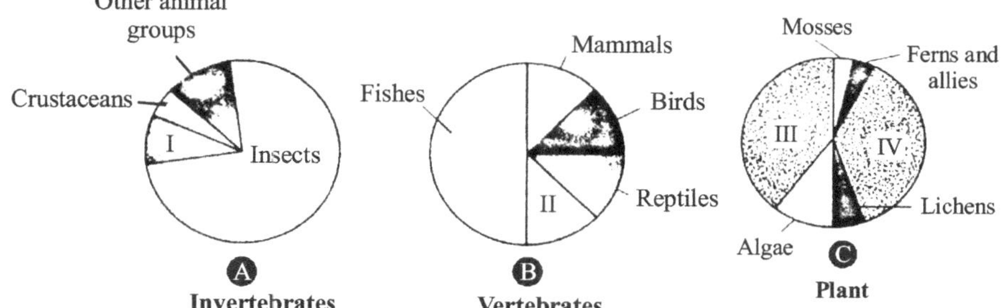

(a) I- Molluscs, II-Amphibians, III-Fungi, IV-Angiosperms
(b) I- Molluscs, II-Amphibians, III-Angiosperms, IV-Fungi
(c) I- Hexapoda, II-Amphibians, III-Fungi, IV-Angiosperms
(d) I- Turtles, II-Amphibians, III-Fungi, IV-Angiosperms

13. Given below is the representation of the extent of global diversity of invertebrates. What groups the four portions (A-D) represent respectively?

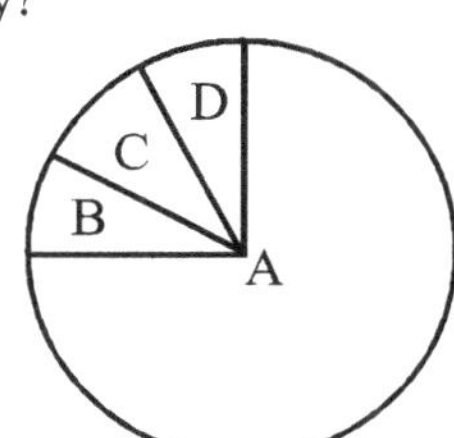

	A	B	C	D
(a)	Insects	Crustaceans	Other animal groups	Molluscs
(b)	Crustaceans	Insects	Molluscs	Other animal groups
(c)	Molluscs	Other animal groups	Crustaceans	Insects
(d)	Insects	Molluscs	Crustaceans	Other animal groups

14. Which of the following boxes show maximum, greater and minimum diversity ?

A				B				C		
Animals	Species	Members		Animals	Species	Members		Animals	Species	Members
Bird	I	1		Bird	I	2		Bird	I	2
Bird	II	1		Bird	II	2		Mammal	II	2
Bird	III	4		Mammal	III	2		Insect	III	2

(a) A- Minimum diversity, B - Greater diversity, C - Maximum diversity
(b) A - Maximum diversity, B - Greater diversity, C - Minimum diversity
(c) A - Maximum diversity, B - Minimum diversity, C - Greater diversity
(d) A - Minimum diversity, B - Maximum diversity, C - Greater diversity.

15. Match the following and choose the correct option.

	Column-I		Column-II
A.	Narrowly utilitarian argument	I.	Conserving biodiversity for major ecosystem services
B.	Broadly utilitarian argument	II.	Conserving biodiversity for philosophical or spiritual need to realise that every species has intrinsic value and moral duty to pass our biological legacy in good order to future generation.
C.	Ethical argument	III.	Conserving biodiversity for direct economic benefits like food, medicine, industrial products etc.

(a) A – I, B – II, C – III

(b) A – III, B – I, C – II

(c) A – II, B – I, C – III

(d) A – I, B – III, C – II

16. Match the following.

	Column-I		Column-II
(A)	Ranthambore National Park	(i)	Assam
(B)	Kaziranga National Park	(ii)	Rajasthan
(C)	Jim corbett National Park	(iii)	Orissa
(D)	Nandan kanan zoological Park	(iv)	Uttarakhand

(a) (A) - (i), (B) - (ii), (C) - (iii), (D) - (iv)

(b) (A) - (ii), (B) - (iii), (C) - (iv), (D) - (i)

(c) (A) - (ii), (B) - (i), (C) - (iv), (D) - (iii)

(d) (A) - (iii), (B) - (ii), (C) - (i), (D) - (iv)

Solutions

1. **(d)** 2. **(a)** 3. **(d)** 4. **(c)** 5. **(b)**

6. **(c)** 7. **(a)**

8. **(d)** Arthropoda is the largest phylum of Animalia which includes insects. Over two-thirds of all named species on earth are arthropods. They have organ system level of organisation. Mollusca is the second largest animal phylum. They are terrestrial or aquatic (marine or fresh).

9. **(b)** 10. **(a)** 11. **(a)**

12. **(a)** In the given pie diagrams (A, B and C), the proportionate number of species of major taxa of invertebrates, vertebrates and plants respectively marked as I (mollusca), II (amphibians), III (Fungi), IV (Angiosperms)

13. **(d)** Arthropoda is the largest phylum of Animalia which includes insects. Over two-thirds of all named species on earth are arthropods. They have organ system level of organisation. Mollusca is the second largest animal phylum. They are terrestrial or aquatic (marine or fresh).

14. **(a)** A, B and C respectively show minimum, greater and maximum diversity. Since the number of individuals in all the three boxes are same but the variety of animals in all the boxes are different, like box A shows diversity of single animal - bird, box B shows diversity of birds and mammals whereas box C shows diversity of three animals - birds, mammals and insects.

15. **(b)** A - III, B - I, C - II

16. **(c)** Ranthambore National Park is a vast wildlife reserve near the town of Sawai Madhopur in Rajasthan, northern India. It is a former royal hunting ground and home to tigers, leopards and marsh crocodiles. Kaziranga National Park is a protected area in the northeast Indian state of Assam. It is a home to tigers, elephants and the world's largest population of Indian one-horned rhinoceroses. Jim Corbett National Park is a forested wildlife sanctuary in northern India's Uttarakhand State. Rich in flora and fauna, it is known for its Bengal tigers. Nandankanan Zoological Park is a 437-hectare zoo and botanical garden in Bhubaneswar, Orissa, India. It serves the first captive gharial breeding center of India.

Environmental Issues

39. Match the following columns.

Column I	Column II
A. Suspended solids	I. Nitrates ammonia, phosphate sodium calcium
B. Colloidal matterials	II. Faecal matter, bacteria, paper and cloth fibres
C. Dissolved materials	III. Sand, silt and clay

(a) A–I; B–II; C–III
(b) A–II; B–III; C–I
(c) A–III; B–I; C–II
(d) A–III; B–II; C–I

35. Match the sources of solid waste in Column A with the type of solid waste in column B.

Column I	Column II
A. Old newspapers	I. Municipal solid wastes
B. Construction site	II. Industrial solid wastes
C. Discarded medicines	III. Hospital solid wastes and syringes

(a) A–II; B–III; C–I
(b) A–I; B–III; C–II
(c) A–I; B–II; C–III
(d) A–II; B–III; C–I

5. Identify the correctly matched pair.
(a) Basal Convention   -   Biodiversity Conservation
(b) Kyoto Protocol   -   Climatic change
(c) Montreal Protocol   -   Global warming
(d) Ramsar Convention   -   Ground water pollution

13. The below diagram shows a scrubber. Identify A, B, C and D.

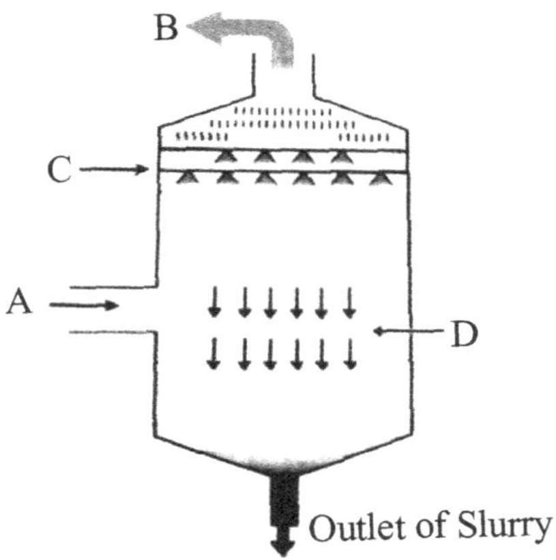

(a) A-Particulate matter, B-Clean air, C-Dirty air, D-Dust particle
(b) A-Dirty air, B-Clean air, C-Water lime spray, D-Slurry outlet
(c) A-Slurry outlet, B-Dirty airm, C-Particulate matter, D-Clean air
(d) A-Dust particle, B-Clean air, C-Particulate matter, D-water spray

27. Match the following items in column I with column II and choose the correct answer.

Calumn I	Column II
A. Arsenic	I. Minamata disease
B. Nitrate	II. Itai-itai
C. Mercury	III. Blue-baby syndrome
D. Cadmium	IV. Skeletal fluorosis
E. Fluoride	V. Black-fool disease

(a) A–II; B–III; C–V; D–I; E–IV
(b) A–V; B–III; C–I; D–II; E–IV
(c) A–III; B–IV; C–V; D–I; E–II
(d) A–V; B–IV; C–III; D–II; E–I

41. Match the following columns.

	Column I		Column II
A.	Particulate pollutants	I.	Hydrogen sulphide
B.	Gaseous pollutants	II.	Carbon monoxide
		III.	Metallic particles
		IV.	Dust particles
		V.	Soot
		VI.	Aerosol
		VII.	Smoke
		VIII.	Nitrogen dioxide
		IX.	Sulphus dioxide

(a) A–III, IV, V, VI, VII; B–I, II, VIII, IX
(b) A–III, IV, V, B–I, II, VI, VII, VIII, IX
(c) A–III, IV, V, VI; B–I, II, VII, VIII, IX
(d) A–I, II, III, IV; B–V, VI, VII, VIII, IX

7. Match the following and select the correct option.

	Column I		Column II
A.	Emphysema	(i)	Increase in the concentration of non-biodegrable substances in food chains
B.	ADA deficiency	(ii)	a-1 antitrypsin
C.	Eutrophication	(iii)	Bone marrow transplantation
D.	Biomagnification	(iv)	Nutrient enrichment of water body

(a) A-(iii), B-(ii), C-(iv), D-(i)
(b) A-(ii), B-(iii), C-(iv), D-(i)
(c) A-(i), B-(iii), C-(ii), D-(iv)
(d) A-(iv), B-(ii), C-(iii), D-(i)

8. Match the column I with column II and choose the correct option:

	Column I		Column II
A.	Environment Protection Act	1.	1947
B.	Air Pollution and Control of Pollution Act	2.	1987
C.	Water Act	3.	1986
D.	Amendment of Air Act to include noise	4.	1981

(a) A-3, B-4, C-1, D-2
(b) A-1, B-3, C-2, D-4
(c) A-4, B-1, C-2, D-3
(d) A-3, B-4, C-2, D-1

9. Match the columns I with column II and choose the correct option:

	Column I		Column II
A.	UV rays	1.	Biomagnification
B.	Biodegradable organic matter	2.	Eutrophication
C.	DDT	3.	Snow blindness
D.	Phosphates	4.	BOD

(a) A-2, B-1, C-4, D-3
(b) A-3, B-2, C-4, D-1
(c) A-3, B-4, C-1, D-2
(d) A-3, B-1, C-4, D-2

10. Match the column I with column II and find out the correct combination:

	Column I		Column II
A.	Ozone depletion	1.	Thickness of ozone
B.	Greenhouse gas	2.	CFCs
C.	Decibels	3.	Units of sound
D.	Dobson units	4.	Methane

(a) A-2, B-3, C-4, D-1
(b) A-2, B-4, C-3, D-1
(c) A-3, B-2, C-4, D-1
(d) A-4, B-2, C-3, D-1

11. Match the items given in Column I with those in Column II and select the correct option given below

	Column-I		Column-II
A.	Eutrophication	i.	UV-B radiation
B.	Sanitary landfill	ii.	Deforestation
C.	Snow blindness	iii.	Nutrient enrichment
D.	Jhum cultivation	iv.	Waste disposal

	A	B	C	D
(a)	ii	i	iii	iv
(b)	i	iii	iv	ii
(c)	i	ii	iv	iii
(d)	iii	iv	i	ii

12. Identify the correctly matched pair.

    (a) Basal Convention - Biodiversity Conservation

    (b) Kyoto Protocol - Climatic change

    (c) Montreal Protocol - Global warming

    (d) Ramsar Convention - Ground water pollution

13. Which one of the following pairs is mismatched?

    (a) Fossil fuel burning - release of CO_2

    (b) Nuclear power - radioactive wastes

    (c) Solar energy - green house effect

    (d) Biomass burning - release of CO_2

Solutions

1. **(d)** Suspended Solid - Sand, silt and clay Colloidal Materials -Faecal matter, bacteria, paper and cloth fibres Dissolved Materials-Nitrates. ammonia phosphates, sodium and calcium

2. **(c)**

3. **(b)** Kyoto Protocol (1997) : International conference held in Kyoto, Japan obtained commitments from different countries for reducing overall greenhouse gas emissions at a level 9% below 1990 level by 2008-2012.

Montreal Protocol (1987) : Industrialized countries agreed to limit production of chloroflourocarbons to half the level of 1986.

4. **(b)** **5.** **(b)**

6. **(a)** Particulate pollutants, metallic particles, soot aerosol, smoke and dust particles. Gasesous pollutants Hydrogen sulphide, carbon monoxide, nitrogen dioxide and sulphur dioxide.

7. **(b)** **8.** **(a)** **9.** **(c)** **10.** **(b)**

11. **(d)** Snow blindness, also called arc eye or photokeratitis, is a painful eye condition caused by overexposure to ultraviolet (UV) light. When too much UV light hits the transparent outer layer of your eyes, called the cornea, it essentially gives your cornea a sunburn. Snow blindness symptoms can be disorienting.

12. **(b)** Kyoto Protocol (1997) : International conference held in Kyoto, Japan obtained commitments from different countries for reducing overall greenhouse gas emissions at a level 9% below 1990 level by 2008-2012.

Montreal Protocol (1987) : Industrialized countries agreed to limit production of chloroflourocarbons to half the level of 1986.

13. **(c)** Solar energy coming to the earth is not responsible for green house effect. It is the increase in green house gases in atmosphere like CO_2 which is released by complete combustion of fossil fuels or biomass in industries or transportation vehicles that prevent the reradiation of infrared radiation from the earth and result in increase in temperature of the earth.